DATE DUE

BRODART.   Cat. No. 23-221

We Answer Only to God

We Answer Only to God
*Politics and the Military
in Panama,
1903–1947*

Thomas L. Pearcy

UNIVERSITY OF NEW MEXICO PRESS
Albuquerque

Library of Congress Cataloging-in-Publication Data

Pearcy, Thomas L., 1960–
    We answer only to God : politics and the military in Panama,
1903–1947 / Thomas L. Pearcy. — 1st ed.
        p.   cm.
    Includes bibliographical references and index.
    ISBN 0–8263–1841–X (cloth)
        1. Panama—Politics and governments—1903–1946.   2. Panama—
Politics and government—1946–1981.   3. Panama. Guardia Nacional—
Political activity—History.   4. Civil-military relations—Panama—
History.   5. Social conflict—Panama—History.   6. Panama—
Relations—United States.   7. United States—Relations—Panama.
I. Title.
F1566.5.P43   1998
972.8705—dc21   98–14669
                                                                      CIP

Contents

꙳

Illustrations

Maps

Figures

Tables

☙

Foreword

As Panamá entered the 1930s, this young republic experienced steady social, political, and economic changes. The political influence of Colombian institutions and the "Próceres" generation came to an end. The old distinction between "intramuros" and "extramuros" became meaningless with the appearance of Exposición and Bella Vista as the new residence of Panama's elite and the emergence of new popular "barrios" of El Chorrillo, Marañón, Boca La Caja, and so forth. The composition of urban society also changed. There was a growing presence of American officers and European businessmen. The transformation of the "arrabal" occurred through immigration of West Indians and migration of Panamanian peasants from the countryside.

The ascent of radical ideologies and parties, as well as the growing participation of middle classes and labor organizations, compelled the traditional oligarchy to look for new means of political control. Constitutional reforms and professionalization of the armed forces were some of the measures taken in the face of these new challenges. By the 1950s, Panama's social and political structures had undergone profound changes, and the configuration of social forces and political actors for the next three decades had been laid down.

In this book, Thomas L. Pearcy accomplishes a penetrating and suggestive analysis of a fascinating period of Panamá's contemporary history. Employing new documents and innovative methodology—including the demographic program Populate—he provides a provocative interpretation of the evolution of Panamanian society in which internal factors play a fundamental role.

A very important lesson revealed by this work is that historians interested in Panamanian republican history need to fully acquaint themselves with our national repositories. For the study of the twentieth century, Panama's Archivos Nacionales, Archivos del Ministerio de Relaciones Exteriores, Archivos del Registro de la Propiedad, and Archivos del Registro Público hold an abundance of primary sources. Research in these collections will foster greater insight into Panamá's institutional and political history. Also, the Contraloría General de la República, parish records, and clinical archives of Hospital Santo

Tomás and Caja de Seguro Social preserve a wealth of basic data that will further our understanding of social and demographic trends. In addition, Universidad de Panamá "Simón Bolívar" library and national library "Ernesto J. Castillero Reyes" preserve a rich collection of Panamanian newspapers, journals, and magazines that can provide a distinctive view into the meaning of everyday activities and the impact of extraordinary events on the urban society at mid-century.

One of the strengths of this book is Pearcy's recognition of the significance of these sources. He carefully and thoroughly researched this book. As a result, he uncovers a complex picture of the evolving social forces that emerged in Panamá since the 1930s, in a background characterized by the rise of nationalism, the ascension of militarism, the growth of internal migration, and the beginning of industrialization. He utilizes his new evidences and findings to formulate an innovative theoretical framework, which adds a fresh perspective to the discussion of mid-century Panamá. Pearcy's interpretation not only offers a rational explanation for the period, but also provides new insights into the intricate social and political circumstances of Panamá today. Without any doubt, this book represents an extraordinary contribution to the study and comprehension of Panamá's contemporary history.

FERNANDO APARICIO
History Department
Universidad de Panamá

Preface

Since the independence of the isthmus from Colombia in 1903, its peoples have played a pivotal role in their nation's development. They have responded to imperialism, political corruption and repression, economic collapse, social stratification, and racism by voting, migrating, protesting, organizing, and as a last resort, taking up arms. Despite this resourcefulness on the part of Panama's citizens, until recently scholarship dealing with the country during the first decades of the twentieth century focused principally on Panama's role in international commerce and military affairs. As a consequence, historiographical analyses have tended to portray the isthmus as a reflection of the Panama Canal and of United States foreign policy rather than as a sovereign and autonomous nation. This trend, known by some scholars in Panama as "geographic determinism," has painted a misleading picture of Panama, one that depicts its people as passive objects of change, an ancillary component of the nation's history.[1]

This perception began to change in the 1960s, and since that time Panamanian historical scholarship has been frequently in a state of flux. In a 1964 outburst, Canal Zone troops killed twenty-four Panamanian high school students; then in 1968, General Omar Torrijos led a successful coup d'état against the nation's civilian government. With these events, a new generation of scholars began rethinking the way it had portrayed Panamanian history. General Torrijos's policies drew attention to the common citizen. This shift in governmental policy translated into a change in direction for some scholars who, along with Torrijos, began to focus their attention on domestic issues.

One new genre of literature with origins in the 1960s was a series of studies centering on Panama's National Police. Steve Ropp, Marco Gandásegui, Renato Pereira, Richard Millett, and a number of other observers in Panama and the United States traced the Torrijos government as it evolved. While these studies varied widely and frequently disagreed with one another, collectively they have provided considerable insight into the genesis and operation of Panama's recent military leaders.[2]

Simultaneously the tumultuous sixties gave rise to a second revisionist school. Rather than focusing on the development and evolution of the military, this second group of analyses concentrated more on historical methodologies. In their 1980 work *La historia de Panamá en sus textos*, for example, Celestino Andrés Araúz, Carlos Manuel Gasteazoro, and Armando Pinzón called for researchers to go beyond the use of "geographic determinism" to interpret Panamanian history, relying instead on census data, tax records, immigration information, and other public and private materials to explore the characteristics and development of Panamanian society. According to these writers, a whole generation of earlier scholars wrongly portrayed the canal as if it constituted the whole of the republic. In the wake of the 1968 revolt, the institutionalists had made the military the subject of their studies, replacing the canal with the National Guard as the topic of academic inquiry. Araúz, Gasteazoro, Pinzón, and their colleagues called for a corresponding shift in historical methodology.

In this vein, Omar Jaén Suárez and Alfredo Figueroa Navarro led the drive to reevaluate Panamanian history. In 1982 the third edition of Figueroa Navarro's work *Dominio y sociedad en el Panamá Colombiano, 1821–1903* became the definitive example of this school of thought. Figueroa Navarro, Jaén Suárez, and their peers in the social history movement provided valuable insight into the forces that fashioned nineteenth century Isthmian society, focusing primarily on people rather than on geography or institutions. Published shortly after Torrijos's tragic and untimely death, *Dominio y sociedad* has provided the methodological blueprint for a new generation of researchers interested in exploring the innermost workings of life on the isthmus.

This new social history has largely emphasized the effects of international change on the people of Panama. These works have gone beyond the narrower topical scope of earlier analyses that revolved exclusively around the canal. They have also transcended the narrower chronological confines of the institutionalists to depict a nineteenth century Isthmian society weakened by external economic factors and increasingly vulnerable to what Figueroa Navarro dubbed "Americanization." This scholarship has pointed to the increasingly visible role of Colombian and North American troops in late nineteenth century Panama as evidence for what they have regarded as the degeneration of Isthmian sovereignty. For example in a recent work, Andrew Zimbalist and John Weeks commented that "if anything, the control of Panama's elite over the political system grew weaker" following Panama's independence from Colombia in 1903.[3]

By emphasizing "Americanization," these studies imply that the expanding foreign presence in Panama in the nineteenth and early twentieth centuries signaled progressively less autonomy for Panama. Accordingly this decline in Isthmian autonomy opened the door to foreign imperialists. In taking this

approach, these authors overlook historical trends that have shaped Panamanian society for centuries. Throughout the nineteenth century (and, for
that matter, since the early sixteenth century), Panama's urban elite relied
on foreign troops to suppress political and social unrest. In 1903 the United
States replaced Colombia as the insurer of the elite's position in Isthmian
politics and society. The Progressive administrations of Theodore Roosevelt,
William Howard Taft, and Woodrow Wilson provided Panama's wealthy
with more military might than Bogotá or Spain had ever been capable of
offering. Rather than leading to an erosion of elite status and Isthmian sovereignty generally, independence from Colombia in 1903 reinforced the
pattern of social and political evolution on the isthmus that had begun during
the colonial period. Events since then, including Panama's recent authoritarian
regimes, have served to reinforce the pattern of government by force, a pattern
that has characterized Isthmian politics for more than 170 years.

Triggered in part by the 1968 revolt, these two trends in analyses of
contemporary Panama underscore the frequently problematic association
between Panama's governments and its peoples that lies at the core of Panama's
recent authoritarian regimes. Why have Panamanians become increasingly po-
liticized? How has the government responded to this marked increase in political activity among the masses? Why have rising levels of political activity among
the Panamanian people and the government's response to that activity translated into an authoritarian state?

The North American invasion in December of 1989 gave rise to yet another revisionist school, the third analytical shift to occur since the 1968
revolution. In the wake of the North American invasion, scholars began to
reevaluate the role of the military in Isthmian society. These most recent
analyses have sought to combine the social history approach of Figueroa
Navarro and his colleagues with the institutional approach of Pereira and
his counterparts—giving rise to the social institutionalist approach to recent
Panamanian history. In his 1990 article "Panama: Obstacles to Democracy
and Sovereignty," George Priestly challenged the institutionalist practice of
focusing on the police to the exclusion of the rest of the nation. Priestly
called for new studies of Panama's police that "analyze the interests and
roles of all relevant sociopolitical and economic forces in Panama."[4] In a
more recent article, "Explaining the Long-Term Maintenance of a Military
Regime: Panama before the U.S. Invasion," Steve Ropp singles out several
characteristics of Isthmian society that help "explain the Panamanian
military's ability to sustain itself far beyond its anticipated life expectancy."
The Priestly article identifies the historiographical problem: narrow analyses that focus on one component of Panamanian society to the exclusion of
all others. The Ropp article provides a much-needed new approach to Pana-

manian scholarship, one that incorporates what Priestly earlier referred to as "relevant sociopolitical and economic forces."

These two articles provide more recent examples of the revision in Panamanian historiography that began in the sixties and continues today. Going beyond what earlier scholarship had denounced as "geographic determinism," Priestly and Ropp provide a healthy reexamination of Panamanian society while framing the police within the broader sociological context of a sovereign republic. Both authors challenge scholars to take an alternative approach to Panamanian history, one that couples social history with institutional analyses.

This is where the present study fits into the ongoing analysis of contemporary Panama. The social analyses of Figueroa and his colleagues focused largely on the nineteenth and early twentieth centuries, concluding sometime around independence and painstakingly avoiding narrower institutionalist topics. In the meantime, while the institutionalists endeavored to place the military in historical perspective, most began their studies at or near independence, in 1903 (in *Panamá: Fuerzas armadas y política*, for example, Renato Pereira begins his analysis of the police in a section titled "Período de la policía colonial, 1904–1931"). I will connect the social history literature with the institutional literature, using a combination of methodologies and entirely new primary source materials to situate the military more fully within the broader context of a sovereign, independent republic.

Acknowledgments

I BEGIN BY THANKING MY WIFE, SHAUNA HOLT PEARCY. AS I PREPARED THIS manuscript we traveled the length and breadth of Panama, from Cuna burial grounds deep in the Darien rain forest to the highlands of Boquete, in the process gaining a mutual appreciation for Panama and its peoples. Together we have tried to inculcate in our three children a deep reverence for other peoples and lands. With much love, appreciation, and admiration I dedicate this book to her. I also wish to thank my three children, Morgan, Trevor, and Ethan. They helped make this book possible by continually reminding me what really matters. Ani peh mar sabe buki dara.

Many scholars contributed significantly to this work as it evolved from a doctoral dissertation to conference papers, published articles, and a book. Oakah Jones, Robert Jackson, Steve Stein, Robert Levine, Bill Smith, Michael Krenn, Thomas Cowger, Frederick Nunn, Steve Ropp, Mike Conniff, Mark Grandstaff, Kendall Brown, Sharon Phillipps Collazos, Enilsa E. de Cedeño, Fermina Santana, Fernando Aparicio, Pantaleón García, Alfredo Castillero Calvo, Alfredo Figueroa Navarro, David Acosta, and Ambassadors Ambler Moss and Jack Vaughn each gave valuable criticisms and recommendations at key stages of my research and writing. Though I bear sole responsibility for any factual or interpretive errors contained herein, I sincerely appreciate the encouragement and collegiality I received from each of these colleagues.

Beyond family and colleagues, numerous other friends in Panama contributed to and facilitated the successful completion of this project. The staffs of the Archivos Nacionales, Archivo de Relaciones Exteriores, Archivo de la Presidencia, Contraloría General de la República, and the Biblioteca Nacional gave selflessly of their time and resources. Similarly, I owe a heartfelt *abrazo* to my colleagues and to their students at the Universidad de Panamá's central campus in Panama City and its regional campuses in Coclé and Santiago, in addition to the faculty and students of the Universidad Autónoma de Chiriquí. My interaction with these people enabled me to see the human costs of militarism in Panama. Por eso les agradezco sinceramente. Also in Panama I wish to thank Amy Margaret Bliss, United States Cultural

Affairs Officer in Panama, whose generosity and professionalism made my experience as a Fulbright Scholar in Panama wonderful and rewarding.

In the United States numerous people also helped me at various stages of this project. The excellent staffs of the National Archives and the Library of Congress in Washington, DC, particularly Mr. Ed Reece of the Military Records Department, made relatively quick work of a project that may have dragged along endlessly with the guidance of less experienced or less knowledgeable archivists. Moreover, Joseph Dane Hartgrove of the archives' Civil Reference Branch painstakingly provided me with dozens of corrected citations in accordance with the archives' own research guidelines.

Many other friends and organizations contributed significantly to the completion of this book. In the history department at the University of Miami, Lenny del Granado, Ada Orlando, and Jesús R. Sánchez-Reyes supported me and gave me encouragement to complete my graduate training. At Brigham Young University, Mariel Budd and her successor, Julie Radle, helped me meet deadlines and keep on track with editing, revisions, and other fine tuning. I also wish to thank the Theodore Parker Pre-Dissertation Committee and the Fulbright Scholarship Committee for their financial support. The generosity of these two granting agencies facilitated a number of research trips to Washington and Panama.

Finally, I conclude by acknowledging with great respect and *cariño* my students and my colleagues at the Universidad de Panamá's central campus in Panama City. Watching as a visiting professor while the National Police teargassed and shot at you reminded me painfully of how little separates dictatorship and representative government in Panama—and how fragile human rights are there. As we learned in the United States with Kent State, elected officials have no right to turn a nation's soldiers on its own people. My thoughts and those of my family will be with you in the coming months and years as you continue to make your voice heard. ¡Ni un paso atrás!

Introduction

In July of 1981 General Omar Torrijos died when his airplane crashed into the rugged Panamanian countryside. This tragic event closed a remarkable epoch in Panama's history. Following the successful revolution that carried him to power in 1968, Torrijos almost single-handedly altered Panama's power structure, while recasting the nation's future at home and abroad. In 1972 his government enacted a dramatic new constitution and new labor legislation that included sweeping labor and housing reforms aimed, among other things, at improving the circumstances of the nation's poor. Then in 1978, Torrijos achieved his greatest success with the Torrijos-Carter Treaties, historic pacts that established Panama's control of the Panama Canal, effective December 31, 1999.[1]

General Torrijos's success as a leader stemmed from his function as the dynamic and widely popular commander of Panama's powerful National Guard.[2] Torrijos had a magnetic personality like few other public figures in American history. He mesmerized audiences with his strident patriotism. His refreshing appeal to the common folk and his willingness to confront without hesitation the United States earned him widespread accolades, and his circle of friends consisted of some of the world's prominent scholars and leaders, including Mario Vargas Llosa, Gabriel García Márquez, Felipe González, Carlos Andrés Pérez, Daniel Oduber, Julio Cortázar, and Graham Greene.[3]

Nevertheless, contrary to what scholars and others (including those who knew him best) have written about this magnetic statesman since his death, neither Torrijos nor his successor, Manuel Noriega, made the police Panama's dominant political force.[4] Rather, Torrijos and his colleagues capitalized on an extant military infrastructure whose formation over the decades prior to 1968 reflected profound changes that had taken place in society. Despite the flood of attention they have received since the 1989 invasion, including the blitzkrieg of narratives inevitably generated by a tragedy like Just Cause, Torrijos and Noriega are simply the most visible recent manifestations of circumstances that have existed in Panama for decades.[5] Recognized in this light, Panama's recent military governments are not historical aberrations; rather, they both embody and epitomize the dynamic convergence of social, economic, and political forces that has occurred in Panama since independence.

When and how, then, did the military begin dominating Panama's government? I will argue here that this occurred with the Filós-Hines Treaty debacle of December 1947. Prior to that time, Panama's military had intervened in the nation's political affairs on behalf of the governing elite. Then in December of 1947, Panama's police became a dominant arbitrating force in the nation's affairs, when a series of events propelled it into the center of the political realm.[6] How did this happen? In his award-winning discussion of militaries in Latin America, Professor Mario Esteban Carranza notes that when a country's civilian rule becomes jeopardized, a "state of exception" results, wherein a "crisis in hegemony" forces the police to play a more prominent role in civilian affairs, in order to help resolve the crisis and to restore the regime's dominance and authority. While Carranza's discussion fails to delineate clearly the domestic forces that underlie the phenomenon he addresses, his hypothesis correctly identifies the proclivity of Panama's police during times of crisis to intervene in civilian matters.[7]

Using Carranza's analysis as his theoretical point of departure in explaining Panama's recent bout with military regimes, political scientist George Priestly has argued that Panama experienced its definitive "crisis in hegemony" in the 1960s, a critical juncture that spawned the 1968 putsch and elevated Panama's police in the nation's power structure.[8] This recent academic attention to the Torrijos and Noriega regimes correctly underscores the transition of the police from moderator of political affairs to a governing body—a transition completed by the October 1968 putsch. However, my own research challenges the tendency to portray Panama's military-dominated governments either as essentially post-1968 phenomena or as circumstances rooted in events beyond Panama's control. Instead, since its earliest formative years, Panama's population and economy have grown and diversified, sometimes with startling rapidity. The establishment by the United States of the canal enclave during the period 1904–14 gave rise to numerous labor associations and civic action groups that organized to protect and improve the working and living conditions of the nation's workers, particularly those affiliated with the waterway. Then in the twenties and thirties, financial difficulties, caused first by the end of World War I and then by the Depression, precipitated the establishment of various new political parties and civic action groups that gave voice to Panama's expanding middle class. Finally, when he founded the National University in October of 1935, President Harmodio Arias provided the ideological bases for the powerful nationalist crusade that would come to dominate much of intellectual and political life on the isthmus.

These events magnified and exacerbated deep-rooted fissures in Isthmian society reminiscent of those divisions described by political scientist Samuel Huntington in his discussion of praetorianism. Beginning in the 1950s, at the onset of the Cold War, with his seminal work *The Soldier and the State*, Huntington and others began to study civil-military relations in developing nations. Of such countries Huntington noted, "politics [there] lacks autonomy, complexity, coherence, and adaptability. All sorts of social forces become engaged directly in general politics."[9] According to Huntington and others, this lack of cohesion in political and governmental concerns translated in practical terms into political chaos similar to that of ancient Rome during its long decline, when political discord prompted "a progressive assumption of political power by the soldiery."[10]

This accurately describes twentieth-century Panama. Distrust of foreigners on the one hand and the desire to capitalize on the potential of the isthmus as an emporium of world commerce on the other divided Panamanians along economic, social, and political lines throughout the period from 1903 to the 1940s. Frequently these divisions produced confrontations among a growing cadre of competing, frequently armed elements whose diametrically opposed agendas left Panama's political and social groups "fragmented and incapable of unified political action other than resistance, violence, defiance, and terrorism."[11]

Under the best of circumstances, these clashes tended to undermine the government's ability to manage the nation's affairs. In reality, as the Republic of Panama took shape, its government repeatedly demonstrated an acute inability to manage the nation's affairs—an inability that frequently reached crisis proportions reminiscent of Carranza's "states of exception" when Panama's police have stepped forward to moderate a crisis and to restore relative calm. Gradually this repeated crisis intervention by Panama's police provoked a subtle shift in the nation's balance of power. Formally Panama's constitution charged the president, the legislature, and the courts with governing the republic. Informally, however, circumstances in Panama throughout the period from 1903 to the midforties gave the police increasing power to mediate politics and to act unilaterally within the realm of civilian affairs.[12] As described by political scientist Amos Perlmutter in his discussion of military regimes that moderate versus those that rule, Panama's police was by the conclusion of World War II rapidly approaching the point at which it could unilaterally moderate the nation's political affairs.[13] Commenting on the advent of military regimes in modern developing nations, Perlmutter has noted that "an army becomes praetorian when a small group of officers, a few key activists, succeed in propelling the military into politics."[14] By the time World War II ended, all that remained to complete

Panama's transition from civilian rule to a system of praetorian governance based largely on police moderation was a state of exception of sufficient magnitude to trigger a true crisis in civilian hegemony, thereby "propelling the military into politics."

This watershed occurred in December of 1947. At that time, officials from Panama and the United States renegotiated their 1942 military base accord, a pact that had given North Americans permission to occupy dozens of bases outside the Canal Zone in order to defend the canal. By renegotiating the 1942 treaty, the regime of President Enrique Jiménez blatantly disregarded overwhelming popular opposition to extending the expanded American military presence on the isthmus. This remarkably cavalier disregard of popular sentiment by a Panamanian president provided the motivation for a massive, surprisingly cohesive opposition front that transcended race and class lines, reaching deep into the nation's interior provinces. The clash between this substantial opposition front and the Jiménez regime caused a decisive showdown (Carranza's "state of exception").

Ultimately this confrontation developed into a pivotal confrontation, when Panama's legislators, under enormous popular pressure, rejected Washington's petition to extend the 1942 Defense Site Agreement between the two nations. Unlike previous "states of exception," the police in this instance actually failed to quell opposition to the 1947 accord. An unprecedented nationalist front forced Panama's legislators to reject it, producing a veritable crisis in civilian hegemony.

At first glance the outcome of the Filós-Hines debate appears to have been a stunning, overwhelming victory for Panamanians who opposed the treaty and rallied against it. Yet closer examination refutes this initial conclusion. Significantly, in the weeks following the resolution of the debate, the opposition front dissipated to the point of extinction. Much like the women's movement in the United States following the passage of the 19th Amendment (1920), the largest political front in Panama's history fragmented into myriad civic and political interest groups once they no longer had a common cause to bind them together. Despite the ephemeral unity generated by the widespread perception of a common foe, Panama remained primarily a state where praetorian guards with competing agendas dictated the nation's domestic agenda. Moreover after enduring severe internal dissension and even the resignation of a key cabinet member during the base agreement debacle, the Jiménez administration emerged from the fray too divided to govern effectively.

A historic turning point ensued in the nation's balance of power, as civilian rule yielded to military dominance. During two weeks of heated clashes that involved Panama's government, its police, and a massive opposition front, the young republic completed its transition from formal rule to informal control by a praetorian guard with an autocrat at its head. Of those sides involved in the debate, only the police emerged sufficiently intact to arbitrate unilaterally the affairs of the nation.

The extent of the fissures fragmenting both the Jiménez government and the surprisingly ephemeral opposition front became apparent in the months following the confrontation. First the police completely dominated the 1948 presidential campaign and election. When activist candidate Arnulfo Arias won, First Commander Remón intervened, destroying thousands of ballots and causing enough chaos to skew the electoral process. Remón then appointed Arias's aged opponent, Domingo Díaz, president of the republic.[15]

In 1948 another incident further accentuated recent changes in the nation's balance of power: the two governments began negotiating an unpopular treaty regarding commercial air traffic in Panama. The accord, first introduced in 1946, called for a joint commission of Panamanians and Americans to oversee the management of Panama's new airport at Tocumen. This commission would govern the handling of baggage, traffic control, customs, mail, and sanitation. Final say in the commission's decisions rested with its North American members, who would dominate the governing board. As historian John Major has noted, this was one more way for Washington to keep "Panama on its traditional leash" in times of peace.[16]

Negotiations for the aviation accord eventually fueled the first violent confrontation between the police and activists since the Filós-Hines impasse. When an opposition front began clamoring against the aviation agreement, the police enacted a three-month state of siege and brutally suppressed the opposition, killing two individuals and injuring dozens in the process. Power in Panama now clearly rested with the police, a fact made manifest through flagrant electoral manipulation and equally conspicuous political repression.[17]

Beginning with the 1948 presidential election, events in the months and years following the base agreement episode repeatedly accentuated the police's dominant role in Panamanian politics. From 1949 to 1952, the police seated and then unseated five different presidents. In one particularly heated, divisive, and telling week in November 1949, First Commander Remón placed three different men in the presidency in a five-day span, with no regard for the unconstitutionality of his actions. While Panamanian law placed formal control of the nation in the hands of its elected officials, Remón now informally dictated government policies; the convergence of forces provoked by the base negotiations had completed Panama's decades-long transition from formal governance to informal rule and occasional informal tyranny.

Regarding the current state of civil-military relations around the globe, one political scientist recently posed the disquieting question, "are we doomed to be united only in war?" Of recent Panamanian history one might well ask, "are Panamanians doomed to be united only in their disdain for the United States?"[18] By the onset of World War II, Panamanians had failed to achieve unified political action and governance beyond intermittent isolated cases of resistance, violence, defiance, and terrorism—activities usually aimed at undermining complicity between wealthy Panamanians and their associates in the United States. Response to these circumstances in the late 1940s elevated the National Police to the position of national arbiter and initiated Panama's decades-long involvement with the sort of praetorian rule described by Huntington in lieu of a common thread that might have united disparate sectors of Isthmian society in a cohesive administrative bloc.[19]

This study accepts Huntington's premise that badly fragmented societies have difficulty governing themselves. The disequilibrium triggered by war, the canal project, and the Depression precipitated political and economic circumstances under which Panamanians frequently took up arms to fight other Panamanians. These skirmishes accentuated fissures that had characterized Panama since well before 1903. Consequently, relying largely on available literature to construct this first portion of my study, this book begins with a brief narrative discussion of Panama's decisive eighty-two-year annexation to Colombia (1821–1903). Since Europeans first arrived there, early in the sixteenth century, successful government in Panama had hinged on the intervention of Spanish troops to stifle threats to the colonial status quo. After 1821 two large waves of West Indian immigrants, drawn to Panama by the railroad and canal projects, upset the delicate nineteenth century ethnic and social milieu of the isthmus. Moreover wealthy merchants in Panama City sent their children to schools in Europe, and when these children returned, they brought with them the liberal ideas of the Enlightenment. These returning youths subsequently provided the tiny nucleus for a disproportionately influential nationalist crusade based on the ideals of nineteenth century European liberalism.

Continuing the Spanish tradition of rule by force, the Colombian government relied on its army to perpetuate its control of the isthmus, despite the challenges posed by significant demographic and social changes occurring there after 1821. Colombia's deployment of troops in this fashion underscored its selective application of European liberalism: Colombians implemented ideas that benefited them and discarded those that did not. Whereas liberal European institutions such as the Masons largely objected to rule by military abuse, "enlightened" Colombians disregarded this principle of liberalism and used their troops to control Panama.[20] The ingredients of Panama's later praetorianism and widespread political militarism—labor unrest, nascent nationalism, and government by troop deployment—actually flourished in nineteenth century

Panama. During the late nineteenth and early twentieth centuries, circumstances in Panama caused the convergence of these factors, giving rise to military government there in the late 1940s, not just in or after 1968.

Chapter 2 examines Panama's independence from Colombia and its subsequent emergence and development as a republic. This chapter focuses specifically on the competing agendas that emerged from the preindependence period to give shape and substance to the nascent republic. Unable to perpetuate itself through constitutionally appointed electoral means (formal power), Panama's urban elite, consisting primarily of wealthy merchants and landowners, had to find another way to secure their hold on "the capacity to control the behavior of other people."[21]

Relying largely on primary sources, chapter 2 demonstrates that the construction of the canal caused massive demographic and social upheaval, drawing rigorous protests from Panama's expanding urban working class and members of its dynamic middle class, many of whom emphatically opposed the expanding North American presence caused by the canal project. Coupled with the other demands of governance, these canal-related difficulties impelled Panama's first presidents to rely heavily on the National Police. Particularly helpful at election time, the police served to intimidate opponents at balloting sites and to sway election results by threatening voters, destroying ballots, and casting multiple votes. In this way Panama's first presidents artificially skewed the new republic's balance of power in their favor, commonly (and illegally) using the police to generate the veneer of popular support. This worked until an expanding, increasingly organized labor force, a more competent middle class, and an increasingly autonomous, powerful police rendered obsolete this old-style politicking, a fact manifested glaringly in the early morning hours of January 2, 1931, when middle-class activists overthrew the government and initiated a decade of nationalist rule.

Chapter 3 focuses on the ten-year reign of Panama's revolutionary "Generation of '31." Analyses of Panama during the thirties tend to focus on the antielite platform of these revolutionaries.[22] Yet this literature ignores the fact that governments in the thirties elevated the police to its role as political moderator on the isthmus—a short step from the politically dominant role it would ascend to in October 1968. A January 1931 coup had overthrown the elite administration of Florencio H. Arosemena. The successful insurgents promised relief for the nation's farmers, new jobs and higher pay for the country's laborers, and increased autonomy from the United States. Yet fluctuations in the standard of living among the nation's poor, identified and described here using deviations in demographic, economic, and legitimacy data, underscore the fact that nationalist presidents in the thirties failed in their efforts to alleviate the effects of the Depression. To make matters worse, they continued to practice the political favoritism they had promised to abolish when they ousted Arosemena.

Faced with chronic economic and social difficulties caused largely by the Depression, from 1931 to 1941 Panama's leaders instituted a series of measures aimed at making the nation's police force a more formidable obstacle to would-be opponents. To begin with they built new police facilities and furnished police officers with commissaries to provide them with necessities at a reduced cost; this proved to be particularly popular among police personnel and their families during the Depression. Second, Panama's presidents also began to place large groups of their own armed supporters within the ranks of the police, to neutralize any dissension within the police force. Finally, in 1935 President Harmodio Arias established the National University in Panama City, to "preserve Panamanian nationality" as part of the patriotic reclamation process. As Jorge Conte-Porras notes in his insightful book on Panama's students, *La rebelión de las esfinges*, university officials encouraged students to maintain a state of "constant rebelliousness" in opposition to United States imperialism.[23] With its graduates teaching at rural schools and with student and teacher groups organizing throughout the republic, the National University had become by the late 1930s the patriotic heart and soul of nationalist activity in Panama.

Beyond promoting an esprit de corps among police officers and an attitude of "constant rebelliousness" among Panamanian students, technological advances of this period, particularly in armaments, increased the police's institutional autonomy and made it an increasingly difficult organization for civilian administrations to control. New and better weapons, combined with new police facilities in Panama City and elsewhere in the republic, made the police an increasingly daunting component of the federal bureaucracy. Moreover while these efforts during the Depression to modernize Panama's police greatly enhanced its capacity to function in a military manner, these steps also developed the officer corps professionally and engendered a profound sense of camaraderie among its officers, producing in them what one scholar has rather dryly dubbed an "acute awareness among the officers of their messianic vocation."[24] During dire crises, Panama's police could now step in and save the republic from opportunists and would-be antagonists.

These changes backfired, however, in October 1941. At that time a "state of exception" occurred, when ardently nationalist president Arnulfo Arias enacted a series of totalitarian-style reforms that alienated many people, including several influential police officers. Under these circumstances, the police stepped in and overthrew Arias, ending the ten-year reign of the nationalist Generation of '31 and reversing the results of the 1931 uprising. However, at that time no crisis in civilian hegemony existed, at least formally, and the police consequently returned control of the nation's government to the urban elite.

Chapter 4 relies on government documents from the United States and Panama to chart a complex series of political changes that consolidated the police's ability to moderate informally the affairs of the Panamanian government, nearly completing a change in the balance of power that had been developing over several decades. The October 1941 police coup, Panama's first, had ended the ten-year reign of the nationalist Generation of '31. With the support of the United States, the police then appointed two consecutive interim presidents, Ricardo Adolfo de la Guardia and Enrique A. Jiménez, to govern the nation during the remainder of the World War II. These appointments triggered six years of violent political confrontations involving the pro-American elite, the police, and thousands of Panamanians who opposed the elite and its blatant complicity with the United States.

By appointing interim regimes, the temporary police-elite coalition circumvented the opposition's ability to check electorally the political hegemony of the status quo. In doing so, the dubious coalition further alienated nationalists and workers, providing an adhesive of sorts as disparate groups began banding together to oppose a common foe—the police-appointed interim regimes of de la Guardia and Jiménez. Further complicating these volatile circumstances, both de la Guardia and Jiménez lacked tenable bases of popular support with which to counter spiraling opposition to their administrations. Moreover having been appointed rather than elected, neither man commanded any substantive influence with the nation's electoral boards.

Unable to generate any pretense of an electoral mandate, and faced with an opposition front that was slowly increasing in size, sophistication, and intensity, de la Guardia and Jiménez lacked even the façade of popular support that had sustained several of their predecessors. In fact both presidents' notorious lack of popularity significantly increased opposition to government policies. More than any of Panama's earlier presidents (and much like Panama's latest American-appointed interim president, Guillermo Endara), de la Guardia and Jiménez were socially and politically isolated from much of the rest of the nation. Likewise more than any of their predecessors, these two interim presidents needed the police to sustain their highly vulnerable administrations.

As might be expected, modernization of the police proceeded at a feverish pitch from 1941 to 1947, as de la Guardia and Jiménez scrambled to bolster their administrations. Both presidents cooperated fully with Washington in an effort to augment wartime security of the canal. The United States government responded by increasing military assistance to the Panamanian government. These factors made the police an increasingly viable

instrument of political control. They also contributed to the institutional autonomy of the police, solidifying the esprit de corps among its officers and
corroborating their shared sense of their "messianic" role in Panamanian society—a perception intensified by the evolving conflict over the base treaty.[25]

Chapter 5 also utilizes government records in Panama City and Washington to examine the culmination of the rise to political preeminence of the
National Police. At stake during the Filós-Hines negotiations in December
1947 was whether a Panamanian president could blatantly legislate against
the will of the people. Scholars have dismissed the National Assembly's rejection of the Filós-Hines Treaty as either an economic blunder or a short-
lived nationalist victory. However, I contend that the treaty and its rejection
caused a historic convergence of forces that had combined to change Panama
socially, economically, and politically since 1903 and before: between 1903
and 1931, presidents had coupled their political longevity with police intimidation to control Panama's rapidly changing populace. Then between
1931 and 1941, nationalist presidents responded to a surprisingly diverse,
resilient opposition by restructuring the police and making that institution a
quasi-military extension of the executive branch of government. Expanding
on a practice that emerged between 1903 and 1931, nationalist presidents
in the 1930s elevated the use of police intimidation for partisan purposes to an
executive ritual. Finally, by appointing and backing two consecutive interim
presidents in the forties, the National Police and their associates disenfranchised
those Panamanians who objected to the Jiménez administration and its policies,
setting the government and its opponents on a decisive collision course that
would determine Panama's balance of power for the next half century.

The increasing politicization of women, workers, and high school students in the twenties, thirties, and forties formed the basis of a rapidly expanding movement that opposed both elite government and North American
imperialism. Moreover the establishment of the National University in the
thirties provided an intellectual and organizational nucleus to the growing
protest. While Panama's legislature debated ratification of the Filós-Hines
agreement (December 10 to December 22), widespread violence erupted in
the capital city. Recently formed high school student organizations served
as conduits to transmit the protest deep into the Panamanian countryside.

On December 12, 1947, dissension between the government and its opponents reached its apogee when President Jiménez unleashed a startling
display of police brutality in an attempt to forcibly quell opposition to the
treaty. The president's one-time use of force backfired miserably. Shocked
by the government's disregard for public sentiment, thousands more Panamanians joined the opposition front. Although Jiménez did not deploy the
police again, his use of violence united Panamanians from disparate back-

grounds and interests, many of whom had not previously associated with the antibase movement. Now protestors in cities throughout the republic used strikes and walkouts to bring the nation to a standstill.

With this flare-up in activist activity, disagreement over the base accord had evolved from a nationalistic campaign against North American imperialism into a decisive struggle between the people of Panama and their government. Although overlooked by scholars, circumstances surrounding the rejection of the Filós-Hines Treaty redefined the role of the police in Panamanian society. First Commander Remón's own election to the presidency in 1952 reaffirmed the police's stronghold on the nation's political system. It also cemented its political hegemony, a legacy which General Torrijos capitalized on sixteen years later.

One observation should be made regarding the focus of the present study. Unquestionably the United States has had a significant effect on the development of the Panamanian republic, including its recent bout with authoritarian governments. Nevertheless Washington played at most an ancillary role in these affairs. Of primary concern here are the various domestic factors, in addition to the international ones, that converged in the late 1940s to result in Panama's recent military-dominated governments.

I must here adjoin a methodological caveat. While I have borrowed, sometimes extensively, from the literature in relevant fields, my analysis is intentionally brief and consequently lacks depth in the areas of marginality, political power, and diplomacy, to name a few. Moreover, due largely to my own rather unorthodox approach to Panama's police, I have included few comparative comments tying Panama into the broader literature on militaries in Latin America. While there are many excellent studies on other countries in the region, their methodologies differ sufficiently from my own so as to render useless any attempt to draw comparative analogies, although there is a definite need for further analysis.

I

A Legacy of Conflicting Agendas, 1821–1903

PANAMA'S INDEPENDENCE AND SUBSEQUENT DEVELOPMENT AS A STATE revolved around several pivotal social and political characteristics that emerged during the tumultuous eighty-two-year annexation of the isthmus to Colombia: a politically dominant urban elite, rapidly expanding lower and middle classes, and a permanent foreign military presence. Throughout the nineteenth century, these factors frequently pitted elements of Panamanian society against each other and threatened elite hegemony with social unrest, racism, nationalism, and later, anti-Americanism. The result was a fragile status quo, whose perpetuation relied on the intervention of foreign troops to stifle opponents of the urban elite.[1]

Thus well before Panama's independence from Colombia in 1903, a pattern of government had emerged. This style of leadership revolved around the principle of armed perpetuation of privilege, contingent on foreign military intervention. While much of the literature in both Panama and the United States portrays military-dominated governments in Panama as historical aberrations, Panama's twentieth century police-dominated regimes are only the most recent manifestations of an intricate series of social and political phenomena that have their roots in the nineteenth century.

In this chapter, I briefly analyze several characteristics of nineteenth century Panama, which considered collectively, provided the basis for Panama's twentieth century dictatorships. This allows the establishment of a conceptual framework within which to analyze the origins and context of armed force—or threat of it—in twentieth century Panamanian politics. Labor unrest, a changing middle class, and governments that bullied their constituents—each of these existed in nineteenth century Panama, and following independence, circumstances forced the gradual convergence of these forces. This in turn precipitated the advent of military governments, as officials sought to contain worker unrest and middle-class agitation. Considered in this light, Panama's recent autocratic governments are not recent or incomprehensible; rather, their roots are deep in Panama's rich national history.

Changing Masters: From Spanish Colony to Colombian Vassal

In November of 1821, thirty-one of Panama's leading landowners and merchants convened in Panama City and declared Panama's independence from Spain. They then annexed the isthmus to Simón Bolívar's Gran Colombia. This new union, born out of Panama's inability to defend itself militarily, reflected the mutual interests of wealthy merchants in Panama City and government officials in Bogotá, both of whom intended to capitalize on the Spanish withdrawal to profit from the transport and freightage of commerce across Panama's narrow waist.[2]

The new government immediately began to promote the interests of Panama's wealthy merchant elite. It enacted a commercial regulation that allowed merchants in Panama City and Portobelo (Colón) to trade freely with friendly nations. The same edict established laws for handling cargo crossing the isthmus and for controlling contraband.[3] While its alliance with administrators in Bogotá benefited Panama's small merchant elite, the coalition set the new government in Bogotá at odds with much of Panama and the remainder of Colombia's restive Caribbean coast. In those areas Black majorities favored states' rights, racial equality, and laissez-faire economics and therefore objected to the powerful centralized Creole government in Bogotá. The fact that Panama's population was predominantly Black framed this centralist-federalist debate in racial terms on the isthmus.[4]

To further complicate Panama's delicate social and racial balance, two massive waves of immigrant laborers arrived during the nineteenth century to work on the railroad and canal projects. These demographic shifts greatly increased the number of Black urban workers, expanding Panama City's shantytowns (known as the *arrabal*) and worsening living conditions there. Moreover by enlarging Panama's population of nonelite, non-Creole residents, they also increased the number of Panamanians who opposed Colombian centralism and therefore aggravated the centralist-federalist struggle, further jeopardizing Panama's status quo. The evolving conflict between nineteenth century Panama's small Colombian-backed urban elite and the remainder of its population resulted in a pattern of government that endured throughout the nineteenth century and eventually figured prominently in the formation of an independent Panamanian republic. Confronted by federalism, nationalism, anti-Americanism (following the railroad project), and racial divisions that favored Panama's expanding urban masses, administrators relied on electoral fraud and foreign troops to extinguish political opposition and to suppress social unrest. Thus well before it emerged from the independence process in 1903, Panama had a government that depended on the intervention of foreign troops for its political longevity.[5]

Colombia's conservative-liberal struggle reached its apex with the Thousand Days' War (1899–1902); and Panama's urban elite, now at odds with their former allies in Bogotá, capitalized on the confusion by declaring Panama's independence in 1903.[6] The urban masses and the nationalist bloc of its middle class—those urban merchants opposed to foreign intervention altogether—had unsuccessfully attempted independence on several previous occasions, including 1830, 1831, 1840, and 1861.[7] While their independence attempts were thwarted, these groups did achieve a degree of autonomy for Panama as a federal state in the United States of Colombia by the mid-1850s. How did the 1903 attempt differ from previous efforts? Why did it succeed where the others had failed? Given the particularly belligerent nature of Colombia's Conservative Regeneration (1885–95), what had changed during the nineteenth century to facilitate Isthmian independence, despite more rigorous opposition from Bogotá? Most important, how did those changes contribute to the formation of the nascent Panamanian republic?

In their recent study of Panamanian politics, political scientist Andrew Zimbalist and economist John Weeks argue that Panama's urban elite lost power toward the end of the nineteenth century, thus clearing the way for United States imperialism and triggering decades of North American intervention. This argument accurately depicts the enormous influence of the canal, yet despite its political appeal, it essentially removes the Panamanian element from that nation's history. Long before, the events that culminated in Panama's independence altered the character of the urban elite and actually strengthened its hold on power. In return for the complicity of a few wealthy Panamanian merchants in connection with the canal, the United States set about helping those merchants establish an administrative infrastructure that would enable them to preserve their social and economic status; this system has endured in one form or another throughout the twentieth century.[8]

Three nineteenth century events contributed to the formation of an independent Panamanian republic in 1903: the consolidation and perpetuation of elite privilege, the emergence of anti-Americanism as a political currency, and the replacement of Colombia by the United States as Panama's principal foreign patron. These events helped translate nineteenth century elite privilege into twentieth century political power, framed social mobility in racial terms, and established a pattern of government that depended increasingly on the forcible subjugation of political opponents.

A brief summary of some major events of the nineteenth century illuminates this evolution. First, Panama's independence from Spain benefited its small, prosperous merchant class at the expense of its Black and Mestizo majorities. This injustice triggered the emergence and political expression of a popular class consciousness and led to the racial and social fissures that dominated nineteenth century Panama's political landscape.

Second, in 1846 Colombia and the United States signed the Mallarino-Bidlack Treaty, a pact that gave Washington license to intervene unilaterally in Panama to guarantee the uninterrupted flow of transisthmian commerce. This agreement granted the United States considerable leverage in Panama's economic affairs and formed the basis of an alliance between officials in Washington and elite merchants in Panama City. The United States thus began to supplant Colombia as the principal arbiter in Panamanian affairs, and Panamanian nationalist animosity toward foreign intervention began shifting from Bogotá to Washington.

Finally, the decline of Colombian conservatism in the 1840s ushered in three decades of federalist liberalism that stressed states' rights and laissez-faire economics—critical issues to merchants in Panama City, whose fortunes depended on the unfettered transportation of commerce across the narrow isthmus. However, when the Colombian economy collapsed in the late 1870s and early 1880s, a conservative crusade known as the Regeneration (1885–95) ended the nation's thirty-year experiment with liberalism, reversed its federalist policies, and sought to extinguish forcefully the nation's liberal movement. This radical conservatism alienated many former proponents of a strong central government and set the stage for the Thousand Days' War and Panama's independence from Colombia.

Modern Panama's Governing Elite

Toward the end of the eighteenth century, the Spanish and Portuguese monarchies enacted sweeping administrative realignments aimed at streamlining colonial bureaucracy. Besides loosening trade restrictions, these changes, known respectively as the Bourbon and Pombaline reforms, reserved the highest colonial administrative posts for *peninsulares* and *reinóis*—those persons born in Spain and Portugal. Thus when the colonies achieved independence, only Brazil, which had hosted the Portuguese royal family when it fled from the Napoleonic invasion, escaped the dissolution of its government. Throughout Spanish America, the lack of experienced American-born personnel to staff the new governments provoked a power struggle, as the region's small Creole class (Whites born in America) rushed to capitalize on the vacuum created by the expulsion of Spanish officials.[9]

This dearth of upper-level government experience among most of Latin America's postindependence governors laid the foundations for narrowly based autocratic regimes that moved immediately to exclude most of their respective citizens from their countries' nascent political circles. Such was the case in Panama, where Creole officials considered the majority of the population—Blacks, mulattos, and Indians—inferior peoples incapable of governing themselves. Following independence, Bolívar and his appointees based suffrage on property requirements, thus perpetuating the colonial legacy of political proscription of non-Creoles, while cementing the status of the White minority. This frustrated Panama's large Black population, most of whom belonged to a movement known as the "Black Liberals," workers of Caribbean extraction who lived along Colombia's northeastern coast and who favored states' rights and racial equality.[10]

In the decades following independence, class and race problems manifested themselves in Panama's considerable civil strife, which regularly pitted Panama City's *intramuros* (Whites living within the city's walls) against the *extramuros* (the rest of Panama City's population, which was almost exclusively non-White).[11] These problems placed Panama squarely within Gran Colombia's postindependence conservative-liberal struggle, a debate with race and class overtones that revolved around the question of political enfranchisement. In 1826 for example, the liberal constitution of Bolivia set off an intense debate in Panama regarding slavery and political privilege based on race and class distinctions. The Bolivian charter abolished slavery and extended suffrage to all persons who could read and write, thus theoretically revoking economically based voting requirements. Although much of Bolivia's non-Spanish-speaking population remained politically disenfranchised by the 1826 pact, and the results were therefore more conjectural than real, the statute nevertheless triggered a chain reaction through Gran Colombia, including Panama, where workers equated their circumstances with those of their Bolivian peers and began to clamor for similar legislation.[12]

This controversy was the first sign of a popular class consciousness among lower-class Panamanians, an awareness that soon produced Panama's first mass political activities. In 1830 a mulatto, José Domingo Espinar, began a separatist movement among the poor in Panama City. Espinar, formerly Simón Bolívar's private secretary, used the political acumen he had acquired while serving under the Liberator to fashion Panama City's masses into a powerful, well-organized group with common goals. Espinar drew on his sizable popular backing to declare Panama's independence on September 26, 1830, and he actually achieved control of the government in Panama City for several months.

However, in addition to the growing suspicion of Espinar's ties to the centralist Bolívar regime in Gran Colombia (late 1820s), Panama City's White population feared a repeat of the Black uprising in Haiti. Conservative Governor José de Obaldía even accused Espinar of attempting to carry out a "caste war" against Panama's White population. Espinar scoffed at Obaldía's

charges, adding in response that the governor "must have recently undergone a profound organic alteration of the brain."[13]

The repression of Espinar's movement was not a simple matter. Unlike
elsewhere in Spanish America, where ownership of the means of production
afforded the elite direct control over the livelihood of the masses and therefore provided a coercive means of resisting demands for democratic reforms,
merchants in Panama City had no equivalent form of persuasion.[14] Consequently their influence over the city's masses derived from their ability to
draw on the armed support of those who controlled commerce across the
isthmus, in this case Colombia, to stifle political resistance. When faced
with the decision between intercession by Colombian troops and widespread
violence among the city's large Black population, Panama's wealthy favored
the former. Espinar's ephemeral tenure came to an abrupt end in 1831,
when troops under the direction of Colonel Juan Eligio Alzuru overthrew
his government. For the first time in the history of independent Panama,
foreign troops had intervened to salvage elite supremacy.[15]

Colonel Alzuru's defeat of Espinar and his followers closed the first of
what would be various chapters in the nineteenth century struggle between
the urban masses and wealthy merchants in Panama. While the victory solidified elite claims to power, it also constituted a triumph of sorts for Espinar
and his defeated masses. For the first time, *arrabaleros* (persons from Panama
City's lower-class neighborhoods, the arrabal) had organized their opposition to class-based government. The fact that so many persons acted in con-
cert for a common cause underscored the presence of a sense of collective
identity, an adhesive that would bind the community together during future
confrontations with what Espinar dubbed Panama City's "aristocratic party."[16]

Finally, while Espinar's ouster reversed much of the headway made by
lower-class Panamanians during the first decade of independence, shifting
political currents in Bogotá less than two decades later provided renewed
hope among arrabaleros. By the late 1840s, the gradual demise of Colombian
conservatism gave leaders of Panama City's masses enough political latitude to
organize once again, and the group's developing sense of collective identity,
combined with a universal male suffrage law passed in Bogotá in 1853 and the
influx of additional thousands of workers at midcentury, made the urban poor
an increasingly significant component in Panamanian politics.[17]

Anti-Americanism as a Viable Political Currency

Foreign intervention was another factor that played a decisive role in
Panama's nineteenth century development. The unfolding Industrial Revo-

lution had placed a premium on access to foreign markets and raw materials, and as the site of the shortest distance between the Atlantic and Pacific Oceans, Panama became the focus of considerable diplomatic attention. An agreement between Colombia and the United States in 1846 shifted effective control of commerce crossing the Panamanian Isthmus from Bogotá to Washington. Soon thereafter the construction of the Panama Railroad by North American financiers resulted in an influx of West Indian laborers to construct the passageway. Finally, a few decades later, the Frenchman Ferdinand de Lesseps began digging a canal across the isthmus, again introducing large numbers of Caribbean laborers into Panama's delicate social structure.[18]

The rapid growth of urban Panama triggered by these two construction projects worsened class, race, and political distinctions in Panama. At midcentury events surrounding the construction, completion, and use of the Panama Railroad also caused virulent anti-Americanism, as Panamanian hostility toward foreigners shifted from Colombia to the United States. As the United States assumed effective control of commerce crossing the Panamanian isthmus, the small merchant elite in Panama City now had to forge ties with Washington to solidify their position, in the face of deteriorating urban conditions caused by the large influx of foreign workers and the persistent challenge they posed to the region's narrow, class-based political system.

At least partially in response to the activities of Europe's Holy Alliance after 1815, United States President James Monroe issued the Monroe Doctrine on December 2, 1823. This dictum, intended to prevent further European offensives in the Americas, failed miserably. British, French, German, Spanish, and Italian incursions throughout the remainder of the nineteenth century underscored the impotency of nascent American hemispheric hegemony.[19]

For twenty-two years after Monroe issued his confrontational edict, the United States remained essentially uninvolved in the affairs of Latin America. Then in December of 1846, the United States and the Republic of New Granada (Colombia) signed the Mallarino-Bidlack Treaty. Through this pact, New Granada granted Washington license to intervene militarily and unilaterally in Panama, to assure the free and uninterrupted flow of commerce across the isthmus. This treaty, the result of Colombian fears regarding European aggression, provided the United States with the perfect opportunity to stake its claim to Isthmian affairs.[20]

In addition to triggering a stormy relationship between Panama and the United States that continues today, the Mallarino-Bidlack Treaty had a profound effect on the Creole patricians who controlled Isthmian politics. Many merchants began to see large returns on their investments when the railroad project commenced. As a consequence, they favored the expanded North American presence brought about by the 1846 accord, and an alliance formed

between officials in Washington, who wanted to establish United States hegemony over a possible canal route, and merchants in Panama, who prospered economically and politically from the expanded North American
presence. Between 1855 and 1903, Washington landed troops twelve times
in Panama to protect this merger of interests.[21]

However, some members of Panama's expanding middle class opposed
the spiraling North American presence at midcentury as a violation of Panamanian sovereignty. Particularly, those middle-class professionals most influenced by the spread of European liberalism opposed foreign intervention
of any type, including that which involved North Americans. Increased levels of commercial activity after the turn of the century and the spread of
European liberalism among Panama's intellectuals had gradually divided
Panama's expanding middle class into two principal subgroups: moderate
liberals (persons with economic ties to foreign business, who consequently
favored the expanding North American presence) and nationalists (those persons opposed to foreign intervention in Isthmian affairs, including Panamanian
intellectuals). Following completion of the Panama Railroad in 1855, this latter
derivative of the liberal bloc became synonymous with anti-Americanism.

The most visible member of this group was Justo Arosemena, an outspoken lawyer from Panama City whose familial renown (his father, Manuel
Arosemena, had been one of the leaders of the federalist movement following independence) and aggressive personality elevated him to prominence
among Panamanian nationalists. Like his famous father, Arosemena considered Panama a potential emporium of world commerce. He consequently
opposed Colombian economic and political jurisdiction in Panama. He felt
that officials in Bogotá siphoned off profits from transisthmian commerce
that rightfully belonged to merchants in Panama City. He called for an autonomous Panamanian government that could administer the legal and economic affairs of the isthmus and keep profits from Panama's transportation
and freightage industries in Panama City.[22]

When tens of thousands of North Americans descended on the isthmus at
midcentury, en route to California, Arosemena and his associates cast nationalist dislike for foreigners in anti-American terms. In light of the William Walker incident in Central America and the Watermelon Riot in Panama
City (discussed later in this chapter), Arosemena argued in a vitriolic 1856
article that only a "free, civil, pacific, and *federal*" Colombia could "stop the
Yankee conqueror" from occupying the whole of the Americas. Thus anti-
Americanism emerged as a political currency on the Panamanian Isthmus.[23]

The debate between Panama's politically and economically dominant merchant elite and the more nationalistic members of its expanding middle class at
midcentury caused a conflict in Panamanian politics that centered largely on the

expanding North American presence on the isthmus. Following the Mallarino-Bidlack Treaty, the United States replaced Spain and Colombia as the focus of growing nationalist efforts to rid the isthmus of empire-building foreigners. While the merchant elite successfully thwarted nationalist challenges to the status quo until 1931, politics in Panama have revolved around the large United States presence since the construction of the Panama Railroad.

The Elite's Increasing Economic and Military Dependency

Postindependence Panama had no equivalent of the landed oligarchies found elsewhere in Latin America, where landownership gave the wealthy control of peasants' livelihoods and, consequently, a mechanism with which to resist popular pressure for political reform. Instead, beyond the sums they earned exporting and reexporting South American goods through the first decades of independence, Panama's urban elite earned a meager existence by supplying housing and services to the occupying Colombian army, which in turn stifled opposition to elite hegemony.[24]

However, in the 1850s, Panama's upper class began to diversify the economy. Its members began assuming administrative positions with the railroad company while investing in rental properties and related service sector industries to capitalize on market expansion caused by the California gold rush. This diversification integrated more fully the interests of Panama's small merchant elite with North American business. It also made them more dependent on traffic generated by gold fever.[25]

Initially this diversification generated great wealth for the native financiers. Large waves of immigrant laborers and "forty-niners" caused rental prices to soar, giving landlords unprecedented returns on their investments. The promise of higher returns triggered a housing frenzy among the urban elite, who began purchasing properties in the arrabal for resale or rental. Moreover merchants all along the trade route prospered from the vastly expanded markets generated by the construction of the railroad and by the gold rush. This flurry of activity continued throughout the next decade and caused what one Panamanian scholar has labeled "a false sense of prosperity."[26]

Indeed the prosperity proved short-lived. When California's gold veins dried up, the number of persons crossing the isthmus slowed to a trickle. Panama's economy lapsed into a recession as the housing and service markets contracted, and returns on goods and services dropped in proportion to the diminishing demand triggered by the end of the gold rush. The speculative tertiary investment of the gold rush years made Panama more vulnerable than ever to fluctuations in world commercial activity, and as the country's economy collapsed during the 1860s, the sense of prosperity yielded to a sense of frustration, desperation, and anger.[27]

The boom-bust economic cycle triggered by the gold rush accentuated the elite's tenuous position within the broader social context. For their part, British and American financiers controlled Panama's freightage and storage industries at midcentury, and their investments revolved around world commerce generally, not just the gold rush. Consequently these two industries continued to flourish when the flow of prospectors tapered off. Panamanian capital, on the other hand, had been invested primarily in the housing and service industries, both of which depended heavily on the flow of forty-niners for sustained growth.

In addition to this economic dependency, the bust that followed the gold rush posed another serious threat to Panama's urban elite. Panama City's 1843 population of 4,897 had been augmented by the influx of 20,000 laborers to build the railroad.[28] With control of the nation's primary resource—the transportation and storage of commerce—in foreign hands, regulation of the rapidly expanding popular sector's livelihood also remained largely outside the elite's sphere of influence. Thus in lieu of a coercive labor system that might afford substantive control of the nation's masses, Panama's urban elite relied increasingly on Colombian troops (and American soldiers following the 1846 treaty) to suppress popular opposition to elite domination. The gold rush ultimately meant increasing economic and military dependency for Panama's small merchant elite.[29]

If Panama's midnineteenth century boom proved fleeting for the urban elite, its demise devastated the remainder of Panama's population. For the 20,000 Black laborers who immigrated to Panama and constructed the railroad, its completion meant unemployment or underemployment and hard times. Once it transversed the whole of the isthmus, the railroad shortened travel time for forty-niners, and in the process displaced hundreds of muleteers, oarsmen, and workers of many other professions who had earned their livings in the prerailroad transportation industry.

Despite hard times, many West Indians remained in Panama City following the completion of the railroad, simply because they lacked the funds to return to their Caribbean homes. Trapped by their circumstances, these workers perpetuated the crisis their arrival had triggered within the arrabal community. Not unlike contemporary Panama City's *barriadas brujas* ("bewitched shantytowns"), living conditions in these nineteenth century lower-class neighborhoods worsened with the influx of additional workers during the construction boom and remained at deplorable levels following the railroad's completion. Symbolically and literally, the wall surrounding Panama City's upper- and middle-class neighborhoods separated the city's large working class from the medical and food supplies and other amenities found within the city wall. Mortality rates soared within the arrabal, and living conditions among Panama's urban poor remained below acceptable levels throughout the remainder of the century (see appendix A).

To make matters worse for the city's poor, the tens of thousands of North Americans who crossed the isthmus on their way to California were racially intolerant of the area's large Black population. White North Americans kept to themselves or interacted only with White Panamanians during their transit, and Black hostility toward both groups understandably grew at an alarming rate. These tensions climaxed on April 15, 1856, when Jack Oliver, a North American, refused to pay for a piece of watermelon he took from Panamanian vendor José Manuel Luna. As the confrontation escalated into the now infamous Watermelon Riot, the United States landed one hundred and sixty troops to control the crisis, thus making clear its willingness to use military force in Panama. The Watermelon Riot also underscored the inability of White Panamanians to control the urban masses without the assistance of foreign soldiers; and for the first time, the troops came from North America instead of Colombia.[30]

Finally, in addition to adversely affecting Panamanians of diverse social position, completion of the railroad also served to intensify the animosity between Panama City and Bogotá. Railroad officials paid $250,000 per year to the Colombian government for the land and necessary rights to operate the railroad, but Bogotá sent only $25,000 of the money to Panama. This amount seemed entirely too little to many Panamanians. Much of Panama clamored for an end to this economic irritant, and anti-Bogotá campaigns resulted in dozens of insurrections among Isthmians over the next fifty years. These popular movements later triggered repeated North American and Colombian military interventions to perpetuate elite hegemony and Colombian supremacy on the isthmus.[31]

Thus while the construction of the railroad temporarily benefited those few merchants who effectively tapped into the profits to be made from the gold rush, it also caused overcrowding and unemployment, while worsening nationalist animosity toward Bogotá and introducing anti-Americanism as a nascent political currency on the isthmus. These circumstances prompted a resurgence of political activism among Panama's masses at midcentury reminiscent of the 1830 movement. Under the direction of another dynamic leader of West Indian extraction, Buenaventura Correoso, residents of the arrabal used their decisive demographic advantage to control the presidency of the Federal State of Panama for a decade in the 1860s and 1870s.[32] For the second time, a popular *caudillo* capitalized on the demographic strength of Panama's rapidly expanding urban masses to gain control of the government in Panama City. Correoso used his large constituency to exploit the latitude provided for in Colombia's 1863 constitution—one of nineteenth century Latin America's most liberal—to win control of the local government despite intense opposition from the city's White merchants and landowners. However, in a theme that has repeated itself throughout much of nineteenth and twentieth century Panamanian history, White nationalists refused to lend their support to Correoso for racial reasons, thus denying the rebel leader valuable middle-class links to Colombian bureaucracy that might have provided him with the military, electoral, or administrative means of consolidating his rebellion.

As witnessed by the virulent renters' strikes by Canal Zone employees in the 1920s (see chapter 2), racism continued to segregate Panama's middle-class nationalists from popular movements well into the twentieth century. Throughout the nineteenth and twentieth centuries, the unwillingness of White nationalists to merge their protests with those of the masses cemented the urban elite's hold on power and secured the role of the United States as power broker on the isthmus.

From Colombian Vassal to United States Colony

The prosperity Panama experienced in the 1860s with the completion of the railroad paralleled similar economic expansion elsewhere in Colombia. Coffee prices were high, as were returns on Colombia's other cash crops— indigo, tobacco, and rubber. This economic stability seemed to substantiate the liberal policies of laissez-faire economics, and in 1863 officials in Bogotá enacted one of the most liberal constitutions to appear in all of nineteenth century Latin America. Buoyed by a hardy economy, their policies appear to have carried the day.

However, by pushing states' rights so emphatically, the federalists severely limited Bogotá's ability to govern the nation's hinterlands, particularly the residents of the Colombian coastal states of Bolívar, Magdalena, and Panama. Regionalism reached crisis proportions in the late 1870s and early 1880s, when a decline in world prices for coffee, indigo, tobacco, and rubber triggered widespread unrest among the agricultural workers who had lost their jobs or had had their wages cut because of the downturn in prices.

In Bogotá, this emergency prompted a conservative campaign to end liberalism, known as the Regeneration (1885—95). Under the direction of liberal-turned-conservative President Rafael Núñez, conservatives in Bogotá sought to regain effective control of all of Colombia by reversing the federalist decentralization outlined in the 1863 constitution. Núñez increased taxes and carried out systematic forced loans to finance the government. As far as Panama was concerned, he established customs houses on the isthmus, a practice outlawed in March of 1835, when officials in Bogotá had established a system of free ports in Panama in response to demands by Panama City's merchants. He also enacted strict antivagrancy laws, to be enforced by expanded police and military garrisons on the isthmus. Finally, Núñez disenfranchised much of the nation's masses by basing suffrage on literacy and property qualifications, thus ending universal adult male suffrage in Panama.[33]

From 1885 to 1888, much of Panama's oligarchy supported the Núñez administration, despite widespread Panamanian resentment of his policies. Under the direction of French engineer Ferdinand de Lesseps, the Compagnie Universelle du Canal Interocéanique had begun to construct a canal across the isthmus in 1880. While the project moved forward, merchants and landowners in and around Panama City, who were prospering from the renewed economic activity, could afford to pay the high taxes imposed by officials in Bogotá. The benefits they received from the French venture outweighed elite resentment of *bogotano* intervention.

However, when the French effort failed in 1888, the ensuing economic crisis encompassed much of the isthmus and made it very difficult for Panamanians of all classes to meet Bogotá's fiscal demands. Consequently, as the urban elite watched profits from the canal project disappear, their support for the French canal company waned, and their disdain for Núñez transcended any stability he might have offered them in their quest to perpetuate their privileged status. After 1888 Panama's dominant merchant elite understood that they could no longer rely on Bogotá to suppress opposition to elite hegemony on the isthmus, and this breach of confidence, combined with Bogotá's increasingly recalcitrant centralist tactics, caused Panama City's merchants to look for another ally with enough military strength to sustain their dominance in the face of mounting popular and middle-class opposition. Thus continuing merchant interest in seeing the canal project through to fruition, combined with the maturing alliance with Washington begun with the Mallarino-Bidlack Treaty, pushed Panama's elite toward closer diplomatic ties with lawmakers in Washington. Alienated by the Regeneration's centralist platform, the powerful Panama City merchant elite turned to Washington to bolster its social status.

Unlike some of their upper-class contemporaries, Panama's poor opposed the Regeneration from its inception in 1885. Living conditions in the lower-class neighborhood of Santa Ana were already considerably worse than circumstances in the elite neighborhood of San Felipe when the Regeneration began (see appendix A). In Santa Ana mortality rates far exceeded those of San Felipe, and residents of Santa Ana had a much shorter life expectancy at birth. The large disparity between gross and net reproduction ratios also attests to much higher levels of infant mortality among the poor. Núñez's tax increase pushed living conditions in the arrabal to the crisis stage. Furthermore his vagrancy and suffrage laws were aimed particularly at Blacks along Colombia's politically active northern coast, including Panama.

Under these circumstances, the Regeneration triggered strong resistance among Panama's expanding, predominantly Black urban masses, who revolted shortly after the Regeneration began, in early 1885. Mulatto leaders Rafael Aizpuru and Pedro Prestán forcibly took control of Colón and Panama City, with the support of the lower class populations of both cities. However, Núñez's troops, with the approval of Panama's merchant elite and the support of twelve hundred North American soldiers, put down the uprising and hanged Prestán in August 1885. This reversal, the third such setback since 1830 to be suffered by Panama's urban masses at the hands of White Panamanians and foreign troops, essentially ended nineteenth century arrabal political agitation.[34] By 1890 conditions in Panama had reached critical proportions. The failure of the French canal enterprise had dashed the economic aspirations of Panama's merchant elite while intensifying the suffering of its urban poor. Moreover the Regeneration had alienated both working-class Panamanians and Panama City's urban elite, who had previously looked to the Núñez administration as a stabilizing force with which to counter political opposition.

Conclusions

For Panama, the nineteenth century brought sweeping changes. Two large waves of foreign workers, foreign capital, and foreign technology permanently altered Panamanian society, while setting the stage for Isthmian independence and self-government.[35] Why did independence occur in 1903 and not during an earlier campaign? Why was a successful independence campaign led by the elite instead of by the nationalist bloc of the middle class or Panama City's expanding masses, groups that had lobbied for autonomy and independence throughout much of the nineteenth century? What part did foreigners play in these processes? Finally, what legacies did the events of the nineteenth century bequeath to the Republic of Panama after its independence from Colombia in 1903, and how did those legacies affect the formation of the new republic?

First, independence from Spain frustrated the aspirations of Panama's large working class, which found itself forcibly subjected to elite rule after 1821. With control of Panama's principal resource and the livelihood of much of its urban masses firmly in foreign hands, wealthy Panamanians lacked a vehicle of coercion with which to stifle popular demands for democratic reform. These circumstances triggered economic and military dependence, first on Colombia and then on the United States; this reliance cemented elite hegemony when two immense waves of immigrants came to Panama as part of the North American and French railroad and canal projects.

Second, anti-Americanism became a common political currency in Panama following the completion of the railroad, in 1855. Rapid increases in the flow of international commerce and the spread of European liberalism following independence produced a middle-class group of nationalists who opposed foreign intervention in Panamanian affairs. In the mid-1850s, Justo Arosemena and other intellectuals directed nationalist rhetoric against foreign intervention, specifically by the United States.

Finally, the Núñez-led Regeneration provided the impetus for Panama's move toward independence after the turn of the century. By forcibly suppressing the Prestán movement, Colombia (and the United States, under the guise of promoting uninterrupted transportation and freightage of commerce across Panama) had helped Panama's merchant elite eclipse the last significant popular uprising of the nineteenth century. With working-class unrest checked in this fashion, antipathy toward Colombia grew among wealthy Panamanians, a group that increasingly resented Bogotá's intervention in their affairs. Furthermore, now distrustful of Colombian officials, Panama's wealthy looked to Washington for the support Colombia had once provided.

When Colombian officials rejected the Hay-Herrán Treaty in 1903, and thus refused North Americans the right to complete the defunct French canal project, Panama's merchants invoked their evolving alliance with the United States. On November 3, 1903, with the help of the United States, Panama declared its independence from Colombia. The country's merchant elite immediately negotiated away control of the nation's economy—the canal—for Washington's support in the face of spiraling popular opposition and the threat of Colombian retaliation. Panama had itself another de facto viceroy.

Consequently early twentieth century Panamanian history repeated the pattern of the nineteenth: a small group of wealthy merchants intent on perpetuating their privileged circumstances, economic and military dependence on a foreign nation, and a large foreign military presence whose two-tiered mission included cementing elite privilege and securing control of Panama's transportation and storage industries. However, the United States had now replaced Colombia as Panama's foreign patron, and the emergence of a new republic afforded the elite a unique opportunity to translate their privileged status into political power. Following independence, elite response to problems generated by the American canal project led to a government based on police repression.

ॐ

2

Vying for a Place in the Emerging
Panamanian State, 1903–1931

THE END OF THE NINETEENTH CENTURY BROUGHT TO PANAMA WIDESPREAD
change that uprooted the lives of thousands of its citizens. The failure of the
French canal project in 1888 resulted in lost investments and widespread
unemployment all along the proposed waterway, as Panama's service-sector
economy constricted and the value of land and property along the route
depreciated drastically. Members of Panama's large urban labor force found
themselves struggling to survive. Meanwhile aggressive efforts by the Conservative Núñez regime in Bogotá to alleviate the nation's economic misfortunes intensified the crisis, triggering a wave of unrest throughout much of
Colombia, including Panama, and setting the stage for the latter's successful
independence campaign of November 1903.[1]

Coming in the wake of the French canal debacle and Colombia's bloody
Thousand Days' War, the establishment of an independent, sovereign republic in Panama occurred amidst much diplomatic turbulence and domestic squabbling. Officials in Panama City had to deal with repeated emphatic
protests from Colombia, frequent intervention by the United States, and
deep social, racial, and ethnic schisms that had divided Panamanians peri-
odically since the sixteenth century. Fashioned by these circumstances,
Panama's first administrations took a series of steps to neutralize internal
dissension while securing Panama's status as a sovereign republic.[2] As they
did so, these early leaders began the new nation's historic gradual shift away
from reliance on foreign military intervention, laying the basis for a native
police force that would eventually dominate twentieth century Panamanian
politics the way foreign troops had controlled the isthmus from the sixteenth through the nineteenth century.

This chapter examines several elements of the dynamic relationship between Panamanians and their leaders, an association that ultimately produced a series of military-dominated regimes, including those of José Remón,
Omar Torrijos, and Manuel Noriega. The Thousand Days' War provides a
window through which to study Panamanian society at the turn of the century. As Panamanian sociologist Alfredo Figueroa Navarro has suggested in

his watershed work *Dominio y sociedad en el Panamá Colombiano, 1821–1903*, this conflict underscored the urban elite's hold on power. Bolstered by an influx of wealthy immigrant families during the French canal debacle (1880–88), Panama City's wealthy emerged from the war with enough political and diplomatic clout to secure Panama's independence from Colombia the following year—a feat that had been attempted unsuccessfully many times since 1821. The advantageous conclusion of the civil war and their own successful bid for independence gave Panama's urban elite dominion over the new nation as it took shape. They would chart the future of the new republic, and the pattern they established has dominated Isthmian politics since that time.

Next follows an examination of the republic that appeared after independence in November 1903. The nineteenth century dealt a series of decisive blows to Panama's poor. Moreover the war partially silenced the militant component of Panama's nascent middle class. Nevertheless, despite their previous setbacks, members of these two groups became increasingly active following independence, and their persistent agitation after 1903 required the immediate, uninterrupted attention of the nation's new government. In light of these circumstances, and with the financial and military support of the United States, Panama's rulers began fashioning a governmental bureaucracy that could administer the turbulent affairs of the new nation despite worker unrest and a burgeoning middle-class opposition movement. This strategy worked until January of 1931, when middle-class activists had regrouped sufficiently from their humiliating defeat in the Thousand Days' War to topple the elite regime of Florencio Harmodio Arosemena.

The Thousand Days' War and Independence: A Reaffirmation of Panama's Status Quo

Colombia's bloody Thousand Days' War pitted Colombians who favored a highly centralized government (conservatives) against those who advocated states' rights (liberals, or in Panama's case, nationalists—those Panamanians who wanted to sever ties to Bogotá). As the fighting spread to the northernmost Colombian province of Panama in 1900, it accentuated changes there that had occurred during the nineteenth century. Having been defeated militarily at least three times since 1821, Panama's urban masses played only a minor role in the war. Moreover Panama's small but powerful urban elite remained largely aloof from the conflict. Instead the wealthy focused their attention on protecting their investments and on defending the Panama Railroad, their economic lifeline.

With much of Panama's urban masses and its rich either unable or unwilling to declare war on Colombia, an array of Panamanian doctors, lawyers, educators, intellectuals, and merchants took up arms to break Panama's political ties to Bogotá. These individuals envisioned Panama becoming an emporium of world commerce with the profits remaining in Isthmian hands, and they intended to use the confusion caused by Colombia's civil war to achieve Panamanian independence. Estranged from Bogotá by the latter's determination to capitalize on commodities crossing the isthmus, the rebels contended that Panamanians needed absolute control of the nation's commercial activities. Distinguished from the rest of Panamanian society by their vehement opposition to foreign intervention in Isthmian affairs, these activists provided all the leadership and much of the manpower for an independence movement of unprecedented scale. They also established a basis for Panama's diverse twentieth century nationalist movement.[3]

Yet without the support of Panama's wealthy and its massive population of urban poor, these nationalists lacked a cohesive, unified front that could transcend race and class divisions. Consequently during the Thousand Days' War they did not have the numbers or the military means to remove Panama from Colombian political jurisdiction. Similar ethnic and social divisions had in fact undermined several nineteenth century popular uprisings in Panama, including those of José Domingo Espinar (1830) and Buenaventura Correoso (1860s and 1870s). This time, however, it was the nationalist component of Panama's White middle class that succumbed to a combination of social fragmentation and foreign troops.

Despite the nationalists' ultimate failure to achieve their objectives, their struggle to separate Panama from Colombia profoundly affected Isthmian society. Beginning in July 1900, Emiliano J. Herrera and Belisario Porras led the nationalist campaign to force the withdrawal of Colombian troops from the isthmus. Beginning in the city of David in northern Panama, Porras, Herrera, and their troops advanced southward until they arrived on the outskirts of Panama City. From there one thousand rebel soldiers launched an offensive on the capital. Government forces engaged the nationalists as they entered the city at Calidonia Bridge, and the well-trained and better-equipped Colombian troops exacted a heavy toll on the insurgents. More than four hundred nationalists were injured or killed, while government forces suffered only ninety-eight casualties. After two days of fighting, the rebels surrendered on July 26, 1900.[4]

Thus ended the first of a series of nationalist military forays deep within Panamanian territory. Porras, who fled to Central America following the debacle at Calidonia, tried again unsuccessfully in 1902–3; his legendary tenacity earned him the leadership of Panama's liberal movement following independence. Despite the fact that the liberal cause survived to fight another day, the victory of government troops over rebel forces at Calidonia established (or expanded on) a precedent for elite hegemony in Isthmian affairs that carried over into Panama's national period. While Porras, Herrera, and their men had the support of much of rural Panama, they lacked even the rhetorical support of a cohesive popular front and consequently failed to seriously challenge government forces.

Close examination of the pivotal clash at Calidonia Bridge can tell us much about Panamanian society and politics at the turn of the century. What did not happen at Calidonia is perhaps more important than what did happen there. For decades foreign transportation projects, civil war, Colombian and American military subjugation, and worsening social stratification had uprooted Panama's poor. In the wake of these divisive events, Panamanians of diverse social, economic, and ethnic backgrounds had little reason to cooperate; no "positive motivation to conformity" existed to attract the masses to the nationalist cause.[5] Instead in the working-class neighborhoods of Panama City and Colón, soaring illegitimacy levels and the nation's worst standards of living attest to the wretched condition of Panama's urban working class at the turn of the century (see table 1). These people had been forcefully subdued for decades by Panama's wealthy urban landowners and their merchant counterparts, both of whom relied heavily on foreign troops to stifle popular unrest along Panama's commerce route. Consequently when the confrontation at Calidonia Bridge occurred, very little tied them to the rebellion, and this lack of a substantive unified front severely weakened the rebel cause.[6] With the vast majority of Panama's workers noticeably absent, Calidonia became essentially a battle between White Panamanian nationalists with middle-class leadership and Colombian troops who had the backing of an urban elite bent on protecting its investments.[7]

Panama's urban wealthy fared notably better than did the poor during the period from 1898 to 1902. By this time affluent landowners and merchants in Panama City had clearly gained preeminence in the area's political, social, and economic spheres—factors accentuated by their superior standards of living. While demographic and illegitimacy data underscore the hardships confronting Panama's masses during the critical last years of the nineteenth century and the first years of the twentieth, illegitimacy for Panama's urban rich actually dropped during this important interval and other demographic data, including net reproduction ratio and life expectancy, reflect the comparatively favorable circumstances of Panama's urban wealthy at the turn of the century (see table 1).[8]

Significantly, while control of the railroad clearly gave Panama's wealthy urban aristocracy the upper hand at the turn of the century, Figueroa Navarro

TABLE 2.1: ILLEGITIMACY IN SELECTED PARISHES, 1898–1910

Year	Santa Ana*	La Merced**	Aguadulce	Chitré	David	Las Tablas
1898	84%	61%	65%	46%	71%	n/a
1899	84%	53%	64%	46%	71%	57%
1900	82%	63%	67%	45%	78%	62%
1901	84%	52%	62%	46%	73%	62%
1902	79%	57%	61%	44%	77%	59%
1903	85%	61%	80%	49%	75%	64%
1904	82%	59%	58%	47%	72%	63%
1905	79%	62%	66%	57%	71%	53%
1906	82%	56%	77%	52%	79%	63%
1907	80%	50%	66%	48%	80%	n/a
1908	78%	54%	71%	51%	79%	n/a
1909	n/a	54%	76%	57%	79%	n/a
1910	n/a	53%	71%	56%	77%	53%
Average:	82%	57%	68%	50%	76%	60%

*Santa Ana is a working-class parish in Panama City
**La Merced is an upper-class parish in Panama City
Source: Registros parroquiales from the San José parish in David (LDS films 760741–760747), the San Juan Bautista parish in Aguadulce (films 1809803–1809804), the Santa Ana parish in Panama City (films 1091673–1091675), the La Merced parish in Panama City (films 1094125 and 1094128), the Santa Librada parish in Las Tablas (film 1089178), and the San Juan Bautista parish in Chitré (films 1089485–1089846).

has pointed out that a small rural oligarchy dating from the era of the Bourbon Reforms still maintained considerable influence in the countryside, particularly in the provinces of Chitré and Las Tablas. These families had fled the chaos in Panama City in 1739, when the king of Spain liberalized trade policies and eliminated Panama's port monopoly over the transport of goods between Europe and the Americas.[9] My findings indicate that these families provided a stabilizing element for their respective home districts, where illegitimacy and other demographic data remained constant when compared with other rural provinces during the volatile period from 1898 to 1903. Thus despite the animosity that had developed between Panama's rural oligarchy and its urban elite during the nineteenth century, similarities in their standards of living epitomize the depth and breadth of social fragmentation that existed in Panama at the time of independence.[10]

Given their superior circumstances, Panama's urban elite had little reason to go to war. Instead they distanced themselves from the fighting. Having fostered an alliance with the United States during the latter half of the nineteenth century (and particularly during the Regeneration), they relied on American troops to protect their economically sensitive areas, particularly the railroad. In Panama City and Colón, they even endorsed American intervention to stifle the liberal threat posed by Porras and his followers. At their request the United States landed marines in Colón in November 1901 to retake that city from liberal forces who had temporarily captured it.

Nationalists, meanwhile, continued agitating against foreign domination of the isthmus, even after Porras and Herrera failed. Yet their efforts fell short of effectively challenging Panama's ruling elite. After several additional military reversals, Panamanian rebels surrendered altogether in October 1902, and the next month a ranking representative of Panama's nationalist opposition, General Benjamín Herrera, signed a peace treaty aboard the American battleship *Wisconsin*. This agreement, which ended the war, called for the surrender of all dissidents and the punishment of those who chose not to acknowledge the accord. This latter tenet stirred considerable unrest among certain pockets of the opposition, particularly those troops led by Victoriano Lorenzo, a Guaymí Indian from Coclé in north-central Panama, who had joined Belisario Porras during his second campaign to free Panama City from Colombian rule. Lorenzo's backing of Porras had given sizable organized Indian support to the nationalist cause, while also incorporating a large component of Panama's displaced agricultural sector into the resistance. For more than a year following Porras's failed second attempt, the Guaymí commander and his troops assisted rebel forces with guerrilla tactics that occasionally succeeded in weakening government forces by dividing them into separate theaters of operation.[11]

Besides calling for an end to the fighting, the peace accord signed aboard the *Wisconsin* called for all insurgents to surrender their weapons. Along with his fellow commanders Herrera and Porras, Lorenzo and his men objected to this clause in the pact. However, unlike his Hispanic comrades, the Guaymí commander and his soldiers protested by refusing to relinquish their weapons. Instead of convening with the other officers and helping implement the peace accord, Lorenzo and his modest band of insurgents holed up in the small town of San Marcos, where their presence demonstrated their disagreement with the terms of the accord and their unwillingness to abandon the cause for which they had fought for more than two years.

At that point a small party of liberal and conservative officers, including Lorenzo's former colleague Benjamín Herrera, set out for that city to subdue Lorenzo and his men. Herrera empathized with the Indian leader; he too objected to the humiliating disarmament clause of the treaty. In the end, however, Herrera became "indignant" and "furious" with Lorenzo for inciting rebellion, and it was Herrera who ultimately arrested Lorenzo.[12]

In a rather startling turn of events, on May 15 Lorenzo's captors killed him by hanging. This tragedy brought to an end the Guaymí resistance movement and silenced Panama's impoverished agricultural sector as well as one of its largest, poorest, and remotest indigenous populations.[13] It also triggered a wave of angry protests from nationalists, who insisted that Lorenzo had been murdered for political reasons. Indeed nearly every scholar who has written about Lorenzo's execution has blamed urban conservatives for his murder.[14] This argument makes good political sense, given the rout of liberal insurgents in the Thousand Days' War by a large multinational coalition. Yet the military officer who arrested Lorenzo, Benjamín Herrera, had served as a general in the liberal army, commanding nearly ten thousand nationalist troops. Furthermore the officer who sentenced Lorenzo to death, Esteban Huertas, was later discharged from his military post after Panama achieved its independence for posing a "liberal" threat to the fragile new government.[15] Finally, in addition to animosity toward Lorenzo among Panama's upper class and Colombian troops stationed in Panama, a moderate segment had developed within the predominantly liberal middle class (*rabiblancos*, meaning "pro–North American" or "pro-Yankee"); this segment owed its employment to the elite. It also felt threatened by Lorenzo and wanted him stifled.[16]

The actions of Herrera and Huertas contradict the suggestion that Lorenzo fell victim to a combination of violent Bogotá-based conservatism and North American imperialism. With control of Panama's political and economic spheres hanging in the balance, class and race issues—decisive elements of Panama's emerging social and political systems—ultimately superseded politics, purported ideologies, and any sense of shared sovereign interests. In other words, while conservatives won the war, an alliance of White conservatives and moderate, pro-American liberals had acted together to eliminate Lorenzo as a threat to Panama's status quo.

When the Thousand Days' War ended, so too did the nationalist campaign and the fleeting involvement of Panama's indigenous populations in it. These events further reinforced the political and social hegemony of Panama's Washington-backed urban elite, while strengthening the ties that linked moderate liberals to the elite cause. Meanwhile political agitation among Panama's urban masses and its Indian populations had been muted, and it would be years before any of these groups would recover sufficiently from the Thousand Days' War to challenge the nation's status quo.

The Urban Elite and American Support

Early in 1902 negotiations began between officials in Washington and Bogotá regarding American plans to construct a canal across Panama. Having eliminated the need for British cooperation on a canal project with the Hay-Pauncefote Treaty of November 1901, the United States was ready to undertake unilaterally the building, financing, and fortification of a transisthmian waterway.[17]

In January of 1903, American Secretary of State John Hay and Colombian legation Tomás Herrán signed an agreement to allow the United States to build a canal across Panama. But the Colombian senate rejected the agreement. This angered President Roosevelt, who envisioned the canal as an integral component in the defense of the United States' Caribbean interests following the Spanish-American War. The rejection also infuriated wealthy Panamanian landowners and merchants, many of whom had lost considerable sums of money when the French undertaking failed. In the wake of Núñez's onerous Regeneration, when officials in Bogotá had attempted to remedy the nation's economic woes by taxing its impoverished Pacific coast (including Panama), Colombia's rejection of the Hay-Herrán pact provided a common thread that united the Roosevelt administration and Panama's urban wealthy on the issue of Panamanian independence.

Under these circumstances, several prominent Panama City businessmen began plotting Panama's independence from Colombia. Representing this group, Manuel Amador Guerrero, the medical officer of the Panama Railroad, sailed for New York in August, where he and members of the Roosevelt administration began to conspire regarding the future of the isthmus and the role the United States would play in it. Meeting with Secretary of State John Hay and with Phillipe Bunau-Varilla, a representative of the defunct French project, Amador obtained American support for an independence campaign in exchange for agreeing to American terms for the canal project.

In keeping with sociologist Talcott Parsons's theory regarding "the optimization of gratification" by competing forces in a given society, Amador's part in this plot emphasized the determination of the elite to preserve at any expense their control of Isthmian politics and society. Amador was one of their own; after migrating to the isthmus from Colombia in 1855, he received his medical degree, went to work for the railroad, and began a long career with Panama's pro-American conservative movement. He had been the heir apparent to the presidency of the Federal State of Panama in 1867, before a liberal revolt temporarily forced him from the isthmus, and in 1885 he briefly served as president of Panama, a position similar to that of provincial governor elsewhere in the region. With this record Amador emerged as the leader of the elite bloc after the conservative victory in the Thousand Days' War. These circumstances placed him in line for the presidency of the republic following Panama's successful bid for independence.[18]

In one of the ironies of twentieth century Panamanian history, the successful revolutionary junta appointed Bunau-Varilla, a non-Panamanian, as their minister plenipotentiary to the United States.[19] This appointment, made because Amador and his fellow revolutionaries feared the United States might withdraw its promise of support if they did not select the Frenchman (a fear planted by Bunau-Varilla), set the stage for the Hay–Bunau-Varilla Treaty of 1903, the single most controversial (and hated) piece of legislation in the history of the Panamanian nation.[20] As British historian John Major has noted, there is disagreement regarding the role the Frenchman actually played in the treaty. Nevertheless there remains little doubt that he signed the agreement against the wishes of the junta, and by so doing granted the United States many concessions that exceeded those approved by his Panamanian superiors. In a fitting end to this diplomatic coup d'état, Bunau-Varilla also recovered the forty million dollars that his failed French canal-digging venture stood to lose if he failed to secure a buyer for the defunct project.[21]

The end of the Thousand Days' War, Colombia's rejection of the Hay-Herrán Treaty, and the Bunau-Varilla accord placed Panama's small urban elite coalition of landlords and merchants squarely in control of the new state. As witnessed by the role American troops had played in retaking the city of Colón in 1901, the elite's alliance with officials in Washington had effectively neutralized nationalists. Moreover Lorenzo's death added much of the rural population to the list of Panamanians who had tried unsuccessfully to challenge conservative elite rule.

Panama thus began its republican era with a system of government that revolved around a small urban elite whose ability to govern hinged on foreign military support, a pattern that had endured in one form or another since Europeans first arrived on the isthmus. This time, however, American troops succeeded Spanish and Colombian troops as Panama's political arbiters. Beginning with the nation's first legislative elections in 1906 and including every legislative and presidential election through 1918, the United States either sent or was asked to send various officials to oversee Panama's elections.[22] Deceptively, American troops did not invade Panama as they had Nicaragua, Haiti, Mexico, and Cuba. Yet beginning soon after independence in 1903, thousands of United States soldiers remained permanently in Panama, officially to defend the canal, a distinction often blurred by reality. Authorized by Article 136 of Panama's 1904 constitution to "intervene in any part of the Republic of Panama to reestablish [sic] public peace," United States soldiers frequently overran the republic in support of Panama's small but powerful class of urban merchants, in the process filling the void created by the disbandment of Panama's own armed forces.[23]

By relying initially on United States troops and capital to secure the presidency, Panama's first presidents, conservatives and liberals alike, evoked massive opposition from middle-class activists. Furthermore by seeking American assistance in quelling strikes and popular unrest, these presidents also earned the wrath of the nation's burgeoning population of urban poor. Confronted with continuing opposition on these two vital fronts, Panama's early leaders became increasingly dependent on the National Police to suppress their opponents, and in so doing they gradually altered the role of the police in Isthmian society. In his analysis of ineffective political systems, Joel S. Migdal, professor of international relations, has noted that "in states with limited abilities to apply rules and mobilize support," one or more government agencies tends to administer the nation's affairs, filling the void created by the central government's deficiencies.[24] Professor Migdal's work accurately describes Panama during its earliest formative years, when the National Police began a decades-long journey to the forefront of Isthmian politics. Although it would be years before the police could impose their will unilaterally on Panama's elected officials, the genesis of this gradual shift nonetheless marks a significant break with Panama's past.

After Independence: Police as Power Brokers

Panama's three-man revolutionary government ruled until February 16, 1904, when the National Assembly unanimously elected the archetypical conservative Manuel Amador Guerrero first president of the republic. Amador's election, coming on the heels of the controversial Bunau-Varilla pact, placed the new administration directly at odds with the recently defeated nationalist faction led by Belisario Porras. Porras, whose position as spokesman of Panama's Liberal party was cemented by his role in the Thousand Days' War, opposed both the 1903 treaty and Amador's election. He and his followers argued that both the treaty and the president's appointment sacrificed Panamanian sovereignty and national integrity for the economic objectives of a few wealthy Panamanian merchants. However, still effectively detached by class and race disparities from substantial segments of the population, nationalists lacked the wherewithal to effectively challenge Amador and his followers, and conservatives dominated the decisive first years of the new republic.[25]

With the Thousand Days' War and a successful independence crusade behind him, Amador first sought to identify and neutralize any vestiges of political opposition on the isthmus. Most notably the new president needed to control Belisario Porras and his nationalist followers, who were known as

Porristas. To accomplish this, Amador began with the nation's armed forces. Samuel P. Huntington has noted that "any further reduction of military power beyond the point where professionalism is maximized only redounds to the benefit of some particular civilian group and only serves to enhance the power of that group in its struggles with other civilian groups."[26] Certainly this applies to postindependence Panama, where, lacking a tenable response to the military potential of General Esteban Huertas and his soldiers, Amador disregarded Huertas's striking display of loyalty during the independence movement and declared the general a liberal threat to the new nation. He then suggested to an American legation in November 1903 that "Panama would benefit by the disbandment of the army," a move shrewdly calculated to get Washington to disarm the president's political enemies under the guise of defending the proposed canal.[27]

Amador's proposition enjoyed considerable appeal in Washington, where official interest revolved around securing the nascent Canal Zone. With the full cooperation of the United States, President Amador disbanded the military altogether in 1904. Publicly Huertas refused the monthly pension of five hundred dollars Amador offered him when he resigned on November 18; a few days later, however, he quietly accepted the sum and retired to his hometown of Aguadulce.[28] With Huertas out of the way, both governments agreed that American soldiers would fill the void created by the demise of Panama's military. The intent was to buoy up Amador's fragile presidency while enhancing the United States' presence in, and control of, the Canal Zone and adjoining areas.[29]

Having eliminated the military as a potential vehicle of political mobility and having placed the defense of the country formally in Washington's cooperative hands, Amador focused his attention on the nation's modest police force.[30] The new president clearly understood his tenuous position and the resultant need for a loyal police force capable of quelling popular unrest and thwarting opposition to his administration. Accordingly he again turned to the United States for help, and in 1905 the Amador administration hired Samuel B. David, a New York City police officer, to provide Panama's newly organized National Police with "adequate scientific instruction." Previously the lack of a substantive local military capability had precipitated the direct intervention of Spanish, Colombian, and North American troops in Panama to regulate Isthmian affairs. However, by hiring Samuel B. David, the Amador administration began Panama's subtle shift away from reliance on foreign military intervention toward dependence on an increasingly proficient native police force to do the administration's political bidding. Significantly, by the mid-1940s the professionalism that Amador and his successors courted would engender in the police a sense of collective identity and political cohesion capable of dominating an otherwise fragmented state.[31]

Immediately the president began using these officers to counter working-class unrest and nationalist opposition. In May of 1906, for example, George W. Jiménez, another New York City police officer working for the Amador administration, reported that "explicit directions have been given to the police to prevent by every means in their power the success of the Liberals, who, in a fair election, would overthrow the Amador government by one hundred to one."[32] By 1906, then, the police had become a band of armed partisan supporters, whose primary responsibilities at election time included intimidating would-be opponents at polling sites and "refusing a large number of people the opportunity of casting their votes," while casting multiple votes themselves and otherwise skewing election returns in favor of the president's party.[33] Meanwhile, despite this conspicuous disregard for the political rights of his enemies, Amador's overtures toward the government of the United States presented members of the Roosevelt administration with an opportunity they would not forego. Amador was a political crook, but he was the United States' crook.

By securing training for police officers, Amador secured the loyalty of members of the police force, many of whom owed him their jobs. With the military disbanded, a loyal police force in place, and the endorsement of the Roosevelt administration, Amador became increasingly bold in his attempt to crush the nationalist movement permanently. In 1905 he stripped Belisario Porras of his Panamanian citizenship for "not approving of the separation" from Colombia. Although Porras regained his citizenship and became president of Panama in the second decade of the century, Amador's temporary disenfranchisement of the nation's leading nationalist highlighted the many competing factions and interests that divided Isthmian politics. Moreover by stripping Porras of his citizenship with the tacit support of the United States, Amador also heightened antipathy among many Panamanians for the dominant elite–North American coalition.[34]

The presidency was fast becoming the country's largest cash cow and distributor of political spoils. In addition to requiring police officers and other civil servants to contribute 2.5 percent of their incomes to party coffers (a sum raised to 5 percent by the Porras administration in May 1924), the government regularly permitted its agents to pocket 10 percent of this "party fee" in exchange for a particular favor or endorsement. This provided considerable "informal" influence, particularly in remote areas where party allegiance was minimal. Meanwhile, in addition to coercing funds from supporters, Panama's first presidents controlled an increasing number of lucrative jobs as well as massive government contracts, many of which were related to the huge Canal Zone enclave. In a comprehensive 1929–31 study of Panama's economy commissioned by the Panamanian government, George

E. Roberts noted that nepotism and the exchange of jobs and contracts for political support were frequent in Panama. Roberts, vice president of the National City Bank of New York, reported that presidents throughout the 1920s regularly padded government payrolls by granting family members and friends multiple federal jobs, sometimes as many as four per person. This illegal practice added much to the bureaucratic inefficiency of the government, while artificially augmenting the prestige of the presidency.[35]

Certainly Panama's presidents did not have a monopoly on political vice and partisan chicanery. Nevertheless, as the Canal Zone construction progressed and expanded, so too did the president's bargaining power; as witnessed by the downturn of the midtwenties, this left officials in Panama City particularly vulnerable to shifts in Canal Zone employment practices and fluctuations in world commerce.[36]

As Panama's population grew and new financial prospects arose, Amador and his benefactors continued to try to mask their abuse of the presidency behind a façade of politically charged, conservative-versus-liberal rhetoric. Seeing through this political rhetoric, a Panamanian journalist wrote in 1919 that the country's political parties would better be described as "the party within" (bondholders, landowners, and wealthy merchants) and "the party without" (the working classes, the guilds of artisans, teachers, etc.).[37] In a similar vein, William Jennings Price, American Minister to Panama, noted in May of 1919: "In Panama there are no political parties as such, and the Liberal and Conservative nomenclature means absolutely nothing . . . Thus on one side there are the large landowners . . . against another group represented by Belisario Porras, which in theory at least appeals to the masses."[38] By disbanding the military and cultivating a newfound sense of professionalism and esprit de corps among law enforcement personnel, Amador began to neutralize antiadministration forces. The opposition found itself largely excluded from the nation's political circles.

With the military dismantled and otherwise stalemated by the Amador regime, administration opponents lacked a tenable response to the president's partisan use of the police. Having had their activities checked in this fashion, Belisario Porras and his followers turned to the nation's electoral board for recourse. Established by the government to distribute voter eligibility cards (*cédulas*) before and during elections and to count votes once the process concluded, the board represented a viable alternative agent of political leverage, largely because the distribution of its members throughout the republic made them nearly impossible to regulate.

The earliest partisan use of the electoral board amounted to little more than exchanging public allegations of electoral indiscretions. In 1906, for example, Porristas charged the conservative Amador regime with using the electoral board to illegally manipulate voter registration, thereby minimizing liberal representation in the pending vote. (It merits noting here that the police provided Amador with a fail-safe mechanism: even if any liberals were able to register, the police were instructed to turn back as many as possible without allowing them to vote.) Similarly, in 1908 a coalition of conservatives and moderate liberals known as La Coalición Republicana (The Republican Coalition) charged the Amador government with fixing the election through fraudulent voter registration, a charge that elicited a warning from the United States government: "If fraud is to intervene in the election, so that a dispute arises as to who are the lawful elected authorities, then it becomes necessary for the United States, in discharge of its treaty and constitutional duty, to determine who are the lawfully elected officers, in order that we may recognize them and deal with them as such."[39]

Although the 1906 and 1908 electoral board controversies amounted to little more than partisan quarrels, jockeying for control of these boards became increasingly vicious and decisive as time passed, particularly as the presidency became more associated with large Canal Zone contracts and jobs.[40] One practice that grew out of this maneuvering was the *paquetazo*, which amounted to stuffing the ballot boxes with ghost votes (or votes otherwise falsified), thereby giving the party that controlled the board a landslide victory in a particularly difficult to monitor, remote part of the country. One of the more blatant cases occurred in 1924. On March 19 of that year, the administration of Belisario Porras issued decree no. 38, extending suffrage to the Kuna Indians of the San Blas Islands. Under Panama's constitution, these people already had the right to vote; decree no. 38 merely symbolized the administration's attempt to legitimize its electoral abuse of the Kuna. One year earlier the president had stationed police among them to enforce what anthropologist James Howe has labeled "a full-scale program of coercive acculturation." Chiari, the administration's hand-picked candidate, easily won the 1924 election, including a landslide margin among the indigenous people of San Blas. There police intimidation resulted in a margin of 594 to 17 in favor of Chiari.[41]

As Panamanian scholar Jorge Conte-Porras noted in his 1990 book *Requiem por la revolución*, paquetazos and other forms of fraudulent vote counting have characterized many of Panama's elections. During the 1936 election, for example, Conte-Porras notes that the liberal administration of Harmodio Arias "falsified the triumph of the popular vote" in the district of Veraguas in remote north-central Panama, giving the official candidate Juan Demóstenes Arosemena a vote count there that "exceeded all predictions"— and possibilities.[42] In this way the party that controlled ballot distribution and counting could effectively challenge, if not decide, the outcome of an election even before the vote took place. And when electoral boards occasionally failed to provide an effective alternative path to power, armed paramilitary civilian groups sometimes resorted to arms, as they did in January 1931. In fact Conte-Porras noted that in the 1930s and 1940s, these groups regularly engaged in urban warfare, with bands of praetorian guards vying for dominance in Isthmian politics.[43]

After Amador: Populist Appeal Versus Political Pragmatism

When he left office in 1908, Amador had accumulated an impressive list of accomplishments that gave shape and substance to the emerging state. The new country had its own constitution, an established, stable system of currency, a federal bureaucracy capable of administering both domestic and international affairs, and a relationship with the United States that had cemented Panama's independence from Colombia.[44]

By 1908, however, cracks began to appear in Amador's powerful conservative coalition. During the late nineteenth and early twentieth centuries, the traditional elite of landowners and wealthy merchants had been fused with an increasing number of rich foreigners and successful middle-class merchants. The resulting hybrid party called itself La Coalición Republicana. Going beyond the narrower ideological confines of the Amador camp, La Coalición merged the interests of many urban middle-class merchants with the pursuits of Panama City's small urban elite. These two groups set aside their differences to capitalize on the financial bonanza offered by the emerging Canal Zone. This marriage of ideas as well as interests reached fruition in 1908, when José Domingo de Obaldía won the presidency with its support.[45]

Despite the fact that his candidacy partially bridged the gap between the upper and middle classes and consequently blurred conservative and liberal designations, Obaldía's election failed to bring a truce between the nation's political elite and nationalists, many of whom objected to what they perceived as the conservative, pro-American qualities of his platform. Seen in this light, Obaldía's presidency becomes a critical juncture in contemporary Panamanian social and political history. His platform alienated the nationalist element of Panama's emerging middle class, which helped set the stage for later administrations that were dominated by disgruntled middle-class activists with popular appeal, leaders such as Belisario Porras and Harmodio Arias. Equally important, the Obaldía administration failed to alleviate the crises facing Panama's expanding class of urban workers, choosing instead to use the police to forcibly suppress strikes while ignoring the conditions of the urban poor. Sociologist Ernesto LaClau has noted that in Latin America the masses become disgruntled and begin clamoring for change when a "collapse in transformism" occurs. In Panama this collapse began when the Obaldía administration merged certain middle- and upper-class interests while forcibly preventing the amelioration of working-class conditions. In this way Obaldía redefined slightly the nation's status quo, while simultaneously setting in motion the further organization of labor on the isthmus.[46]

Faced with persistent worker unrest and continued opposition from the nationalist camp, Panama's second president attempted to consolidate the elite's hold on power by further institutionalizing the role of the National Police as a vehicle of political control. In 1909 the Obaldía government followed up on Amador's hiring of Samuel B. David by requesting the assistance of the United States in locating an official of that government to "assist in the instruction and possibly the reorganization of the Panamanian police . . . some person who was or had been in the service of the American government and who was competent to discharge in Panama the duties of Instructor General of the National Police."[47]

According to the Obaldía administration, this position would grant significant authority to an American, who would help in the administration of Panama's peacekeeping forces:

> The Instructor General of the National Police Force, who has been asked for of the American government, shall be one of the chiefs of the force; for better efficiency in the discharge of his duties he may impose punishment, adjudge the awards set forth in the decrees of the National Police and shall be under no superiors [other] than His Excellency the President of the Republic, the Secretary of Government and Justice, and the Chief of Police of the National Police Force [sic].[48]

In response to this petition, the State Department sought the advice of the War Department, which proposed retired Major Wallis B. Clark for the appointment. Clark's nomination met with resounding approval within both the State Department and the Obaldía administration. His tenure as a United States military officer affirmed Clark's loyalty to North American objectives in Panama. It also assured the experience sought by the Panamanians.

Yet officials in both countries had underestimated the level of anti-Americanism in Panama. Unlike Samuel B. David, Wallis B. Clark was a career military officer. Moreover the United States government essentially nominated Clark for the position, a move perceived as intervention by many Panamanians. Native-born officers deeply resented their professional subjugation to another North American, and frequently they simply disregarded his orders. After a few short months, this resistance had fully undermined Clark's attempts to restructure the police force, and he resigned in frustration.

The remainder of Obaldía's term passed without securing a replacement for Clark. Meanwhile the approaching 1912 presidential election once again focused attention on the nation's electoral board. The largest group of conservatives, calling themselves La Unión Patriótica (The Patriotic Union), accused presidential candidate Belisario Porras and his liberal associates of fraudulently using the registration of voters to upend the Unión's campaign for the presidency: "The Liberal Party, which holds absolute control of all electoral colleges—as they are constituted by a majority of members elected ad-hoc from that party—is making a list of voters so as to favor its followers and hurt its opponents by excluding under more or less veiled pretenses many of the members of the Unión Patriótica."[49]

Liberal candidate Belisario Porras enjoyed widespread support among the Obaldía camp, and this gave him significant influence among members of the nation's electoral board as well. It also assured him the support of the National Police, whose principal role during these early years was to support and enforce administration policies. These circumstances in effect gave Porras an insurmountable candidacy, and he easily won the 1912 election.[50]

The new president expanded the boundaries of the capital city, established Panama's Public Registry and its National Archives, and nationalized the nation's lottery. He further bolstered his stock in the eyes of his constituency by continuously bombarding his opponents with vitriolic rhetoric aimed at incriminating them for their alliance with the United States. One of Porras's sons, Camito, owned a share of the nationalist daily *Tiempo*, and this newspaper provided the president with a useful medium through which to promulgate his nationalist agenda. Known in Panamanian historiography as the nation's leading "neoliberal," Porras is remembered by Panamanian nationalists for preserving the integrity of Panama's government, despite opposition from both North American imperialists and the nation's powerful urban elite.[51]

Yet Porras's political pragmatism ultimately outweighed his anti-Americanism. As president he demonstrated a profound awareness of the political benefits to be derived as host nation to the canal, and he never pressed the nationalist question to the point of jeopardizing the support of the United States. On the contrary, he actually broadened Panama's ties with the United States. In 1912 and 1913, President Porras petitioned Washington for tactical and hardware assistance in updating Panama's National Police. In 1916 his administration allowed Americans to partially disarm the National Police, following a confrontation between Panamanian police officers and Canal Zone police; North Americans confiscated 941 rifles, leaving only 390 rifles for use in law enforcement in the rural provinces.[52] Then in 1921 President Porras called upon Canal Zone troops to save his second administration from a massive protest. Meanwhile, like his predecessors, Porras failed to form a significant link between his administration and the large working populations of Panama City and Colón, both of which remained largely alienated from Panama's decision-making circles.[53]

Porras's requests both delighted and concerned the United States government. Washington did not want to provide a nationalist president with a political scapegoat to vindicate his political activities. Nevertheless, despite Porras's nationalism, North Americans viewed these recurrent appeals as prime opportunities to expand U.S. claims in Panama "in connection with the authority conferred upon the United States by Article VII of the Treaty of 1903."

Porras's successor, Ramón M. Valdés, continued to use the police force to consolidate political power on the isthmus. In 1917 Valdés hired A. R. Lamb, a member of the Washington, D.C., Metropolitan Police Force, as Instructor General of the National Police. Panama's political elite, now an amalgamation of upper- and middle-class politicians from the conservative and moderate liberal camps (all rabiblancos), was developing response mechanisms capable of thwarting potential popular opposition and curbing political hostility, thus keeping order in its own house. Lamb's tenure (1917–27) accentuated the role of the police in that development.[54]

In Washington officials viewed the appointment of an American citizen to the position of inspector general as a way to secure American interests by using Panamanian soldiers in addition to North American troops. The United States government immediately began lobbying Panamanian officials to extend Lamb's influence. Earlier the onerous Taft Agreement of 1904, negotiated to ameliorate relations between the two countries following the divisive inception of the canal project, had given Washington control of Canal Zone customs and related duties. With this agreement in effect, the administrations of Amador, Obaldía, and Porras had all appointed United States citizens to many administrative posts within the new government, including advisor in the Department of Public Works, comptroller general in the nation's accounting office, director of public instruction, director of the National Institute, director of the Trade School, superintendent of Santo Tomás Hospital, and head of that facility's nursing school.[55]

Lamb's appointment fit nicely into Washington's efforts to maintain order in and around the Canal Zone. Conveniently North American objectives complemented the needs of Panama's early administrations, all of which actively sought North American cooperation in administering the new republic. Faced with increasing union activity, labor unrest, and a resurgence in nationalist activity, Panama's leaders attempted to capitalize on their longstanding alliance with Washington in order to thwart antiadministration activities.

The First Vestiges of Cohesive Opposition Activity

Beginning with the death of Pedro Prestán, in 1885, minorities and the poor remained noticeably ostracized from Panama's political arena throughout the formative years of the republic.[56] While Amador and his successors consolidated their grip on political power and wealth on the isthmus, much of the nation's poor, including its sizable Black population, continued to live in the most desperate of circumstances.[57] Throughout the first three decades of the twentieth century, Panama's urban Black population, which constituted nearly 20 percent of the entire populace in 1920, lived in the capital's densely populated, unsanitary arrabal.[58]

In 1920 resentment among Panama's urban poor reached a critical level. That year seventeen thousand West Indian Canal Commission employees belonging to various labor organizations carried out the first general strike in the nation's history (many strikes occurred from 1903 to 1920, but these earlier actions lacked the breadth of participation that characterized the 1920 demonstration). Angered by their deplorable living conditions as well as by the commission's racially biased "gold" and "silver" pay scales (where Blacks received their wages in silver while Whites received theirs in gold) and Jim Crow employment practices, they called for sweeping changes in pay and benefits and for an end to the squalid circumstances of the arrabal.[59]

Despite the size of the demonstration, the strike ended quickly and in failure. Rural laborers who migrated to the city did so to find work, and in their critical circumstances they were willing to accept the meager wages the Canal Commission normally paid its black employees. When these migrants broke the strike by accepting jobs previously held by the protesting West Indians, the walkout came to a rapid end. Moreover, with the latitude given them by the strike breakers, Canal Commission authorities began firing the strikers and evicting them from their Canal Zone residences, with the tacit approval of Panamanian officials.

This triggered a crisis among the country's urban laborers. When they lost their jobs, many West Indians living outside the capital began migrating to Panama City, and this exacerbated the situation of those workers already living in the capital's shantytowns. This demographic shift is critical to our understanding of urban life in Panama in the 1920s. In Colón, much of the population decline of the twenties occurred when labor unrest and job loss drove Black laborers and their families to Panama City in search of work. The resulting population influx overwhelmed the capital's working-class arrabal. Moreover, in addition to the significant migratory changes, Panama City experienced a notable drop in gross reproduction (children born), beginning in the mid-1920s. These data suggest that declining standards of

living caused many people, Panamanians and West Indians alike, to put off
having children after arriving in the capital—one of the symptoms of a society in crisis (see table 1 and figures 1 and 6).[60]

In addition to its economic and demographic implications, the failed 1920
renters' strike profoundly affected ordinary Panamanian citizens. The strike
underscored the fissure that divided Black and Whites in Panama, a division
that dated largely from the nineteenth century railroad and canal construction projects. Moreover the 1920 renters' dispute increased unrest in Panama
City and Colón by expanding the population of Panama's urban shantytowns,
where deplorable conditions fueled increased social agitation, as reflected in
higher crime rates. Finally, by providing Canal Zone officials with inexpen-
sive labor, migrant laborers nullified the labor scarcity created by the strike
and eliminated any leverage the strike might have given the West Indian
community. Rather than presenting even a remotely unified front, Panama's
labor force remained highly divided, and these conflicting interests rendered
the protest a failure, leaving Black employees of the Canal Commission increasingly at the mercy of their employer.[61]

Besides unrest among the nation's predominantly Black working class,
problems also developed within the ranks of the country's comparatively
small group of White workers and the expanding nationalist element of its

Figure 1
Illegitimacy in Santa Ana Parish, Panama City, 1898–1930

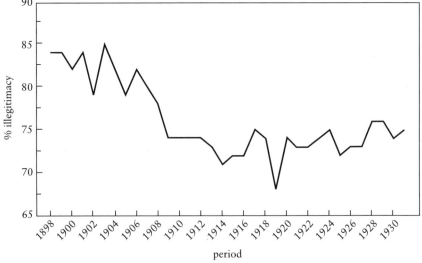

Source: Santa Ana church parish records, vols. 1–7 LDS films 1091673–1091676, 1090674–1090678

Figure 2
Illegitimacy in La Merced Parish, Panama City, 1898–1910

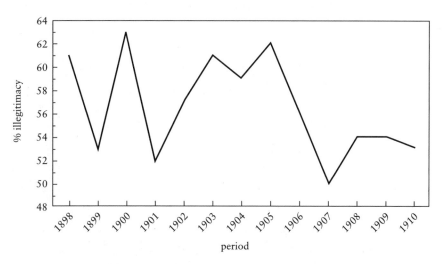

Source: La Merced church parish records, LDS films 1094125 and 1094128

Figure 3
Illegitimacy in San Juan Bautista Parish, Aguadulce, 1898–1932

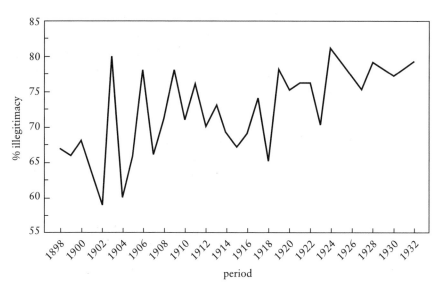

Source: San Juan Bautista parish records, vols. 12–20, LDS films 1809803 and1089804

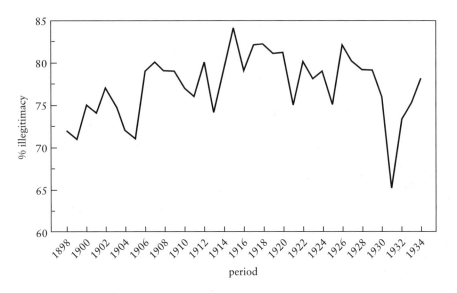

Figure 4
Illegitimacy in San José Parish, David, 1898–1934

Source: San Jose parish records, vols. 6–20, LDS films 760741–760747

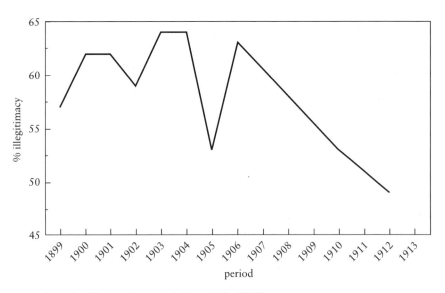

Figure 5
Illegitimacy in Santa Librada Parish, Las Tablas, 1898–1912

Source: Santa Librada parish records, vols. 10–14, LDS film 1089178

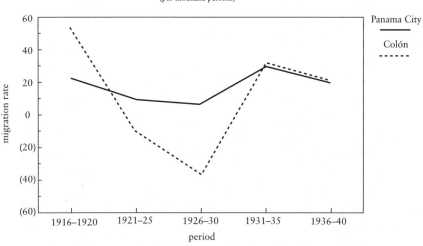

Figure 6
Migration to Panama City and Colón, 1915–1940
(per thousand persons)

Source: *Estadística Panameña* (June 1947), pp. 1–4

middle class. Until July 1921 these groups had organized locally into various small orders that reflected their respective professional pursuits. In Panama City and Colón, for example, butchers, bankers, carpenters, chauffeurs, blacksmiths, typesetters, and various other groups each organized to defend their respective interests. However, such organization lacked any cohesion beyond the local level and therefore undercut the effectiveness of the labor movement as a whole.[62]

In July 1921 leaders from many of these associations united to form La Federación Obrera de la República de Panamá (Panamanian Worker's Federation). This step gave direction and momentum to Panama's Hispanic labor force. The Federación Obrera served temporarily to unite its various sectors into one tightly knit group with shared interests, and it appeared that Panama might have achieved its first cohesive front capable of unified political activity. Leading nationalists viewed the working-class Federación Obrera as a closely knit group through which nationalists might express their own ideas. After all, working-class Hispanics in Panama City and Colón lived under deplorable conditions similar to those of their Black counterparts, and middle-class activists counted on this poverty to bind them together, thus facilitating the nation's first substantive, cohesive political front.[63]

Any hopes for a united front proved short-lived, however. This diverse group of laborers soon divided into two main factions, one radical and one more conservative. By working with Samuel Gompers and his Pan American

Federation of Labor, the Federación Obrera estranged its more ardently nationalist members who, led by Spanish anarchist José María Blásquez de Pedro, branched off to form El Sindicato General de Trabajadores (The General Workers' Union).[64] The predecessor to Panama's Communist and Socialist parties a few years later (1930), the Sindicato favored the use of direct action, including violence when necessary, to oppose North American imperialism and Panama's political status quo, which had now expanded to include both conservative and moderately liberal elements to the exclusion of nationalists, the poor, and minorities.[65]

The construction of the canal and widespread nepotism had greatly expanded the nation's administrative bureaucracy, whereas the canal's completion and the end of World War I eliminated hundreds of jobs and seriously strained the nation's economy.[66] Panama's economy constricted rapidly from 1921 to 1922, when government intake dropped off rapidly, canal traffic decreased slightly for the third time since the waterway opened in 1914, and trade with the United States and Britain, Panama's two largest trading partners at the time, tapered off. Meanwhile, as the economy slowed to a crawl, Panama's presidents continued to use jobs and contracts to reward close associates, and from 1925 to 1929 government spending outran both budget projections and actual receipts (see figures 8 and 11).

Officials in Panama City temporarily offset this fiscal imbalance by taking out a number of large loans from lending institutions in the United States in 1914, 1915, 1923, 1926 (two), 1927, and 1928. In addition to underwriting their own partisan spending, Panama's chief executives used this foreign credit to pay for massive infrastructural growth, including the Chiriquí railroad, highway construction, and an aqueduct in Bocas del Toro. These construction projects revolved largely around the United Fruit Company's massive holdings in northern Panama. However, while government receipts picked up in the midtwenties, these massive loans and the ongoing use of political plums resulted in a spiraling public debt from 1925 to 1929, when shortages of funds forced hiring cutbacks and reduced wages for many of those fortunate enough to retain their positions. In a government that relied heavily on the distribution of jobs as political favors, fewer political spoils translated into nascent antiadministration activity among some of the nation's expanding middle class, who had previously been loyal to the administration.[67]

Provoked largely by the serious fiscal problems that plagued the nation in the early twenties, other middle-class groups sprang up; while less radical than Blásquez and his followers, they nevertheless expressed economic and political dissatisfaction and therefore threatened the nation's political elite. Faced with fewer and lower-paying government jobs and believing that early liberal leaders had abandoned the tenets of the nationalist campaign, individuals such as Eusebio A. Morales, Guillermo Andreve, and José Moscote led a revitalization effort that resulted in a neoliberal movement at the moderate end of the nationalist spectrum, somewhere between rabiblancos and radical nationalists. They organized several groups, including La Liga de Inquilinos (The Tenants' League) and Acción Comunal (Community Action). These groups attempted to reach the nation's masses for the first time and, consequently, to incorporate Panama's urban poor into their own activist agenda.

Since the nineteenth century, the antecedents to these middle-class groups had been marginalized from Panama's power structure and, consequently, from resources generated by activities within the transit area. As noted by Steve Ropp, Omar Jáen Suárez, and Alfredo Figueroa Navarro, this was especially true of the rural middle class—that small group that provided demographic and economic stability to small segments of the Panamanian interior, especially the communities of Chitré and Las Tablas. These rural activists' lobbying activities had increased markedly following the completion of the canal, and in the midtwenties they added their voice to the middle-class dissension that resulted in the formation of activist groups in Panama City.[68]

In 1925 these more moderate groups and their lower-class counterparts began to play a decisive role in Panama City politics. Since independence Panama's government had charged landowners a 2 percent tax on the annual rent they collected from their investment properties. However, in 1925, the Chiari administration passed Law No. 29, a statute aimed at increasing the administration's capital flow by charging landowners an additional five dollars for each thousand dollars of their property's value as listed in the nation's tax records.

Several key leaders of the moderate nationalist movement, including Harmodio Arias of Acción Comunal, owned rental property along the waterway.[69] Upon learning of the pending legislation, the Liga, together with Acción Comunal, organized yet another renters' strike among residents of working-class neighborhoods in Panama City and Colón. The middle class provided the organizational nucleus for this unlikely coalition, and the nation's large West Indian population provided its mass base. This historic arrangement posed a formidable obstacle to the administration's pending tax on landlords.[70]

When the administration proceeded with the tax on October 1, landlords responded by raising rents from 25 to 50 percent to offset the effects of the tax. This increase had drastic implications for Panama's urban poor, particularly in the lower-class neighborhoods of El Chorillo, Calidonia, San Miguel, Marañón, Granillo, Malambo (surrounding Panama City) and Rainbow City and Folk River (on the outskirts of Colón). There such prohibitive rates further aggravated the already intense poverty.[71]

These drastic rent increases and their effects on Panama's urban poor paralleled similar crises in the nineteenth century. During the Regeneration at the end of the century, for example, the Núñez administration had sought to finance much of its reformist agenda by heavily taxing Panama and the rest of Colombia's Caribbean coast, an attempt that triggered massive popular rebellion on the isthmus. The same thing happened in Panama in 1925: the Chiari administration approved the increase on October 1, and a massive tenant strike began eight days later.

On October 10 and 11, violent confrontations between strikers and police resulted in several deaths and much chaos, and on October 12 the tenuous position of the Chiari government became apparent. Stalemated by widespread popular protest, the president invoked Article 136 of the Hay–Bunau-Varilla Treaty and called upon the United States military to defend the government and subdue the opposition. U.S. marines intervened and remained in Panama until October 23. Their occupation spelled defeat for the strikers and resulted in many additional civilian casualties as well as the closing of the Tenants' League office. It also intensified anti-American sentiments among lower-class tenants and middle-class activists.[72]

Chiari's problems worsened following the 1925 strike. In 1926 the administration negotiated the Kellogg-Alfaro Treaty with the United States, a pact aimed at filling the gap created by the abrogation of the Taft Agreement. This new treaty was to be the linchpin of U.S.-Panamanian relations, strengthening the alliance between officials in Panama City and Washington. Unlike its unilaterally formulated predecessor, the final draft of the 1926 accord reflected several years of diplomatic negotiations. Meanwhile, in addition to temporarily allying themselves with the nation's working class, middle-class oppositionists had won several legislative seats in Panama's National Assembly. By the time the agreement came before the legislature, the opposition had achieved sufficient representation in the country's legislature to repudiate it. Still smarting from the North American–assisted collapse of the 1925 renters' strike, nationalist legislators argued that the 1926 pact contradicted Panama's national interests: "Shaped by the press as well as patriotic, cultural, and ethnic interest groups, public opinion had turned in favor of a revision of the 1903 treaty that would restore to our Republic the essential attributes of independence and autonomy".[73] By rejecting the treaty, nationalists asserted their power to check the president's control of the nation's legislative processes. The rejection also constituted a retaliation against United States interference in Panama's affairs.

Coming as it did on the heels of a massive renters' strike, the rejection of the 1926 treaty marked a crisis in Panama's political development. While the ability of members of the elite to rely on foreign troops still secured their place in Panamanian politics (a reality soon changed by the Good Neighbor

Policy), they faced a significant challenge from nationalist sectors of the country's expanding middle class, who were now firmly entrenched in the nation's legislative processes and associated, at least temporarily, with the nation's large lower class. This temporary fusion of interests would end in the 1930s, when nationalist landowners such as President Harmodio Arias (1932–36) deemed it no longer in their interest to incite tenant strikes to protest government policies, once they were in office.

The twenties concluded with one more decisive political confrontation between elite politicians and their political opponents, an event that highlighted continuing divisions among liberals despite their relative cohesion in the midtwenties. In 1928 President Chiari, himself a Panama City landowner, wrested control of the Liberal party apparatus from Belisario Porras. The president also controlled four of seven posts on the nation's electoral board. The combination of these two factors gave Chiari nearly insurmountable powers, by severely curbing his opponents' ability to compete effectively in elections, including the pending 1928 presidential contest.[74]

Thus as the new decade approached, Chiari and his hand-picked successor, Florencio Harmodio Arosemena, had isolated the nation's middle sector economically (awarding fewer government jobs and contracts) and politically (controlling the electoral board and the police). While a series of tenuous alliances with urban workers added a collective emphasis to the nationalist agenda, these coalitions did not come close to reconciling the ethnic, social, and political differences that continued to divide antiadministration forces. Neither did they seriously endanger Chiari's grip on the nation's presidency. With control of the electoral board and the National Police firmly in the hands of the president, nationalists lacked the two fundamental options that had allowed them to occasionally bridle the nation's political elite since 1903. A crisis engulfed the republic as a consequence.

This is where Panama's politics and society stood in January 1931, when the moderately nationalist group Acción Comunal took up arms against the Arosemena administration. Unlike their futile campaign during the Thousand Days' War, however, this time nationalists had achieved sufficient collective political mobilization to drive their opponents from office, thereby ushering in a new era, one dominated at least rhetorically by nationalist patriots opposed to Yankee intervention in isthmus affairs.

Conclusions

The nineteenth century bequeathed to postindependence Panama an entrenched political and economic elite, a dynamic middle class increasingly divided over the amount of leverage foreigners should exercise in the new nation's business, and an unwieldy working class that was growing at an unprecedented rate. Throughout Panama's fitful Colombian era, these components of Panamanian society had remained seriously divided along ethnic, social, and political lines, incapable of any coherent activity beyond the scope of their own myopic agendas.

The beginning of a new century did not ameliorate these fissures. Instead the Thousand Days' War, independence, the American canal project, and the economically difficult twenties further divided these groups, resulting in ever more fragmented classes and escalating political mobilization on the isthmus. As the Depression approached and each of these groups pursued its own agenda (Parsons's "optimization of gratification"), successive administrations relied increasingly on the National Police to check antiadministration activity. In the long run this practice marked Panama's shift away from reliance on foreign military intervention for political stabilization. In the short term, however, the police did not complete its transition to independent power broker until after World War II. Meanwhile Panamanian society remained severely fragmented along class and political lines from 1903 to 1931, culminating in the nation's first armed coup in the early morning hours of January 2, 1931. At that time members of the moderately nationalist group Acción Comunal took up arms and forcibly removed the nation's president from office.

Following a brief display of solidarity among these insurgents, however, the decade of the thirties accentuated and reinforced those fissures that had characterized Panamanian society from 1903 to 1931. Nationalism and opposition to the status quo among much of Panama's expanding middle class had bound the insurgent Generation of '31 together long enough to topple the elite, pro-American administration of Florencio H. Arosemena. Yet immediately following the uprising, the insurgents split into competing groups, thereby forfeiting any sense of collective identity they might have temporarily achieved and forcing successive administrations in the 1930s to rely increasingly on the National Police to mend their political fences. Meanwhile presidents in the thirties fielded their own personal armed units of supporters to counter any partisan squabbling within the ranks of the police, and as Jorge Conte-Porras has noted, these paramilitary praetorian squads frequently reduced politics on the isthmus to open clashes in the streets of the capital city.

3

The Generation of ´31

As the 1920s drew to a close and the Depression loomed near, the Panamanian nation approached a critical juncture in its brief history. Since independence in 1903, Panama's ruling elite, mostly urban landlords and wealthy merchants, had attempted unsuccessfully to establish a cohesive front that could effectively govern the new nation. Instead, throughout the first decades of the twentieth century, competing agendas had seriously divided Panamanian society, rendering its various components "fragmented and incapable of unified political action other than resistance, violence, defiance, and terrorism."[1]

When their attempts to control Panama's fragmented political system failed, successive regimes relied increasingly on a combination of police force, political chicanery, and foreign intervention to stifle opposition and to contain unrest. In the short term, this rather informal means of ruling compensated for the elite's lack of a viable political front; it also perpetuated the status quo against increasingly unfavorable odds.[2] However, the combination of the canal project, World War I, and the economically difficult twenties caused a marked increase in social and political fragmentation on the isthmus, and this situation translated into escalating political mobilization from 1903 to 1931, when "all sorts of social forces [became] engaged directly in general politics."[3]

The divisions caused by this sweeping social and political realignment reached their most serious state with the outbreak of the Depression. In Panama's predominantly service-sector economy, the world's financial difficulties in late 1930 and throughout 1931 caused a severe financial recession, a marked rise in unemployment, and further constraints on the distribution of government jobs and contracts. In a nation already seriously splintered into competing interest groups and beleaguered with a severely distended federal bureaucracy, these factors fueled increased political agitation and, in the early morning hours of January 2, 1931, resulted in the nation's first armed coup. At that time disgruntled activists belonging to the moderately nationalist group Acción Comunal took up arms and forcibly ousted the elite regime of Florencio Arosemena.

Declaring their actions "moved by the purest sentiment of patriotism," the insurgents appeared initially to have achieved unprecedented political unity, while gaining access to profitable jobs and contracts previously out of their reach. However, as the change in government unfolded, the rebels fought among themselves, undermining the relatively unified front they had assembled to overthrow the Arosemena government. Within a matter of months following the revolt, the dissidents had divided into various opposition groups, whose agendas often clashed and whose members sometimes even took up arms to oppose their former allies. In the end the same nationalist insurgents who declared themselves "moved by the purest sentiments of patriotism" further divided Panamanian society, using the police to substitute for their own inability to form a united front capable of governing the nation. By relying on the police in this fashion, Panamanian presidents in the 1930s transformed the police force into an institution capable of dominating Isthmian politics the way foreign troops had in decades past. In the process they established a precedent for the later military regimes of José Remón, Omar Torrijos, and Manuel Noriega.

This postcoup splintering proved decisive in the formation of the modern Panamanian state. As in the case of the Populist movement in the United States in the late nineteenth century, common disdain for the status quo among the activists failed to overcome important distinctions among them. In fact in the final analysis, schisms that occurred in Panamanian politics in the 1930s actually transcended those that had developed during the formative era from 1903 to 1931, extending even to the ranks of the police. There several disgruntled officers exhibited their divided allegiances in the months following the revolt when they joined in an attempted countercoup, an effort that quickly failed. A second countercoup attempt occurred in July 1935; this attempt purportedly involved several prominent members of the National Police, including José Remón. Remón lost his job as a result of the 1935 attempt, only to be rehired in November 1940 by president-elect Arnulfo Arias. Moreover, while both attempts failed, they accentuated the severity of the divisions that plagued Panamanian society during the Depression.[4]

To determine how the coup and its protagonists changed Panama, particularly with respect to the role of the police in the nation's political affairs, it is important to focus on the 1931 uprising. A close look at this putsch will underscore the depth and breadth of the conflicts that divided Panama socially and politically at the time. Professor Mario Esteban Carranza has noted that when a "crisis in hegemony" occurs within a given government, a "state of exception" ensues, and the military assumes a more prominent role in civil society. Political scientist George Priestly argues further that Panama reached this point in the 1960s. However, while Panama's newly appointed

junta survived a countercoup attempt following the 1931 putsch and pun-
ished its perpetrators, the nation's urban shantytowns continued to over-
flow with laborers who lived in the nation's most squalid, desperate
circumstances. This incendiary combination of middle-class fragmentation
and working-class instability placed a premium on the president's ability to
control the police, the sole armed branch of the nation's government (or, in
professor Huntington's words, the nation's only "distinct class of specialists
in the management of violence").[5] Consequently a crisis in hegemony produced a "state of exception" that triggered "a progressive assumption of
political power by the [nation's] soldiery" in the 1940s, not the 1960s.[6]

With their capacity to govern the nation jeopardized by this upheaval,
especially by the problems within the police force, presidents in the 1930s
organized paramilitary activist groups from the ranks of their own civilian
supporters to subdue would-be opponents. Frequently presidents simply
merged these private armies with the police corps, bolstering the ranks of
the police while eclipsing conflicting allegiances within the officer corps. In
this way presidents from the nationalist Generation of '31 fended off their
political enemies, despite the escalating antiadministration sentiment that
developed and flourished during the thirties. They also made the police the
decisive force in Isthmian politics.

The 1931 Coup

As the 1920s came to an end, many Panamanians found themselves struggling to survive. The nation's growing population of impoverished urban
laborers had organized various strikes in the years after World War I, in an
attempt to improve their living and working conditions. Moreover, as the
nation's budget constricted and successive regimes compensated for the lack
of funds by trimming back hiring practices and public contracts, the more
militant components of the middle class increasingly agitated against the
nation's ruling elite.[7]

Various activist groups emerged from the tumultuous twenties, and collectively these groups formed what Panamanian scholar Jorge Conte-Porras
has dubbed the Generation of '31.[8] In addition to activist elements within
extant political parties, the Generation of '31 included new groups that
emerged in the wake of World War I, groups such as the Federación Obrera
de la República de Panamá (Federation of Panamanian Workers), the
Sindicato General de Trabajadores (General Syndicate of Workers), the Liga
de Inquilinos (Renters' League), the Communist and Socialist parties, and
many others, most notably the moderately nationalist middle-class civic or-

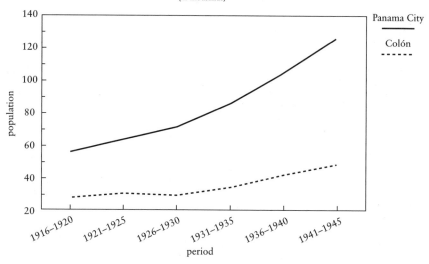

Figure 7
Populations of Panama City and Colón, 1916–1945
(in thousands)

Source: *Estadística Panameña* (June 1947), pp. 1–4

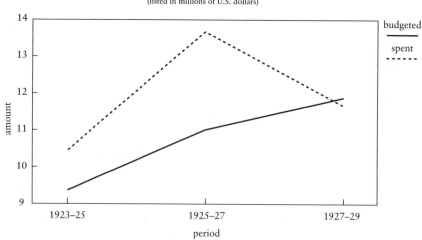

Figure 8
Budgets and Expenses of Panama's Five Government
Ministries, 1923–1929
(listed in millions of U.S. dollars)

Source: George F. Roberts, *Investigación económica de la República de Panamá*, p.25

ganization called Acción Comunal. Historian Ricaurte Soler points out that at the time of its founding, Acción Comunal's membership consisted largely of engineers, lawyers, doctors, and various bureaucrats.[9] Of all the activist groups to emerge during Panama's formative years, only Acción Comunal achieved sufficient solidarity to actually disrupt the nation's ruling class—a group that in the 1920s still consisted primarily of urban landlords and affluent merchants who successfully monopolized the Canal Zone bonanza.[10]

Formed in 1923 largely in response to difficulties caused by the recession of 1920–24 (see figures 7–12), Acción Comunal gave voice to the more moderate elements of Panama's expanding middle class. From its inception, Acción denounced Panama's ruling elite and its compliance with the United States, promulgating instead a "regeneration" of Panamanian nationality and culture based on "patriotism, action, equity, and discipline."[11] Its platform rested on seven basic tenets, which its members declared would "exalt [Panama's] national values" and revitalize the country after years of dishonest government, which they blamed on the nation's pro-American elite. These tenets included the following:

1) Teach your children to love the country.
2) Teach your children to respect the flag.
3) Speak correct Castilian Spanish.

Figure 9

Panama Canal Activity, 1925–1935
(in thousands of vessel transits)

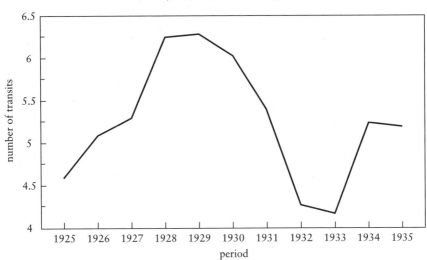

Source: *Estadística Panameña* (June 1952), p. 54

Figure 10

Number of Employees in Panama's Five Government Ministries, 1923–1929
(in thousands)

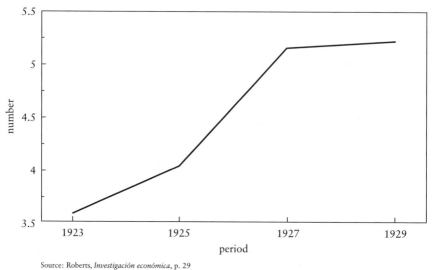

Source: Roberts, *Investigación económica*, p. 29

4) Address foreigners in Spanish.
5) Ask for Panamanian currency [the Balboa] and count in Balboas.
6) Do not make purchases in stores that advertise in English.
7) Do not make purchases in stores that do not employ Panamanians.[12]

Armed with this agenda, members of Acción Comunal encountered their first big test in 1925, when they helped organize a successful tenants' strike among residents of Panama City's impoverished arrabal (working-class shantytown). There deplorable living conditions made life nearly unbearable for thousands of employees of the Canal Commission. The railroad and canal projects had overwhelmed working-class neighborhoods in Panama City and Colón. These realities triggered massive outmigration in the twenties, as people fled urban hardships for the countryside; then, as the Depression began, the pattern reversed itself, as thousands of migrants returned to the cities in search of relief from the nation's devastated agricultural sector (see table 2 and appendix B). This overwhelming return to the city magnified the effects of poverty in the arrabal.[13]

In his study of urban poverty, Alejandro Portes has identified demands for housing and landownership as the two most common reasons for political agitation among Latin America's urban poor. Moreover, Professor Portes's own findings suggest a tendency among other groups, including middle-class observers, to try to incite "vicarious rebellion" among residents of urban

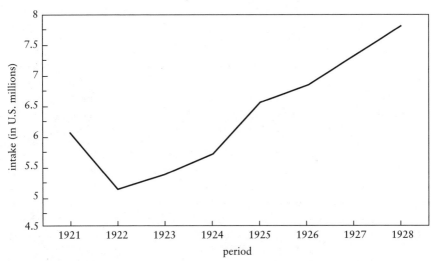

Figure 11
Income of the Republic of Panama, 1921–1928
Including Customs, Taxes, and Public Fees*

*mail and telegraph fees

Source: Roberts, *Investigación económica*, p. 336

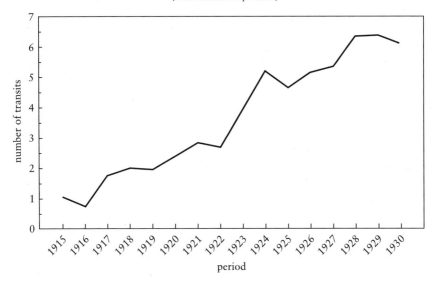

Figure 12
Panama Canal Traffic, 1914–1930
(in thousands of ship transits)

Source: *Estadística Panameña* (June 1952), p. 54

slums.[14] Portes's observations clearly apply to circumstances surrounding Panama's urban poor in the midtwenties: in the wake of the creation of their own organization in 1923, leaders of Acción Comunal saw the wretched condition of the poor as an opportunity. By inciting the strike and then helping organize it, Harmodio Arias and other *comunalistas* (members of Acción Comunal) couched their own disdain for the Chiari administration in popular terms the government could not ignore. The plan worked; the protest stalemated the elite administration of President Rodolfo Chiari and forced his government to call on United States marines to quell the uprising.[15]

Following this successful protest, comunalistas went underground to avoid persecution, but they did not remain there long. In 1926 the governments of Panama and the United States concluded negotiations on the Kellogg-Alfaro Treaty. Officials in Panama City and Washington intended for the agreement to become the linchpin of relations between the two countries. However, Acción Comunal had achieved a viable presence in congress; Harmodio Arias, a brilliant lawyer and strident patriot, was a comunalista and member of congress. Fired by this nationalist presence, Panama's legislature rejected the Kellogg-Alfaro Treaty, arguing in an unprecedented decision that the accord failed to "restore to our Republic the essential attributes of independence and autonomy."[16]

From 1926 to 1930 Acción Comunal's modest membership continued to agitate against the governing elite's complicity with North American imperialists. Nevertheless, until 1929 its numbers remained low and, with the exception of their successes in 1925 and 1926, their influence minimal. Then, as Panama's economy constricted and the fiscal crisis of 1929–30 approached, the group's membership increased from several dozen to more than three hundred members. Most of this growth occurred from July to December 1930, in inverse proportion to the nation's worsening fiscal and political fortunes. Acción Comunal's numbers now included several prominent members of Panama City's middle class, including future presidents Harmodio Arias (one of the earliest members of the group), his younger brother Arnulfo (who joined on November 19, 1930), and Enrique A. Jiménez (whose signature appeared on the group's declaration "To the Panamanian Nation," a manifesto issued immediately following the coup on January 2, 1931; see appendix C for the text of this declaration in its entirety.) These prominent professionals provided Acción Comunal with considerable leadership experience and finesse well beyond that achieved by other segments of the activist Generation of '31, and by late 1930 the society had reached its zenith in terms of size, sophistication, and solidarity.

With Acción Comunal leading the way, opposition to the regime of Florencio H. Arosemena continued to mount, as the nation's fiscal and social conditions worsened. Finally, just after midnight on the morning of January 2, 1931, several dozen comunalistas decided to act on their dislike of the nation's ruling elite.[17] Participating members of the association split up into three regiments, each with a different assignment related to the group's overall objective of toppling the government.[18]

Armed with only a dozen or so shotguns and approximately twenty pistols, the insurgents first cut the city's telephone lines. The initial group, a dozen men under the direction of Roberto Clement, set out to capture the police's cavalry division in the Las Sabanas region of the capital. After quietly arriving at their destination, several of the men went inside and falsely reported an accident in nearby Río Abajo, which they claimed required the immediate attention of the three or four officers on duty. With the phone lines cut, the officers could not corroborate this claim without actually going to the site of the purported mishap. This ruse lured the unsuspecting personnel outside, and Clement and his men then took control of the police substation, meeting only minimal resistance.

Simultaneously a group directed by Homero Ayala P. assaulted the *cuartel central* (police headquarters in Panama City). In a longer, bloodier battle than the one that occurred at cavalry headquarters, Ayala and his colleagues stormed the cuartel, where they confronted much better equipped and better trained police officers. Despite the disparity in armaments and experience, however, the insurgents fought with unflinching conviction, finally capturing the building and jailing those police who survived the onslaught.

The principal objective of the Clement and Ayala groups was to cripple the government's ability to respond to the coup. A third group, this one directed by Acción Comunal's quixotic new leader, Arnulfo Arias, launched a feverish assault on the presidential palace. Arias gained access to the palace by invoking his status as a physician and friend of the administration, claiming the president needed medical assistance. Once inside, Arias let in his fellow conspirators, who then launched an all-out attack on the unsuspecting presidential guard. With Arias leading the way, the insurgents engaged the guard in a bloody fight that lasted several hours. Finally, as daybreak approached, a small rebel detachment reached the president's personal living quarters on the palace's third floor. There, after killing one of the presidential guards, Arnulfo Arias personally captured the president.[19]

This three-tiered attack worked well. With only minimal armaments and training, the rebels daringly engaged government forces for several hours. As the morning broke, dozens of additional observers offered their support for the coup, and these volunteers helped to snuff out the last vestiges of resistance and guard prisoners. Having carried out their attack, the insurgents and their growing crowd of supporters secured control of the executive palace, while taking various political prisoners and forcing the resignation of President Florencio Arosemena and his cabinet.

A total of ten persons died and five fell wounded during the assault. Under the direction of Manuel Quintero, a disciple of Arosemena's arch rival Belisario Porras, this small band of dissidents next issued a proclamation denouncing preceding administrations for "compromising the nation politically, economically, and morally" (see appendix C). After explaining why they had overthrown the Arosemena regime, Quintero and his associates then disclosed what they intended to accomplish in the wake of their successful rebellion: they promised to found "a regime of constitution and law" while reestablishing "the effectivity of republican institutions."[20] In a move aimed largely at legitimizing the coup in Washington's eyes, the insurgents then appointed Arosemena's vice president, former foreign minister Ricardo Alfaro, interim president of the republic.[21]

This coup marked a critical juncture for several reasons. First, as demonstrated by the administration of Harmodio Arias from 1932 to 1936, this uprising gave the activist component of Panama's middle class control of the presidency and, consequently, access to the government jobs and Canal Zone dollars denied them by earlier administrations. In short the coup ended thirty years of elite domination of the nation's government and ushered in a decade of rule by members of the Generation of '31. Second, it revealed a significant shift in United States policy toward Panama. Rather than intervening, American soldiers waited for assurances from the insurgents that they would not impinge the canal's function or security. Having received (and accepted) such reassurances from Arnulfo Arias and his colleagues, American troops opted not to enter the city, remaining instead in the Canal Zone, presumably following President Herbert Hoover's proclivity for noninterventionist diplomacy. Finally, and most importantly, the uprising redefined the nation's political status quo by incorporating middle-class nationalists into the group of Panamanian politicians who, once in office, used the threat of armed force augmented by assistance from the United States to keep the remainder of the nation's population at bay.[22]

Codifying the Coup: The Interim Regime of Ricardo Alfaro

While the revolt toppled the Arosemena administration, it failed to replace the elite's structural hegemony, a fact that severely limited the new regime's effectiveness. Before Arosemena's ouster, *Chiaristas* (followers of Rodolfo Chiari) controlled both the National Police and the electoral board. After the uprising Chiaristas still wielded considerable influence within the police and commanded a majority of votes on the electoral board. This placed them, including members of the ousted Arosemena government, in a position to tamper with the results of the next election, with the possibility of reversing the coup. It also left the new government in a particularly precarious position; lacking an effective grip on both the National Police and the nation's electoral processes, revolutionaries had to confront severe unrest without the political and institutional endorsements, constitutional or informal, that had sustained governments during Panama's first three decades as an independent republic.[23]

Ricardo Alfaro proved himself a willing, capable accomplice in a position that furthered his own political aspirations; in 1940 he would run for president on his own terms. When he took office, one of his first steps was to gain control of the police. The insurgents had begun this process immediately following the coup, when they appointed a number of new officers to replace the ousted Chiarista elements of the officers' corps that had fought openly against the revolt. Eventually these new officers would include José Remón, future first commander of the National Police and president of the republic.

In addition to the new hires made to fill vacancies created by the revolt, on August 17, 1932, Alfaro issued decree no. 142, which incorporated an organized group of his own armed supporters into the National Police force. The merger of this proadministration paramilitary unit with the police gave government officials, known as "administration liberals" to distinguish them from the urban elite, sufficient leverage within the ranks of the police to counter Chiarista influence there.[24] The merger established a precedent followed throughout the 1930s; capitalizing on the noninterventionist policies of Presidents Herbert Hoover and Franklin D. Roosevelt, nationalist administrations relied extensively on paramilitary groups to sustain their governments in lieu of United States troops. Three of the four presidents from the Generation of ´31 formed their own praetorianesque paramilitary organizations to hold the opposition in check and help arbitrate the nation's affairs: in 1932 President Ricardo Alfaro organized La Reserva Nacionalista (Nationalist Reserve) and incorporated it into the National Police with decree no. 142; in 1936 President Harmodio Arias incorporated his own three-hundred-man Guardia Cívica (Civic Guard) into the ranks of the National Police; and in 1940, when the presidential election pitted Arnulfo Arias against former president Ricardo Alfaro the latter reorganized his armed band into La Guardia Cívica Nacionalista (Nationalist Civic Guard) to challenge the Arias candidacy.[25]

As the 1932 election approached and Alfaro's interim tenure drew to its close, administration liberals took additional steps to consolidate their hold on power. Having neutralized Chiarista leverage within the police force, the interim government moved to counter the opposition's domination of the electoral board. To prevent Chiari's followers from voting more than once, the Alfaro administration requested the assistance of the United States in devising a plan to prevent multiple voting; the latter provided the government with an indelible red dye with which to stamp the hands of voters after they had cast their votes.[26]

Election results underscored the extent to which the insurgents now controlled the nation's political machinery. Although Chiaristas did manage to erase the ink and vote more than once, nationalist candidate Harmodio Arias won the election over Francisco Arias by the surprisingly large margin of 39,533 to 29,282.[27]

"El Candidato de los Pobres"

Harmodio Arias came to the presidency in 1932 as the most visible leader of Acción Comunal. Depicted by his followers and in the pages of his own powerful newspaper as "el candidato de los pobres" (the poor man's candidate), Arias ran on the premise of "an absolutely republican government" based on "rights which are inherent in the citizens of the republic." His earlier involvement with Acción Comunal had gained him the support of the nation's large West Indian community; combined with his moderate liberal (nationalist) backing, their endorsement made him the first Panamanian president whose constituency transcended both race and class lines. With the possible exception of Belisario Porras's 1912 campaign, no Panamanian president had ever commanded such widespread backing.

Certainly much of Arias's appeal as a candidate stemmed from the economic crisis caused by the Depression. He promised relief to the nation's farmers, new jobs and higher pay for the country's workers, and increased autonomy from the United States.[28] Despite his initial charm, Arias soon found himself confronted by a growing opposition front, and President Franklin Roosevelt's noninterventionist Good Neighbor Policy made it impossible for him to call on United States troops to save his presidency, as Belisario Porras had done in 1921. Thus caught between mounting domestic opposition and the inability to rely on United States soldiers, Arias responded by depending more than ever on the National Police to settle his political problems.

As historian Michael Conniff has pointed out, Arias's victory in 1932 stemmed from his ability to dovetail his nationalist backing with the interests of Panama's large West Indian community. In 1925 he had gained prominence as one of the organizers of the working-class renters' strike. Then, in

the late twenties, he expanded his ties to Panama City's West Indian workers by serving as their lawyer when the Chiari family tried to prohibit them
from voting in Panama's elections.[29]

Arias's successful representation of the West Indian community marked
the culmination of nationalist efforts, which had begun in 1925, to court
Panama City's large population of Black voters. West Indians expressed their
gratitude by voting for Arias in the 1932 presidential election, thwarting
upper-class efforts to reverse the 1931 coup and giving Arias an unprecedented broad base of support.[30]

Yet as the Arias administration took shape, it began to resemble those of
Panama's earlier elite family regimes. He placed relatives and close friends
in key positions that gave him extraordinary control of the nation's police
force, which he used to manipulate his political opponents. He also used the
presidency to more fully politicize the nation's youth, astutely assimilating
many of them into his own nationalist crusade. His appointments included
the following:

1. Arnulfo Arias, Harmodio's younger brother and Harvard-edu-
   cated physician who had masterminded the 1931 revolt, became
   head of Panama City's Santo Tomás Hospital, director of the
   Sanitation Bureau, and director of the Lucha Anti-Tuberculosa
   campaign. These programs received extensive governmental
   appropriations and did not fall under the fiscal supervision of the
   comptroller general.

2. Tomás Guardia, Harmodio's brother-in-law, served as director of
   the Central Roads Board. Appointed to this position by Arias's
   predecessor, he continued to function in that capacity during his
   brother-in-law's administration. The board received funds directly
   from the road tax that each citizen paid, which varied from three
   to twenty-five dollars annually, and from a four-cent tax on each
   gallon of gasoline sold in the republic. This position answered
   directly to the president and also did not make an accounting of
   expenses to the comptroller general's office.

3. Arias appointed another of his brothers-in-law, Aurelio Guardia
   Vieto, to the posts of Comandante Primer Jefe del Cuerpo de
   Polic'a Nacional (National Police Chief—he served in this capacity from 1933 to 1935) and Inspector General de las Fuerzas
   Públicas (National Police Inspector—he filled this position from
   1936 to 1939). This appointment placed the nation's police force
   and its arms directly under the supervision of the president and
   his family during his administration (and that of his successor)
   and gave Arias another way to counter Chiarista influence among
   the ranks of the police.

4. A third brother-in-law, Octavio Méndez Pereira, became director of the National Institute, giving the president a powerful advocate with the nation's politically active youth. When Arias created the National University in 1935, it expanded his sphere of influence to include the capital city's college-aged students. His appointment of Méndez then secured for him the invaluable support of high school students in Panama City. With these appointments Arias became known as an advocate of the student cause, and this helped more fully integrate Panama City students into the nationalist movement.

5. Finally, Arias appointed yet another of his brothers-in-law to the position of solicitor general.

Much like President Chiari's use of the executive office in the 1920s to secure his family's monopoly on the nation's beef industry, Harmodio Arias also used his position to secure lucrative contracts for friends and family.[31] One of the most flagrant cases of fiscal abuse during his administration was a case involving one of his younger brothers, who received a major government contract to build schools in the nation's interior. None of these contracts required their beneficiaries to report to the General Accounting Office; this type of budget manipulation had seriously compromised Panama's fiscal integrity throughout the twenties, and by granting contracts (sometimes multiple contracts of disproportionately large sums) to family members, Arias perpetuated the serious budgetary problems of the previous decade.[32]

Expanding on Alfaro's creation of a paramilitary force to check resistance within the nation's police force, Arias augmented the National Police with three hundred of his own armed supporters. Known as La Guardia Cívica, these men gave Arias a group of "armed patriots" that increased his leverage against political opponents. Working in conjunction with Arias's brother-in-law, who was serving at the time as the National Police Chief, the Guardia gave the president his own personal army with which to curb political opposition.

Having solidified his control of the police, Arias then began a program of modernization aimed at making that organization a more effective armed regiment that could fill the void created by the Good Neighbor Policy. First, he reaffirmed Panama's sovereign right to enforce its own laws by rearming the police with high-powered rifles that had been confiscated in 1916 by the United States.[33] He then constructed modern police installations throughout the republic, including the new cuartel central in the Panama City suburb of El Chorillo, which served as police headquarters until it was destroyed during the December 1989 invasion. Finally, beginning with José Remón in 1932, Arias began hiring native Panamanian graduates of foreign military schools to fill pivotal positions within the police force, many of which had remained vacant since the 1931 coup.

Hired initially as a captain and assigned to police headquarters in Panama City, Remón's eventful career perpetuated an abiding sense of loyalty among his fellow officers. As his career unfolded, for example, Remón successfully lobbied for both an expansion of the police force and an increase in police salaries—moves that proved particularly popular during the Depression and at the height of the war in the midforties, when jobs in Panama City were scarce.[34] Furthermore, as his superiors promoted him through the ranks of the officers' corps, Remón did not forget his colleagues; rather, he granted vacation leaves to his men and established a police commissary to supply officers with basic commodities at reduced prices. Significantly, when Remón hired new officers, he frequently did so from among members of Panama City's working class, including Blacks. Finally, as first commander, Remón displayed considerable racial acumen when he promoted a Black officer, Saturnino Flores, to the lofty position of third commander of the National Police.[35]

Beyond cementing Remón's status as a prominent police officer, these steps to enhance the professional caliber of Panama's law enforcement agency permanently altered the function of the police on the isthmus.[36] In addition to becoming a vehicle of social mobility for a select few of Panama's urban poor, the refurbished police gave its commanding officers considerable leverage in civilian decision-making circles. Under Harmodio Arias, the National Police began emerging as an alternative to the presidency in the quest for wealth and power on the isthmus, a process that would reach full fruition in the late forties, when First Commander Remón appointed and removed presidents at will.[37]

The Fragmentation of the Generation of ´31

Arias' manipulation of the National Police quickly became a decisive factor in his administration of the nation's affairs, particularly when his base of support began splintering into myriad factions. The president's distribution of political favors alienated some of his middle-class colleagues, many of whom soon began organizing opposition to his regime. These fissures among Arias's middle-class allies deepened as the country's economic circumstances worsened, forcing the administration to pay its upper-echelon employees only 90 percent of their salaries in cash, with the other 10 percent paid in noninterest-bearing treasury certificates.[38] Moreover the elite faction displaced by the 1931 revolt was intent on regaining power, and the threat of a countercoup remained very real throughout the early 1930s.[39] Finally, tens of thousands of the nation's urban workers continued to endure the consequences of life in Panama City's miserable arrabal, and strikes by the poor required the administration's constant vigilance.

This turmoil reached a climax of sorts in 1932, when the new president found himself torn between his purported allegiance to the West Indian community and his own concerns as a landlord and as president. For many Panamanians the first indication of the Depression had been the nation's slumping sugar, coconut, and banana industries in the late 1920s. A diseased banana crop in Bocas del Toro in northern Panama aggravated the region's already precarious situation, and thousands of workers now fled to the city, where their presence further complicated life among the nation's severely distended population of urban poor. Yet the market closures around the world in late 1929 meant sharp reductions in the number of ships using the canal and, consequently, commensurate decreases in jobs, taxes, and capital flow generated by canal traffic.[40]

With their working and living situations aggravated by thousands of new arrivals and the nation's depressed economy, workers in Panama City and Colón began a tenement strike in 1932, reminiscent of the 1925 crusade that Harmodio Arias himself had helped organize.[41] However, as socialist leader Demetrio Porras incisively argued at the time, the president now had little vested interest in the success of a working-class protest. As a landowner who had ascended to the presidency, Arias could hardly be expected to resolve the controversy in favor of the renters.[42]

From 1903 to 1931, little had changed among the nation's urban poor. Shantytowns along the canal still had the nation's most deplorable living conditions—circumstances against which President Harmodio Arias had agitated in 1925. The arrabal had been overrun by the latest wave of migrants fleeing the hardships of life in the countryside, thus reversing the outmigration of the twenties and overwhelming Panama City's working-class neighborhoods.

Along with this population surge came commensurate changes in the standard of living among the nation's urban poor. Unemployment rates increased as canal traffic dropped off markedly. The hardships triggered by the loss of jobs expressed themselves in a number of measurable sociological phenomena. After a downward trend in illegitimacy over several years, the working-class parish of Santa Ana in Panama City experienced a resurgence in the number of illegitimate births (see figure 1). Meanwhile, while crime rates nationwide actually decreased, in working-class neighborhoods along the canal they increased.[43]

This time when the strike began, however, Arias did not side with the urban poor. As Demetrio Porras had predicted, instead he responded by

TABLE 3.1: CHANGES IN PROVINCIAL POPULATIONS, 1911–1940

	(by percentage change between censuses)			
	1911–1920	1920–1930	1930–1940	1940–1950
Bocas del Toro	19.8	−41.8	4.2	33.6
Coclé	29.0	6.9	15.5	30.4
Colón	81.5	−1.9	36.7	14.8
Chiriquí	20.7	0.6	44.6	23.6
Darién	19.3	24.8	11.5	−1.5
Herrera	26.0	7.1	22.8	31.1
Los Santos	15.2	19.0	20.4	23.3
Panamá	58.5	16.4	51.9	42.6
Veraguas	11.7	4.4	22.2	26.1
Republic, total	32.5	4.8	33.2	28.8

Source: República de Panamá, Contraloría General de la Nación, Dirección de Estadística y Censo, Estadística Panameña 10(3) (March 1951):1.

sending in the refurbished National Police to stop the uprising, after piece-meal diplomacy failed. In addition he suspended the strikers' constitutional rights and had their leaders arrested.[44]

Arias' use of violence to end the 1932 renters' strike, combined with widespread knowledge of his political favors to friends and family, caused several rifts within political circles beyond those that had appeared in the twenties. Many of Arias's followers now distanced themselves from the president. Victor F. Goytía, who had helped organize Acción Comunal to "terminate the succession of dishonest governments in Panama" and to "find an honest man of outstanding ability, who was not a politician, as a candidate for the presidency," denounced the 1931 uprising and the Arias administration. He was particularly critical of Arias's use of force against the poor. "There was just a change of power and of men but not of policies. The reigning families continued to reign while the woes of the common people failed to find any remedy whatsoever."[45]

Following the end of the renters' strike, other individuals soon followed Goytía into the opposition camps that were cropping up among disaffected members of the middle class. Correa García, Carlos López, and several other nationalist legislators, all formerly influential followers of Arias, merged their protests into a new opposition front. This group united several estranged moderate factions of the Liberal party, including followers of Francisco Arias, the man Harmodio had defeated in the 1932 election (Francisco's nickname was "Pancho," and his followers referred to themselves as "Panchistas"), the Independent Liberals (Belisario Porras and his devotees—

Porristas), and the ousted Chiaristas. At least twice during Arias's administration, this opposition front attempted to overturn the presidency, once in
the failed counterrevolution of 1932 and then again in 1935. It is possible
that the latter attempt included hostile members of the National Police,
many of whose leaders, including Remón, fell out of favor and were de-
moted or fired for their complicity.

Thus as his tenure in office continued, Arias faced increasing levels of
opposition from various sources. He held a precariously small majority in
the Assembly (18 to 14), and his opponents leveled increasingly acerbic
charges against him for abandoning the poor and for nepotism, practices
contrary to his promise of a democracy unfettered by executive favoritism.

Panama the Victim: Arias and the National Psyche

The forcible subjugation of political opponents in Panama did not begin with
Harmodio Arias or any other member of the nationalist Generation of '31.
Presidents from 1931 to 1941 merely adapted this elite practice to a different
set of circumstances in the thirties, particularly the Good Neighbor Policy.

The 1931 uprising and the subsequent interim administration had challenged elite domination of the presidency. However, it was President
Harmodio Arias who engaged Panama's national psyche, by couching the
change of government in broader terms all Panamanians could relate to. By
rhetorically positioning his own government within a framework of nationalism that included issues such as the fatherland under attack, imperial arro-
gance, and the emotional value of land, ethnicity, and culture, Harmodio
Arias neutralized much of the opposition that might have otherwise undermined his administration.[46]

One of the vehicles Arias used to carry out this strategy was education.
When he took office in 1932, high school and college students already constituted a very active component of national politics. In 1921, for example,
students had organized their own resistance to the United States intervention in the province of Chiriquí, and they communicated regularly with
their peers in Cuba, Peru, Argentina, and Mexico.[47] Student leaders continued to protest North American imperialism throughout the twenties, and in
the thirties they became increasingly involved in politics through the Communist and Socialist parties and the Alianza Revolucionaria de la Juventud
Unida (Revolutionary Alliance of United Youth)—ARJU—the Panamanian
offshoot of Peru's Aprista campaign.[48]

Thus by the thirties, young people already had an active voice in Panama's
political affairs. To tap this ready source of political energy, President Arias

established the National University of Panama in 1935, to "preserve the Panamanian nationality." This move drew support from the Socialist and Communist wings of the liberal bloc and gave a much-needed infusion of solidarity to the president's badly divided constituency.[49]

Arias's appointment of his brother-in-law Octavio Méndez Pereira to the post of director of the National Institute in Panama City had given the president significant leverage with the youth of the capital. From his position as director, Méndez Pereira encouraged his students to maintain a state of "constant rebelliousness" to check the spread of imperialism—and, ostensibly, to support the administration's activities with respect to government contracts, the poor, and so forth. Beyond what it accomplished for the president, this taunting nationalism secured for Méndez the unyielding loyalty of many of his students. In a January 1947 survey conducted among high school students in Panama City, respondents ranked Méndez Pereira as the third greatest living Panamanian. Undoubtedly he played a significant role in the creation and promulgation of a national consciousness among these young people, and this awareness underscored President Arias's overarching efforts to paint the nation's misfortunes in patriotic rhetoric that youth could relate to—rhetoric blaming the United States for the nation's hardships.[50]

This youth support became particularly significant after 1941, when a United States–backed coup returned the urban elite to power and forcibly isolated the presidency from the nationalist component of the middle class. With much of the nation's opposition to the status quo politically blackballed, students played an increasingly visible role in Isthmian politics after 1941, rallying their support for the opposition cause and contributing significantly to the rejection of the Filós-Hines Treaty in December 1947. Rejection of the 1947 accord would force Americans to downsize their military presence in Panama, bringing about a decisive showdown between nationalists and government officials and elevating the police to the role of ruler in Panamanian politics.

Arias also used economic nationalism to check opposition to his administration. Since independence, Panama's economy had relied heavily on the $250,000 annuity the United States paid for the use of the canal and its surroundings. However, this sum had failed to offset the nation's economic hardships, and the country had been forced to take out several large loans in the United States to help underwrite the expense of governing the nation. These loans, totaling nearly fifteen million dollars, required monthly service payments of $182,500, a nearly impossible sum for the nation's depressed economy in the early thirties.[51]

Caught between the threat of financial collapse and mounting opposition, Arias proved particularly astute in his use of the canal annuity issue to

frame the nation's problems in terms that blamed the United States for
Panama's hardships. On October 10, 1933, Arias met with Franklin D.
Roosevelt at the White House in Washington "to discuss the whole question
of Panamanian-American relations." The two agreed to renew negotiations
to resolve differences between the two governments, including the subject
of canal annuity payments, and the presidents then turned negotiations over
to their respective diplomatic corps.[52] However, these negotiations reached
an impasse in 1934, when the United States asked Panama to continue accepting the sum of $250,000 as payment for use of the canal.[53] The Arias adminis-
tration rejected this proposal, Washington refused to increase its payments, and
for the next five years Panama refused to accept the annuity.[54]

Although rejection of the canal annuity aggravated an already stagnant
economy, Arias succeeded in identifying the United States as the nation's enemy
and, implicitly, the source of its economic and social problems. The president's
affront to United States policy provided a patriotic focal point for much of the
agitation that was dividing the nation; in this way Arias ingeniously perpetuated
his administration despite the nation's dire circumstances.[55]

After much deliberation, representatives from the two nations signed the
Hull-Alfaro Treaty on March 2, 1936. This new pact, named for the diplomats who drafted it, accomplished two important things for Panama. First,
once approved by the legislatures of both countries, it would raise the amount
of the canal annuity from $250,000 to $430,000. Second, dubbed by historians as "illusory" because it merely compensated for Roosevelt's 1934 de-
valuation of the dollar, this pending increase nevertheless provided the Arias
administration with the political currency it needed to help counter its opposition. Regardless of its true significance, the 1936 treaty decreased the
pressure on Arias and permitted the president to finish his term in office.[56]

Beyond Populist Appeal:
The Presidency of Juan Demóstenes Arosemena

As the 1936 election approached, Arias sought to avoid a repeat of 1932
conditions, when the opposition's control of the electoral board had jeopardized the revolt. Thus in addition to making the National Police his own
armed deterrent, Arias used his influence as president to dominate the board.
This gave him autocratic control over the nation's political system, reminiscent of the approach of the Chiaristas in the late twenties.

As the 1936 presidential campaign unfolded, the breadth of Arias's control became apparent. Instead of supporting the candidate of his own Partido
Liberal Doctrinario (Doctrinaire Liberal party), the president supported the

candidacy of Juan Demóstenes Arosemena, his minister of foreign relations. This move was a transparent effort on Arias's part to perpetuate his own hold on power, and it bore striking similarities to the Chiarista coalition that had controlled the presidency in the late twenties and ultimately fell victim to the 1931 revolt. Demóstenes Arosemena, a wealthy landowner like Panama's earlier politicians, was particularly unpopular among disaffected nationalists who had fled the ranks of Arias supporters to form part of the opposition front.[57]

In response to the president's brazen inflexibility regarding his choice, the National Electoral Board twice voted 4 to 3 to block Arosemena's candidacy. Cornered by widespread opposition to the president's well-publicized betrayal of his own political loyalties, members of the electoral board based their opposition on Article 72 of Law no. 28 (1930), which prohibited the election of any person who had held public office within six months prior to an election. Demóstenes Arosemena continued to function as part of the administration throughout his campaign, clearly rendering himself constitutionally ineligible to run for public office. Yet with President Arias as his political patron, Arosemena stuck with his controversial, and unconstitutional, candidacy. On election day the administration distributed duplicate cédulas (voter registration cards), destroyed ballot boxes, detained opposing members of the electoral board, and concocted "el paquetazo de Veraguas" (ghost votes from the rural province of Veraguas). The result was a high voter turnout that exceeded all predictions (and possibilities) and that brought Arosemena to the presidency despite his constitutional ineligibility. The president of the National Electoral Board, Rosendo Jurado, protested by resigning his post. Jurado contended that the opposition candidate, Domingo Díaz Arosemena, had won the election. Nevertheless, Arias had the weapons to enforce his selection and had decisively manipulated the electoral board to substantiate it. With Arias's blessing, Juan Demóstenes Arosemena became Panama's next president.[58]

On January 28, 1937, Arosemena formally expressed his gratitude to the nation's armed forces and his affinity for strong public law enforcement when he declared, through Law no. 28, the "Día del Policía" (National Police Officer Day).[59] The next year Panama's National Assembly granted the Arosemena administration one million dollars beyond its regularly appointed budget, to "acquire goods relating to national defense." Thus the Arosemena presidency furthered modernization of the police on the isthmus, and because of these largely partisan gestures, the National Police inched nearer center stage in Panamanian politics.[60]

One pivotal issue confronted the Arosemena administration as it finished out the thirties. The United States Senate delayed its vote on the Hull-Alfaro treaty until August 1939, and Arosemena had to deal with the popular resentment triggered by the delay. Desperate for an agreement, his administration negotiated away any real benefits garnered for Panama by the accord. Final approval by the U.S. Congress in August 1939 hinged on Panama's acquiescence on several key premises written into the original 1936 pact. To achieve ratification, Panama conceded to Washington the right of eminent domain over lands and waters *outside* the canal zone for purposes of defending the canal; the right to intervene unilaterally in the cities of Panama and Colón to preserve order and offset any threat to these vital ports; and the general guarantee of Panamanian independence.[61]

Despite any gains Panama might have achieved with the accord and the political refuge it provided the Arias administration after negotiations began in 1933, this treaty led to future North American intervention and established a legal basis for the United States position in the later Filós-Hines debacle, when American troops occupied an additional 134 bases throughout the republic, under the guise of protecting the waterway. While temporarily abating opposition to President Harmodio Arias, the treaty set nationalists and pro-American forces in Panama on a collision course as World War II approached and Washington became increasingly alarmed by events in Europe and the Pacific. Meanwhile the crucial importance of the canal tempered Washington's enthusiastic regard for diplomatic good neighborliness based on "the rights of others."[62] The 1936 Hull-Alfaro Treaty ended Panama's protectorate status, liberating Panamanians in the same way similar good neighbor diplomacy had emancipated Cubans and Haitians. However, officials in Washington refused to concede their right to intervene militarily in Panama to protect the canal, and the concessions American legislators exacted from Panamanian officials in 1939 to that effect reflected the pragmatic limits of the Good Neighbor Policy in Panama.

As Secretary of State Cordell Hull had pointed out in Montevideo in 1933, President Roosevelt did not intend to leave American interests vulnerable to foreign aggression. Outside the sovereign borders of the United States, the American government and business community had no larger vested interest than the Panama Canal. While American soldiers abandoned other countries in the region, and Roosevelt heralded the dawn of a collective American pact of respect for the sovereignty of other American nations, more than thirty thousand American troops, along with twenty thousand American civilians, remained in Panama to operate, administer, and protect the Panama Canal, America's largest, most strategic foreign interest. There were definite limits to Rooseveltian good neighborliness.[63]

In December 1939 President Arosemena died, and his replacement was none other than former conservative presidential candidate Augusto Boyd.

Boyd continued Arosemena's policy of cooperation with the United States, and he further alienated the nationalist element of Panama's Liberal party. Ironically then, as Panama's decade of "the purest sentiment of patriotism" drew to a close, it ended the way it had begun—under an elite, pro-American regime.

Conclusions

In Panama the formative period from 1903 to 1931 proved to be a volatile one, producing various activist groups whose competing agendas impaired the government's ability to rule. Successive administrations survived this early instability by employing a combination of police intimidation, political chicanery, and foreign intervention to counter political opposition and to offset widespread unrest.

In the short term this rather serendipitous three-tiered strategy enabled elite regimes to dominate the presidency during Panama's formative years. In the long term, however, informal governance failed to ameliorate profound divisions in Isthmian politics and society that had arisen following independence. In fact as the Depression approached and the nation's economic situation grew critical, social and political fragmentation reached its most serious level when members of Acción Comunal overthrew the government and installed a revolutionary junta aimed at "regenerating" democracy on the isthmus.

Despite their initial successes, however, members of the reactionary Generation of '31 soon splintered into various civic and political action groups whose agendas often clashed. With the middle class divided into myriad competing interest groups, and with tens of thousands of working-class Panamanians clamoring for change, fragmentation among the insurgents soon catapulted the police to a position of unequaled prominence in Isthmian politics, a position previously reserved for foreign troops. Now, in lieu of intervening soldiers, Panama's presidents needed capital, technology, and hardware to develop and maintain their own armed detachments and to fend off growing antiadministration activity on the isthmus. This 1930s "crisis in hegemony" established a precedent for the police dictatorships that would dominate life on the isthmus from 1968 to 1989.

The social and political crises of the 1930s culminated with the controversial election of Arnulfo Arias to the presidency. By the time he assumed office the nation's commercial and landowning elite had been out of power for a decade, and their opposition to, and disdain for, the Generation of '31 had grown in intensity. American officials were gravely concerned about Arias's strident nationalism, and his election provided the elite with a per-

fect opportunity to mount a powerful antinationalist campaign that would
have Washington's tacit approval. This bid to recapture the presidency ended
successfully in 1941, when several powerful Panama City landowners and
merchants, working in conjunction with the United States and numerous
disgruntled police officers, ousted Arias and installed a pro-American interim regime reminiscent of the pre-1931 administrations.[64]

Arias's 1941 overthrow would prove to be an ominous harbinger of future events in Panama, most notably the United States' 1989 invasion of
Panama. In both instances Washington helped seat a pro-American interim
administration following the ouster of a nationalist regime. Moreover in
each case the interim regime's ties to Washington seriously undermined its
legitimacy in the minds of the nation's electorate. And finally, as the Panamanian electorate recently demonstrated when it shocked observers by electing
Ernesto Pérez Balladares and returning to power the party of Generals Torrijos
and Noriega, in each instance close ties to Washington stirred renewed nationalist fervor and resentment for the merchant and landowning elite.

4

Status Quo and Radicalized Political Antagonism, 1941–1947

In January 1931 nationalists overthrew the government of President Florencio H. Arosemena and established an administration aimed at reclaiming "Panama for the Panamanians," while "regenerating" democracy on the isthmus.[1] Coup leaders promised sweeping changes, including relief for the nation's farmers, new jobs and higher pay for the country's workers, an end to nepotism, and increased autonomy from the United States. However, in the months after the putsch, the insurgents fought among themselves, forgoing any cohesion they might temporarily have achieved and further fragmenting Panamanian society and politics.

This crisis in Panamanian politics culminated in 1940, with the election to the presidency of a quixotic nationalist leader by the name of Arnulfo Arias.[2] Arias's presidency marked a critical juncture in the nation's history, one that expedited the further political ascension of the National Police. A former ambassador to Italy, Arias's stridently nationalist agenda, with strong racist overtones, angered many Isthmians and alarmed Washington. His aggressive domestic and diplomatic platforms so divided even his staunchest allies that a group of Arias's closest associates overthrew him in 1941. In his stead the rebels installed an interim administration that reflected the status quo's preferences, while also placating Washington.

The choice of Ricardo Adolfo de la Guardia to serve as interim president in the wake of the coup ended the nationalists' ten-year hold on the presidency. The appointment of a member of one of Panama City's most prominent merchant families reversed the outcome of the 1931 uprising, returning to power the elite that had governed the nation during its formative period from 1903 to 1931. Moreover the appointment of the pro-American de la Guardia mollified officials in Washington, where the canal's safety was of special concern during the war. De la Guardia's dealings with North Americans in and around the capital city (through his family's Cervecería Nacional, the National Brewery) made him particularly pro-American.[3]

While overthrowing Arnulfo Arias eliminated the perceived threat posed by his totalitarian agenda, the coup once again failed to address the broader issues that divided Panamanian society. President de la Guardia and his successor, Enrique Jiménez, lacked legitimacy in the eyes of many Panamanians, because they perceived them as Washington lackeys. This lack of support became particularly significant as the war in Europe and the Pacific unfolded. With its service-sector economy linked so intrinsically to world commerce, the closure of many of Europe's commercial markets following Hitler's invasion of Poland dramatically affected life on the isthmus. There the fiscal downturn triggered by German aggression expressed itself through sudden demographic shifts and fluctuating standards of living among the nation's urban poor.

More significant for political purposes in the forties, however, was the general unrest that characterized Panama's expanding middle class. Widespread disdain among students and professionals for these interim governments and their conspicuous complicity with Washington provided a patriotic rallying point that bound together what was arguably the most effective activist front in twentieth-century Panamanian history. By 1947 opposition to the status quo and to American imperialism on the isthmus reached a high point, resulting in the formation of an opposition front of unprecedented proportions, including more than ten thousand women. Temporarily united by their common intense dislike of the elite and its complicity with Washington in the Filós-Hines debacle, students, political groups, and a massive women's movement forced the Jiménez administration to reject the Filós-Hines agreement in December of 1947. In a politically charged environment reminiscent of the 1925 tenants' strike, the 1926 Kellogg-Alfaro fiasco, and the 1936 debate over the Hull-Alfaro Treaty, nationalists had checked elite manipulation of the nation's legislative and diplomatic processes.[4] Seen in this light, the 1941 coup inaugurated a new era in political activity on the isthmus, one characterized both by the migration of thousands of workers out of the cities and an increasingly militant student movement.[5]

Faced with these circumstances and lacking an effective base of support, the interim de la Guardia and Jiménez administrations turned increasingly to the National Police for sustenance. From 1903 to 1931, the police became an increasingly powerful voice in the nation's political arena. The impetus they received from the Generation of ´31 had given its officers a more visible role in the government's decision-making apparatus, and when the elite moved to overthrow the Arias regime in 1941, they did so with the endorsement and support of the National Police. Then from 1941 to 1948, the de la Guardia and Jiménez administrations channeled additional military hardware and capital into the police force in an effort to stem the tide of nationalist opposition while checking unrest among urban laborers.

The heavy reliance on the police in the 1940s made them increasingly capable of unilaterally assuming control of the civilian sector in times of crisis, such as that of December 1947. The vitriolic debate over the Filós-Hines Treaty ushered in an era of police domination of Isthmian politics during the dictatorship of José Remón—Panama's first bonafide political strongman. By the end of the decade, Remón appointed and removed presidents at will, and for the next forty years the police would arbitrate politics on the isthmus just as foreign troops had done prior to the twentieth century.

Panama's 1940 Presidential Election

Following their campaign to "reclaim Panama for the Panamanians" in January 1931, Panama's nationalist presidents spent the rest of the decade consolidating their power. They integrated groups of armed constituents into the National Police to increase their control over that organization, and they took steps to modernize the police and make it a more formidable component of the nation's political infrastructure. They also gained control of the nation's electoral boards during the administration of Harmodio Arias. This gave them control over the 1936 and 1940 presidential elections, while providing increasingly autocratic administrations with a democratic veneer in the late thirties.

However, while consolidating their grasp on the nation's political infrastructure, presidents in the thirties alienated many of their former allies through political favoritism and strong-arm politics—the very things they had condemned their predecessors for doing. By the end of the decade, nationalists had achieved a level of control of the nation's government similar to that of the elite regime they had overthrown in 1931. In response a new opposition front took shape. This front included former allies of the administration in addition to its long-standing opponents. Consequently, as the thirties drew to a close, various middle-class factions competed with one another and with the administration for political power.

Nevertheless, as historian Michael Conniff has noted, "whoever controls the *Policía Nacional* writes Panama's political history."[6] Panamanian presidents' command of an increasingly powerful police force in the thirties made them much more formidable political and economic opponents than their predecessors in the twenties had been. This rendered highly unlikely a repeat of the 1931 revolt, when a small band of armed civilians had ousted an elite administration. More than three decades of reliance on the National Police to stifle political opposition had altered the way government functioned in Panama City, and the expanding opposition front had to find new ways to counter increasingly entrenched executives. As Panamanian scholar Jorge Conte-Porras has noted in *Arnulfo Arias Madrid*, in the 1940s this increasingly vitriolic standoff resulted in urban warfare, as armed constituencies from opposing factions fought each other openly in the streets of the capital.[7]

While opposing bands of urban guerrillas struggled to carve out their places in Panama's decision-making circles, the National Police—the country's best-trained and most heavily armed "paramilitary" organization—emerged during the 1940 presidential campaign as the decisive factor in Panama's political processes. That year the candidates of two opposing splinter groups from the nationalist bloc that had overthrown the Arosemena regime in 1931 faced off. Arnulfo Arias, leader of the 1931 coup, ran as the candidate of a political coalition known as the Partido Nacional Revolucionario (National Revolutionary party), also known as the Panameñista party. Arias's opponent, renowned diplomat Ricardo J. Alfaro, also ran with the support of a coalition of parties, a group known collectively as the Frente Popular (Popular Front).[8]

The campaign for the 1940 election underscored the role of violence as a legitimate political tactic on the isthmus. Each candidate fielded his own personal army. Arias had the support of his older brother's group of "armed patriots," the Guardia Cívica. Moreover, because of the incumbent administration's loyalty to Harmodio Arias, who had handpicked his successor in 1936, Arnulfo Arias had the support of acting President Augusto Boyd. This gave the Arias camp the nearly insurmountable backing of the electoral board and of the National Police (both of which President Boyd controlled), in addition to the Guardia Cívica. Arnulfo Arias also used his older brother's powerful newspaper, *El Panamá América*, to malign Alfaro and to dispute his integrity, painting him as a "representative of selfish and niggardly interests that lack any ideology" (see figure 13).[9]

Alfaro countered with an equally caustic campaign. Previously he had served as interim president, following the 1931 revolt, and as minister to Washington under President Harmodio Arias. Despite Alfaro's political ties to the Arias family, his government experience in the thirties derived only from political expediency. In 1931, for example, the revolutionary junta had appointed Alfaro interim president because leaders of the uprising hoped his upper-class background and laissez-faire bias would placate Washington and prevent the United States from intervening in the insurrection. The strategy worked: the United States did not intervene, and officials immediately granted recognition to the new Panamanian government. President Harmodio Arias's appointment of Alfaro in the midthirties to serve as Panama's ambassador in Washington was intended once again to make use of the statesman's status and influence in Washington.

Indeed the alliance between Alfaro and the Arias family began and ended with political appointments that benefited both parties. As the 1940 cam-

Figure 13
Sueño Diabólico

Este sueño diabólico que en la mente se halla de algunos infelices, no la canta Batalla, el poeta que hoy chilla en Acción Comunal; olvidando, parece, que en no lejano día a los mismos que ensalza sin piedad maldecía con sus ripios de siempre, la intención criminal.

Desolación y ruina, guerra, saqueos, venganza! palabras con que azuzan los que tienen la panza bien llena y aspiran treparse en el barril; sin fijarse que Alfaro al soñar con la silla se ha despertado en tiempo de su cruel pesadilla y en Washington ya piensa con anhelo febril.

No importa que Batalla y otras ranas de charco sigan croando inútiles saliéndose del marco en que los puso el pueblo por su inutilidad. Si Alfaro ya no sueña, si él mismo no se agita, para qué hacerle caso a que enreda la pita con sus estupideces, su odio y su maldad?

Source: El Panamá América (May 22, 1940), p. 4

paign progressed, Alfaro's dislike for the Arias brothers, and theirs for him, became apparent. Alfaro fashioned the band of armed supporters he had originally organized during his interim administration of 1931–32 (the Reserva Nacionalista, or Nationalist Reserve) into a new paramilitary organization known as the Guardia Cívica Nacionalista (Nationalist Civic Guard). This group countered Arias's militarily charged candidacy, and eventually the campaign pitted these two armed camps against each other.[10]

Neither candidate had a monopoly on guns or sizable constituencies. Had the contest been limited to the candidates and their bands of armed followers, the 1940 campaign might have ended in a near stalemate. However, Arias's ties to the incumbent administration and, consequently, to the National Police gave him the advantage over his opponent. Moreover his temporary electoral coalition of liberal parties augmented his support among members of the electoral board.[11]

In the end the changes that had occurred within the ranks of the National Police in the 1930s became a deciding factor in the outcome of the 1940 election. The incumbent Boyd administration used the police to support the Arias candidacy, and law enforcement officers engaged Alfaro's supporters with gunfire and frequently arrested and incarcerated them.[12] As one State Department official in Panama noted in August 1941, "Boyd virtually assured the election of Arnulfo Arias in the recent presidential election by permitting the National Police and other governmental agencies to overawe and intimidate the electorate in favor of Arias."[13]

Despite his rather large following, Alfaro could not compete with Arias's ties to the Boyd administration. On election day the Frente Popular boycotted the election to protest the use of public resources, particularly the police, to support Arias's candidacy, and Arias won an uncontested election. However, while the election reaffirmed the ability of Arias supporters to manipulate the country's political processes, which they had done repeatedly since the 1931 revolt, it also accelerated the political deterioration of the Generation of ´31. That decline was such that by November 1941, the Panameñista movement had almost entirely alienated most of its earlier adherents, and mounting conflicts had dissolved what had previously been a relatively cohesive political front. This situation led members of the National Police to overthrow Arias and install their own choice for president.[14]

Arnulfo Arias: "Solo Dios Sobre Nosotros"

The administration of Arnulfo Arias came to power in 1940 with the nationalist motto "solo Dios sobre nosotros" (we answer only to God).[15] As leader of the 1931 insurrection, Arias had found favor with officials in Washington when he honored Panama's commitment to defend the canal during and after the revolt. However, shortly after this initial contact with American officials, Arias's cooperative attitude toward the United States underwent significant change. As Panama's minister to Italy (1934–38), Arias observed firsthand the development of Italian fascism, and he admired the nationalist discipline of both Mussolini and Hitler. During his time in Europe, Arias's views became increasingly nationalistic and anti-American.[16]

In light of his prominent ties to Panama's ruling Generation of '31, Arias's apparent change of heart and his newly established alliances worried Washington. Officials there found themselves at a loss to explain the former diplomat's radicalized position when he returned from Italy. As one North American military analyst noted, "Those who have known him for years can offer no explanation to the change of sentiment toward the United States other than that he has reached some understanding with the Berlin and Rome Chancellories."[17]

Arias's activities upon returning from his assignment in Italy in 1938 further alienated the United States government, seemingly confirming Washington's suspicions of his fascist ties. In June of that year, American officials intercepted an arms cache destined for "a radical Panamanian named Arias."[18] While apparently fashioning his own armed backing to integrate himself into a political system that revolved increasingly around the threat of force, officials in Washington viewed Arias differently than they did Panama's other bands of armed activists. The Roosevelt administration distrusted Arias's amicable association with Mussolini and Hitler. Over time these associations would prompt Washington to equate Arnulfo Arias with one of the region's other suspected fascists, Juan Domingo Perón of Argentina.

By the time he assumed office in 1940, Arias faced formidable opposition in Washington. The Roosevelt administration viewed him as a distinct threat to the security of the canal and of the United States. Arias also faced considerable opposition at home, particularly from the powerful, elite Chiarista faction of the Liberal party. Having succumbed to Arias's followers during the nationalist coup of January 1931, the Chiaristas, the most organized, powerful bloc of Panama's urban elite, intended to regain control of the government.

President Arias's affinity for the Hitler and Mussolini regimes, and the subsequent threat he posed to the nation's urban elite, caused considerable domestic opposition to his government. As had his brother Harmodio, President Arnulfo Arias alienated many groups that had initially supported his campaign—most significantly the National Police. Yet pivotal to Arias's ability to carry out his extremist platform was his ability to control the police, and he quickly moved to cement his control of that institution. However, increasing opposition to the new administration jeopardized the president's hold on power. After rehiring José Remón in November 1940, President Arias sent him to Fort Riley, Kansas, to participate in a course on basic cavalry; Arias in fact envisioned using a powerful cavalry for crowd control measures in Panama City. However, Remón and others resented the president's interference in police affairs, and dissension grew among many of that organization's ranking officers. In a State Department communiqué dated June 15, 1941, an American diplomat in Panama spoke of this opposition when he said that "it is very probable that a large part of the police force would revolt against the present government if promised American backing."[19]

In what later proved to be a futile attempt to counter police opposition, Arias created the Policía Secreta Nacional (National Secret Police) through Law no. 72 of June 18, 1941. Its charter called for the secret police to be entirely independent of the National Police, answering only to the minister of government and justice (Ricardo Adolfo de la Guardia) and to the president of the republic. Not surprisingly, the establishment of the secret police simply triggered additional antipathy and distrust among the National Police officers' corps, where Remón and his counterparts questioned the president's motives for creating a secretive, independent police force.[20]

President Arias's creation of a secret police force provided a structural pattern for similar organizations in the sixties, seventies, and eighties. However, he had underestimated the National Police in 1941. Years of modernization had resulted in an increasingly powerful organization where the better-trained officers resented the interference of civilian authorities in their affairs. Intended to give the president a tenable response to the growing threat of armed opposition within the ranks of the police force, the creation of the secret police instead created an institutional gulf that separated the chief executive from the nation's law enforcement officers.

As Arias struggled to control the police, he also tried to enact an agenda of sweeping changes that had the effect of polarizing the way many Panamanians felt about their elected officials. Between his inauguration in 1940 and his overthrow one year later, Arnulfo Arias increased the size and the power of the central government in Panama City, in an attempt to counter opposition to his administration. He began by calling a plebiscite to draft a new constitution, which the National Assembly ratified in January of 1941. This new document reflected Arias's favorable perception of European fascism, in addition to the racial and cultural biases of his Panameñista coalition, a movement that claimed to be founded on "a doctrine that synthesizes patriotism, work, and action."[21] For instance, Article 23 of the new code denied entrance to Panama to immigrants "of the black race whose native language is not Spanish, of the yellow race, and the races originating in India, Asia Minor, and North Africa." While aimed at revoking the citizenship privileges, including suffrage, of Caribbean Blacks and other minority groups, this move gained Arias the support of Creoles and Spanish-speaking Blacks in Panama City and Colón, because it protected them from West Indian job competition.[22] Intended to disenfranchise "large segments of the urban working-class, at strengthening Hispanic culture, and at limiting the influence of immigrant shopkeepers," Arias's racist platform earned his administration the support of much of Panama City's White working class community.[23]

By including Panama's large Jewish Syrian population in the list of "foreigners of races the immigration of which is prohibited," the Arias administration assumed an anti-Semitic stance. This threatened to disenfranchise politically and economically Jews living in Panama.[24] On March 24, 1941, the president reinforced these institutional prejudices when he enacted Law no. 24, which forbade the allocation of business licenses to all "prohibited races." Arias then proclaimed the "nationalization of Panamanian commerce," a declaration that closely resembled a similar comment from January 3, 1931, when Arias and his fellow rebels had professed to be "reclaiming Panama for the Panamanians."[25]

Besides disenfranchising what he considered the racially and ethnically "parasitic" components of Panamanian society, Arias used his authority as chief executive to carry out his own version of the New Deal. Arias intended this legislation to undermine the opposition to his administration coming from the Chiari bloc of the Liberal party, which blamed the president for the nation's dismal economic situation. After giving the vote to Panamanian women and attempting to incorporate them into the Panameñista cause, Arias established the Banco Agropecuario (Cattleman's Bank), a social security system, and the Bank of Urbanization and Rehabilitation.[26] He also began a program of import substitution and issued Panamanian currency for the first time (since 1904, Panama's currency had been the United States dollar). These moves were calculated to increase Panama's economic self-reliance while augmenting the nation's flow of capital by making government funds available to persons of "desirable" ethnic and racial backgrounds.[27]

These programs partially offset the capital shortage caused by the president's failure to renegotiate Panama's large foreign debt. They also helped counter mounting opposition to Arias's racism and anti-Semitism, by generating support among Panama's urban Spanish-speaking labor and commerce communities, small farmers, cattlemen, and women. Finally, some measures Arias initiated in 1940–41 endured beyond his 1941 overthrow and formed the basis of a popular legacy that earned him the presidency in 1949 and again in 1968 (see figure 14).[28]

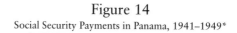

Figure 14

Social Security Payments in Panama, 1941–1949*

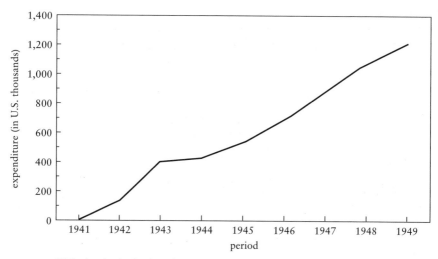

*1949 estimate based on first six months
Source: *Estadística Panameña* (July 1949), pp. 6–7

Beyond his divisive approach to domestic affairs, Arias had the war to contend with, and he tried to capitalize on nationalist resentment toward the expanded American wartime presence the way his brother had in the 1930s. On July 27, 1939, the United States Congress approved the 1936 Hull-Alfaro Treaty between Panama and the United States. American legislators had delayed their decision for three years while they monitored closely the activities of Germans and Japanese in Panama, to learn if those groups threatened the security of the canal. When the two sides finally reached an agreement, American diplomats succeeded in extracting many concessions that had not formed part of the original pact in 1936. Most significantly Panama agreed to allow the United States to occupy land outside the canal zone to defend the canal in the event of war.[29]

A few weeks after the treaty's ratification, on September 1, 1939, the war in Europe began when Hitler invaded Poland. Drawing on the provisions they had extracted from their Panamanian counterparts in the Hull-Alfaro pact, American officials began in January 1940 to fashion their plan to defend the canal from Hitler and his allies.[30] This strategy revolved around the temporary acquisition of lands as provided for in the revised Hull-Alfaro agreement. The defense outline also called for the establishment of military bases on those additional lands, to supplement Canal Zone defenses. In August 1940 Washington officially petitioned Panama for this extra land.[31]

This was the international situation when Arnulfo Arias began his first term as president of Panama on October 1, 1940. These conditions placed the activist president directly at odds with policy makers in Washington. The outbreak of war in Europe intensified North American uneasiness regarding Arias's strident nationalism, and once in office, the newly elected president aggravated those concerns. Refusing to take sides in the conflict, Arias maintained open communications with his former associates in Europe, including Adolf Hitler. On October 18, 1940, for example, Hitler sent Arias the following message: "I am pleased to send my congratulations on the occasion of Your Excellency's inauguration as President of the Republic of Panama. To my congratulations I add my earnest desire that the cordial relations that currently exist between Germany and the Republic of Panama continue during your excellency's administration, and if possible, that they progress even further."[32]

Arias's blatant refusal to back the United States' war effort, combined with his refusal to break off relations with Europe's totalitarians, gravely concerned Washington. Further exacerbating Washington's phobia regarding European aggression in the Americas, President Arias threatened to grant concessions relating to the canal "to other powerful countries that would have the material force to defend it" if the United States did not cooperate with his administration. Given Arias's relationship with Hitler and his continued unwillingness to commit to the Allied cause, the State Department interpreted this as a threat by Arias to allow the Nazis access to the area surrounding the canal. The American government deeply resented Arias's use of the canal as a diplomatic bargaining tool.[33]

Further complicating Arias's relationship with Washington was his need to achieve "tangible benefits" for Panama in wartime negotiations with the United States.[34] The president spoke publicly of what he termed Panama's commitment to cooperate with Washington in the defense of the canal. Privately, however, Arias tied a favorable response to Washington's base petition to a series of concessions from the Roosevelt administration. Obtaining these concessions from Washington would enhance his reputation as a leader who stood up to Washington and would also serve to offset opposition to his own administration. Known as the Twelve Points, Arias' response called for American policemen to carry only billy clubs when outside the Zone. Additionally he demanded that the United States pay Panama an indemnity if the flow of American troops during wartime interrupted regular canal traffic (which it did; see figures 15 and 16); he called for jurisdiction over all roads and highways in Panamanian territory, including those used to transport American servicemen; and he stipulated that the United States stop importing Caribbean Blacks to work in the Canal Zone.[35]

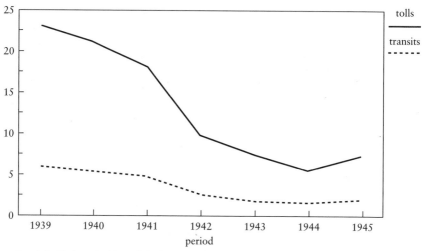

Figure 15
Panama Canal Activity, 1939–1945*

*transits listed in thousands of ships; tolls listed in millions of U.S. dollars

Source: *Estadística Panameña* (June 1952), p. 54

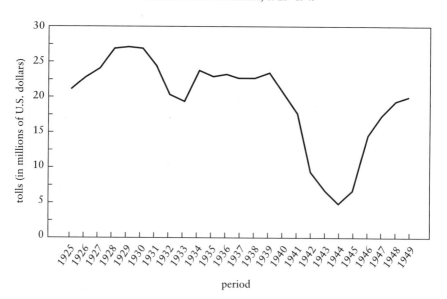

Figure 16
Panama Canal Toll Intake, 1925–1949

Source: *Estadística Panameña*, (June 1952), p. 54

Arnulfo Arias's demands recall a similar tactic adroitly used by his older brother Harmodio during his presidency (1932–36). Harmodio Arias had demanded that the United States raise its annuity payments for use of the canal. However, unlike his younger sibling, Harmodio Arias never threatened the security of the canal. He understood that there were limits to the benefits one could expect as host nation. Conversely Arnulfo Arias insisted that the United States alter its Canal Zone hiring procedures, its law enforcement practices around the Zone, and the benefits it received as operator of the canal, including unrestricted transportation of soldiers and military hardware in time of war. In peacetime these demands would have tested the limits of good neighborliness; in wartime Arias's position simply reinforced Washington's misgivings regarding him.

Following a series of charged diplomatic exchanges with Washington, Arias softened his position and acquiesced to American terms in March 1941, when Washington agreed to consider the proposals he had set forth. (Diplomats from the two countries did not complete the final agreement until 1942, the year after Arias's ouster.)[36] Despite Arias's backpedaling, American officials continued to object to this attempt to use the security of the canal as a vehicle of diplomatic leverage. The United States government concluded that the Panamanian president posed too great a threat to the canal; Arias would have to go. In May 1941 the Office of Naval Intelligence concluded that "the present conditions are considered dangerous to the security of the canal and it is believed that they should be corrected as soon as possible. A local revolution to throw out the crooked pro-Axis officialdom would be preferable to intervention by U.S. forces."[37]

The worsening situation in the Pacific and Europe had placed a premium on the defense of the Panama Canal. With his thinly veiled threats to the United States, combined with his totalitarian domestic policies, Washington felt that President Arnulfo Arias was jeopardizing the canal, something intolerable even for a good neighbor. On October 7, 1941, Panama's controversial leader boarded a Pan American flight for Havana, purportedly to visit a Cuban mistress. Panama's airport was located on an American military base, and American officials recognized Arias, who was traveling incognito. American intelligence officers quietly notified Arias's subordinates of his departure. This gave his enemies the opportunity they had waited for; in his absence his opponents, including José Remón and a large faction of the National Police, invoked Article III of the 1941 constitution to depose Arias. This article required Panama's chief executives to notify the Supreme Court prior to leaving the country. To defend their actions, the National Police cited "popular demand for a change" in addition to a violation of Arias's own constitution. Remón and his fellow police officers then appointed pro-

American businessman Ricardo Adolfo de la Guardia to the presidency. De la Guardia, who was from a wealthy Panama City family with extensive business interests in the capital, was an acceptable choice for Washington. His appointment received rapid approval by relieved officials there.[38]

Thus ended a critical phase in Panamanian history. Arnulfo Arias sought exile in Argentina, where he remained until mid-1945. (Given their evolving concerns regarding the increasingly visible Juan Domingo Perón, a powerful Argentine official with purported ties to European fascists, many in Washington viewed Arias's four-year stay there as a reaffirmation of their suspicions regarding him.) Meanwhile the reign of Panama's nationalist Generation of ´31 ended, Panama's merchant and landowning elite regained control of the nation's government, and Arias's exile propelled Panama's high school and college students, many of them Arnulfistas, to the forefront of the move to oppose elite hegemony and North American imperialism in Panama.

The overthrow of Arnulfo Arias in October 1941 ended a decade of significant change in Panamanian politics. In the quest to perpetuate their hold on power, presidents from 1931 to 1941 had fashioned the National Police into an increasingly powerful branch of the federal government. Armed supporters had become part of the federal payroll. And politicians had expanded the practice of relying on small bands of armed constituents to settle partisan disputes. Arnulfo Arias institutionalized this latter practice when he organized the secret police to protect him from the threat of police reprisal.[39]

A comparison of Arias's ouster with the 1931 coup makes it possible to gauge the extent of change in Panamanian politics during the thirties. Throughout Panama's modern history, Spanish, Colombian, and North American troops had landed repeatedly in Panama to arbitrate Isthmian affairs. In 1931, however, domestic civilian forces toppled the nation's presidency without decisive foreign military intervention. Following the revolt, successive regimes took steps to modernize the National Police, and by the end of the decade that organization had achieved unprecedented institutional autonomy. Never before had a detachment of Panamanian soldiers been capable of shaping Isthmian affairs through the use of overt armed intimidation, independent of foreign intervention. Throughout the first three decades of Panama's republican history, the police had repeatedly served as a political pawn used by incumbent administrations to thwart their political opponents. Nevertheless, never before had the police acted so publicly as the nation's power broker.

Interim President I: Ricardo Adolfo de la Guardia

The abrupt end of the Arias presidency in 1941 accentuated the amount of political influence wielded by the National Police and its civilian administrators. It also underscored the inability of Panama's political blocs to achieve substantive unity and cohesion. Panama's constitution called for one of the ousted executive's two vice presidents to succeed him in office. However, both men declined. With Arias's first two constitutionally mandated successors out of the way, the stage was set for a return to rule by the elite that had dominated Panama politically from 1903 to 1931.

As minister of government and justice during Arnulfo Arias's presidency, Ricardo Adolfo de la Guardia had supervised the National Police. When opposition to Arias mounted among the nation's police officers and much of its civilian population, de la Guardia forged a secret alliance with José Remón, Panama City police chief. The two carefully plotted Arias's overthrow—Panama's first successful military coup.

De la Guardia would eventually use the executive mansion to distribute valuable government contracts and other favors to his closest associates, so as to enhance his political and economic fortunes while expanding and solidifying his base of support. His coconspirator, José Remón, had equally tangible reasons for conspiring against President Arias. After being fired by President Harmodio Arias in 1936 and then sent into what he considered semiexile in the United States by President Arnulfo Arias in 1940, Remón had effectively masked his dislike for the Arias family as he rose slowly through the ranks of the police. After serving in various administrative positions in police headquarters in Panama City, Remón became second commander of the National Police on October 9, 1941, immediately following the overthrow of the Arias regime. With the first commander appointed from among de la Guardia's circle of friends, Remón became the highest ranking officer to have worked his way up through the police.

As Remón rose through the ranks of the officers' corps, he went to great lengths to hire from the city's working class, including Blacks. Occurring as it did at the height of the depression, this policy gave Remón considerable influence among the city's poor and West Indian populations—two facets of society previously excluded from government employment.[40] Remón's popularity among Panama's urban poor in fact led the elite Chiaristas to court the police chief's influence with the masses to counter middle-class activism.[41]

These circumstances made Remón the most formidable opponent of the Arias administration. Having forged an alliance with Remón, de la Guardia emerged from the confusion following Arias's ouster to assume Panama's presidency. Much to Washington's relief, the new president immediately reversed many of Arias's programs. On December 11, 1941, an American official in Panama filed the following report regarding Panama's newest president:

The new administration of Ricardo Adolfo de la Guardia immediately has set about tearing down the totalitarian-like institutions set up by his predecessor. . . . The Arias-inspired organizations and innovations, such as the *Cachorros de Urraca* and the Civic Service Law, were done away with, while freedom of the press was completely restored. The Civil Attaché of the German Legation, undoubtedly the most dangerous Nazi element in Panama, was expelled; the pro-Nazi Panamanian Minister in Berlin was dismissed; the pro-Nazi radio propagandist, Julio Argain, was expelled; and other Nazis . . . left the country, ostensibly of their own accord.[42]

Beyond these steps, the new president reversed Arias's attempts to censure Panama's English-speaking press, recalled the Panamanian paper money Arias had issued to increase Panama's fiscal autonomy from the United States, and immediately ended Panama's neutrality on the war issue. President de la Guardia firmly cast Panama's lot with the United States.[43] Before the Japanese attack on Pearl Harbor, de la Guardia had already agreed to incarcerate all Japanese nationals living in Panama, and his administration declared war on Japan on December 8—the day after the attack on Pearl Harbor.[44]

As he reversed Arias's policies, de la Guardia also set about securing his own hold on power. In the months following the coup, members of Panama's legislature anticipated appointing a permanent interim replacement in 1943 to finish out Arias's term. Yet unlike Ricardo J. Alfaro, who served briefly as interim president following the 1931 revolt and who yielded his temporary administration to an elected president in 1932, de la Guardia intended to lengthen his time in office. On a trip to the Panamanian interior a few months into his term, the new president spoke of his intentions to remain in power: "If the people of Panama desire it, I shall heed their wishes and remain as Chief of State for the remainder of the presidential term [through 1947], since the will of the people, when it is freely and frankly expressed, should be respected."[45]

Like many of his predecessors, de la Guardia used his office to give jobs and contracts to friends and family. For example he lobbied hard for American assistance in establishing a cement plant in Panama. With the United States government considering a new set of locks for the canal and with construction of the Pan- American highway underway, the cement industry had a significant guaranteed market in Panama. De la Guardia's plan called for his old friend and political ally, Augusto Boyd, former conservative president (1939–40), to serve as director of the new plant. The company born out of this executive scheme eventually developed into Cemento Panamá, S.A., one of Panama's seven largest companies by the early sixties.[46]

Much like Harmodio Arias a decade earlier, de la Guardia padded his administration with close personal associates to ensure loyalty in key government positions. In a 1943 State Department memorandum titled "Nepotism in Panama," officials noted that "most Panamanians believe that too many Government positions are being given to members of the favored de la Guardia and Estripeaut [Mrs. de la Guardia's maiden name] families."[47] The most visible examples of this favoritism once again involved the National Police. In addition to his alliance with Remón, de la Guardia appointed Rogelio Fábrega, a member of one of Panama's elite families and a personal friend, to serve as first commander of the National Police. One of the president's brothers, Camilo de la Guardia, was appointed minister of government and justice, an assignment that placed him in control of the National Police. Another brother served as Panama's consul general in New York. Finally de la Guardia's influential brother-in-law, Belisario Porras, Jr., served during his administration as Panama's minister to Cuba.[48]

While using his executive influence to consolidate his hold on power, de la Guardia moved to expand even further the military capacity of the National Police. Assuming office as he did in the wake of a revolt that overthrew the Panameñistas, de la Guardia had a precariously small base of support. Unlike his Generation of '31 predecessors, he did not have the backing of a group of armed followers or of partisan electoral board officials. Moreover he lacked a link to the masses such as those enjoyed by Belisario Porras in 1912, Harmodio Arias in 1932, and even Arnulfo Arias's Panameñista movement in 1940. More than any president in Panama's republican history, de la Guardia's circumstances isolated him socially and politically from the rest of the country. More than any of his predecessors, he needed the police to serve as a mechanism of control.

De la Guardia sought Washington's help as well in consolidating his administration's control of the nation's power structure. His administration requested and received weapons and military advisors from the United States. Following Arias's ouster, Washington wanted to stabilize Panama's political situation as quickly as possible. To this end the United States provided the de la Guardia government with hundreds of automatic weapons and pistols, boats, and other war materials, in addition to a permanent United States military mission to help train Panama's police officers.[49] As a result Panama's police, armed with this American military hardware and technology, stifled the president's opponents and perpetuated his presidency.[50] The most apparent example occurred in September 1943, during an attempted coup. Led by José Pezet, an outspoken opponent of the de la Guardia administration, several dissident police officers and civilians plotted an armed revolt. However, with the tacit approval of the American Embassy (whom Remón informed before the operation), the National Police used the materials it had received from the United States to preempt the coup. The police rounded up the conspirators and arrested them, foiling any threat they might have posed to the administration.[51]

The prompt handling of this uprising convinced officials in Washington that de la Guardia's administration had achieved sufficient stability to protect the canal. One State Department official noted in September 1943 that "no revolution is apt to succeed in Panama so long as the heads of the National Police are loyal to the Government. President de la Guardia has had nothing to worry about on this score."[52] Just as reassuring, de la Guardia's archnemesis and one of the greatest threats to his presidency, Arnulfo Arias, was in exile in Argentina, where he would remain until 1945.

Despite de la Guardia's apparent security and the absence of Arnulfo Arias from the isthmus, opposition from other corners of Isthmian society nevertheless challenged administration policies. Since de la Guardia granted Washington territorial concessions in the 1942 base treaty, students had become increasingly vocal in their opposition to the administration and its complicity with the United States. This heightened opposition reinforced the administration's reliance on the police to settle its political differences, which in turn resulted in additional opposition to government policies. This vicious cycle engendered an increasingly recalcitrant opposition front, unprecedented levels of anti-Americanism, and the institutional ascendancy of the National Police.

The student cause received an additional impetus in 1943. In an ironic turn of events that year, Victor F. Goytía, Minister of Education and one of the founding members of Acción Comunal, threatened to expel any students who protested the government's manipulation of employment practices at the National University. Goytía's attitude toward the students seems confusing, given his proclivity for activism, but it serves to underscore once again the deep fissures that divided Panama's dynamic middle class in the 1940s. In any event students deeply resented Goytía's posture specifically and administrative intimidation generally, and in February 1944 students in Panama City established the Federación de Estudiantes de Panamá (Federation of Panamanian Students—FEP) to help organize their confrontation with the de la Guardia administration. Soon high school students throughout the republic joined the FEP to oppose de la Guardia's *continuismo* (unsolicited continuation in office), and on December 26, 1944, these groups convened the first Congreso de la Juventud (Youth Conference) in the capital to consolidate their efforts. If the 1920s and 1930s marked an era of labor organization and popular unrest, the 1940s were fast becoming a period characterized by the radicalization of middle-class activism, a transition that overshadowed the miserable conditions that persisted in Panama's urban arrabal.[53]

As opposition to de la Guardia spread throughout the country, the president's hold on power began to disintegrate. Several key members of the administration, including the minister of finance, the comptroller general, and the president's financial advisor, resigned their posts to distance themselves from the increasingly isolated de la Guardia administration. Moreover the president's minister of foreign affairs and his minister of education both entertained plans to succeed de la Guardia in the presidency. This political infighting among his closest colleagues badly eroded the president's position by the end of 1944.[54]

Unable to come to a consensus because of partisan bickering, Panama's National Assembly in 1943 had prolonged de la Guardia's administration when it failed to designate an interim replacement (*designado*) to finish out the presidential term. This had given him a legislative mandate by default. However, as opposition to his policies mounted, de la Guardia forced the National Assembly into a crisis in December of 1944, when he abrogated the 1941 constitution and called for a replacement charter that would allow him to continue as president despite mounting protests against his administration.

Opposition to de la Guardia, elite continuismo generally, and North American imperialism came to a head in the early months of 1945. In the face of the expanding protest, the National Assembly, which included a sizable Arias following, voted to unseat de la Guardia. However, Panama's wealthy still wielded sufficient influence in the legislature to dominate the process of selecting a replacement leader, so that Chiarista members of the assembly appointed a proven ally of theirs, Ambassador Enrique A. Jiménez, to serve as president until an elected chief executive could take office in 1948.

Interim President II: Enrique A. Jiménez

During his administration, President de la Guardia had worked closely with Enrique A. Jiménez, another member of Panama's urban political elite. De la Guardia appointed him ambassador to Washington in April 1943. In this position Jiménez loyally carried to Washington de la Guardia's petitions for guns and other military hardware. During his tenure in Washington, Jiménez also worked closely with Augusto Boyd to secure American cooperation in establishing Cemento Panamá. Like Manuel Amador Guerrero in 1904, Jiménez's reputation as a defender of elite interests had positioned him for the presidency in an era of elite political domination.[55]

In Washington, Ambassador Jiménez received a favorable reception, where officials considered him a friend to the United States government, based on his pro-American record. Some North American officials recognized Panamanians' mounting opposition to de la Guardia, and the Roosevelt administration viewed Jiménez as a probable future president of Panama who could be counted on to comply with Washington's wishes: "We may expect the Ambassador to use his present position to enhance his presidential opportunities. More than likely this will lead him to adopt a very cooperative attitude with us and we might bear this in mind and possibly use him more often to carry the ball to the Panamanian government on controversial issues."[56]

By 1943 the State Department planned to use Jiménez and his aspirations to promote United States interests in Panama. Described privately by his American counterparts as "not blessed with a keen intellect," Jiménez eventually became, nevertheless, a linchpin in United States plans to defend the canal, particularly following the conclusion of World War II.[57]

Jiménez became president of Panama in June 1945, when the National Assembly appointed him to replace de la Guardia, and he inherited from his predecessor a nation racked with economic, social, diplomatic, and political problems. His appointment to the presidency by Panama's elite-dominated legislature had circumvented the opposition's ability to check elite political hegemony for the second time in less than four years. The result was increased political unrest among middle-class activists and other opponents of the elite. Further complicating Jiménez's task, Panama's economy had contracted during the war, as world commerce yielded to military traffic in the canal. American military ships simply did not generate the level of commerce associated with Canal Zone traffic. Moreover a general downturn in worldwide commercial activity during the war precipitated less foreign investment, lower real per capita income, plummeting national income (taxes, customs, and general public fees), and increased national deficits.[58] These factors in turn combined to trigger lower wages, lost jobs, and urban-rural migration in Panama, as many urban poor migrated to the interior provinces of Los Santos, Veraguas, Coclé, and Herrera in search of work (see table 3.1). Finally, further compounding the president's problems as the war drew to a close, it became apparent that the United States did not intend to vacate the bases it had been granted temporarily by the 1942 accord. As a consequence nationalists began organizing against the continuation of the expanded American presence.[59]

These worsening social circumstances triggered a crisis in Panamanian politics as the new president found himself confronted with an expanding opposition front. A sharp downturn in the nation's economy, combined with the postwar reversal of wartime migration patterns, caused a significant increase in social and political unrest on the isthmus, particularly in Panama City and Colón. The population of Panama's major urban areas began expanding again, and this growth translated into increased difficulties and lower standards of living for the nation's urban poor (see figures 17 and 18).[60] This fact is reflected in crime data for Panama City for 1945 and 1946, when the number of crimes committed there rose sharply. As Jiménez took office, arrests rose proportionately as the police assumed an increasingly significant role in governing the nation, masking political fragmentation with armed force, while simultaneously checking unrest among the nation's poor.[61]

In addition to marked increases in arrests, civilian paramilitary groups from disaffected blocs of the Liberal party, particularly the nationalist Panameñista movement, began resorting to terrorism to challenge the continuismo of the nation's political elite. Following Arnulfo Arias's return from exile in October 1945, for example, Arnulfistas bombed properties belonging to several of their political opponents, including "restaurants, bars, beer gardens, and other public places," as well as the business of former president de la Guardia.[62]

This augmented crime and the use of terrorism as a tool of political manipulation reached a high point of sorts when Arias and his armed band concocted an elaborate plan, reminiscent of the 1931 coup, to topple the Jiménez regime. On the evening of December 21, 1945, Arias's scheme called for his supporters to gather at strategic locations throughout Panama City

Figure 17
Births and Deaths, Colón, 1916–1945
(five-year averages)

Source: *Estadística Panameña*, (June 1947), pp. 1–4

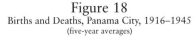

Figure 18
Births and Deaths, Panama City, 1916–1945
(five-year averages)

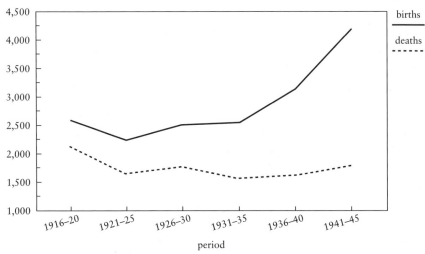

Source: *Estadística Panameña*, (June 1947), pp. 1–4

and Colón. Much like the earlier successful scheme, his plan called initially
for disrupting the government's ability to respond to the crisis, followed by
storming strategic locations in Colón and Panama City. After setting off
false fire alarms throughout Panama City and starting fires in Colón to cause
confusion, Arias planned for his followers to move in and take government
officials hostage, until Jiménez agreed to abdicate. The revolt never advanced
to that point, however. Arnulfistas actually did attack and partially destroy
the police headquarters in Colón, but the National Police foiled the plan
and arrested Arnulfo Arias, who spent several months in jail before being
pardoned by President Jiménez.[63]

The clemency Arias and his followers received from the Jiménez administration following the foiled 1945 revolt reflected the president's initial
attempts to placate the opposition under increasingly difficult circumstances.
However, these efforts to coopt the opposition failed miserably. Arias and
his followers continued their vociferous, frequently violent opposition to
the Jiménez administration.[64] The president responded by reversing his efforts to placate the opposition and denounced Arnulfo Arias in vitriolic terms,
referring to him as a "nazifascista criollo" (a Creole Nazi-fascist).[65] Jiménez
stood to lose a considerable sum of money if the North Americans abandoned their positions, as the opposition demanded. Along with police officers José Remón and Bolívar E. Vallarino Paredes, Jiménez was a "main

shareholder" of the National Cooperative. This government-controlled in-stitution had a monopoly on the slaughter of cattle in Panama City, an in-dustry that had benefited greatly from the expanded North American presence during the war.[66] Indeed while publicly admonishing the United States to abandon the sites before renegotiations began, Jiménez secretly proposed a symbolic return of the bases to Panama, at which time Panama would imme-diately take legislative steps to return the bases to American military con-trol, once nationalist ardor had sufficiently cooled.[67]

Faced with an increasingly hostile opposition that "caused considerable deterioration in the position of the Administration," including jeopardizing the personal fortunes of the president and several senior police officials, Jiménez made two changes aimed at enabling his administration to with-stand its challengers: first, he replaced Panama's controversial 1941 consti-tution with a new document in 1946. When he did so, he did not revoke the right of women to vote, although they had not yet exercised it, because the nation had not held elections since 1940. Jiménez also expanded women's suffrage, by eliminating some education-based requirements that had ex-cluded Panama's lower-class women. In addition the 1946 constitution al-lowed women to vote in presidential and legislative elections for the first time.[68] Jiménez hoped that the new constitution would counter some of the support Panamanian women had given to the Arias camp since the 1940 presidential campaign. However, he underestimated the breadth of popular opposition to a renegotiation of the base treaty.[69]

Second, after assuming office in late 1945, Jiménez set out to make the National Police "an expanded military unit" consisting of a military battal-ion, a military police company, and a horse cavalry company.[70] Jiménez's plans fueled disproportionate growth of the police force when compared with other nations in the region (see figure 19). He also requested materials from the United States to establish "a modest air force," in addition to fifty patrol cars and an expansion of the United States military mission in Panama City. Finally, he assigned his business partner, José Remón, to establish a school to train police officers in military tactics.[71]

These moves further militarized Panama's police force. They also put the administration increasingly at odds with its opponents, further weakening the country's precarious political situation. The depth of the fissures that divided Panama's various politically active groups in the 1940s became ap-parent on the night of June 22, 1946. That evening mounted police used the cavalry training Remón had given them and the equipment they had re-ceived from the United States to disperse a large student gathering. Com-menting on the confrontation, a State Department official noted that "the police carried out their orders with commendable restraint and the Embassy

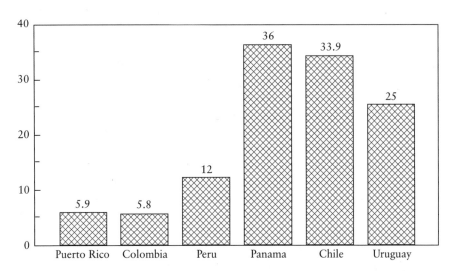

Figure 19
Number of Police Officers per Thousand Persons
in Selected Countries, 1944–1945

Source: Memoria del Gobierno y Justicia, "Policía Nacional" (1945), p. 182

considers it remarkable that there were not severe casualties, inasmuch as mounted police charged with drawn sabers."[72]

State Department officials dismissed the Jiménez administration's partisan difficulties as mere "smoke screens" caused by Arnulfo Arias and other dissident nationalist groups, including the Socialist and Communist blocs of the Liberal party. Writing eleven days *after* the September 1, 1946, deadline Panama had established for the abandonment of all military bases outside the Canal Zone, a State Department official made the following statement regarding the continued opposition in Panama to the expanded North American presence there: "This situation is about 90% smoke-screen put out by the Panamanian opposition. There is no "controversy" between ourselves and the Panamanian government."[73]

While alluding to the gravity of the situation that confronted Panamanian officials, this quote confirms the United States' unwillingness to acknowledge the deep-seated and widespread antagonism the Jiménez administration faced in its efforts to renew the unpopular defense sites treaty.

Finally, by late 1946, the United States government began to take seriously the growing opposition to the proposed renewal of the 1942 base treaty. Beyond supporting the Jiménez administration with military equipment, the United States symbolically returned two of the sites it had received as part of the 1942 accord, Taboga Island and Paitilla, the former being a favorite vacation resort for Panama's wealthy families. Moreover Washington began a propaganda campaign to "prop up" the Panamanian government. As one State Department official noted, the Jiménez administration needed "something to announce to the people . . . we will have to be prepared to approve a loan or build some roads and/or comply with certain other requests."[74]

This same report outlined specific details of the State Department's ongoing efforts to counter opposition to the base treaty. The wording reveals the depth of complicity of the Jiménez administration in these efforts: "Our embassy is to be congratulated for its recent and present continuing strategy, approved by President Jiménez and supported by the press, of publishing every few days statistics which reveal to the surprise of many Panamanians just how much the economy of Panama is dependent upon United States activities on the Isthmus."[75]

Yet despite a propaganda program designed to create favorable public opinion regarding the base issue, officials in Washington and Panama City had underestimated the severity of Panama's political crisis. Nationalist opposition to renegotiation of the 1942 treaty was only the most visible expression of broad social and economic discontent among much of Panama's population. Economic difficulties caused by World War II had triggered demographic shifts and rising crime levels, which in turn had caused increased levels of police activity. Meanwhile the United States' expanded wartime presence on the isthmus had two significant repercussions. It intensified nationalist frustration with the de la Guardia and Jiménez administrations for their compliance with Washington, and it also deepened anti-American sentiment on the isthmus, because many Panamanians now felt that Washington had exploited two consecutive interim presidents to secure an unpopular base accord that would have been impossible otherwise.

The attempt by the Jiménez and Truman governments to prolong the 1942 agreement despite considerable popular opposition provided a common thread that united Panamanians of various political and social backgrounds, much as the opposition front that had formed in the mid-1930s to oppose Harmodio Arias. Consequently, Jiménez's government found itself increasingly at odds with many of the Panamanian people during the first months of 1947. In May 1947, for example, the Frente Patriótico de la Juventud joined forces with the Federación de Estudiantes de Panamá and the Partido del Pueblo (Panama's Communist party) against the proposed base agreement. With Arnulfo Arias in and out of jail for his political activities, this coalition of student groups and political parties became the standard bearer for all Panamanians who had grievances against the Jiménez administration or the United States.

Jiménez's reliance on the National Police became apparent when the National Assembly voted on December 10, 1947, to renew the 1942 accord. By portraying the legislature's decision in patriotic terms, opposition leaders appealed to thousands of Panamanians who were not previously involved in the front. From December 10 to 23, 1947, this unfolding coalition and the National Police faced off in a struggle that permanently redefined the way Panama's presidents interact with the nation's populace. This struggle catapulted the police to a position of political preeminence that would underlie the military regimes of José Remón (1948–55), Omar Torrijos (1968–81), and Manuel Noriega (1983–89).

Conclusions

During Panama's first four decades as a republic, several groups mobilized politically to effect government change on the isthmus. In the teens and twenties, workers—particularly those affiliated with the burgeoning canal enclave—organized to protest their working and living conditions. Then, in the late twenties and early thirties, numerous middle-class civic and political action groups sprung up to lend their respective voices to an antielite, anti–United States movement that gained momentum with the Depression. Finally, precipitated both by the 1941 countercoup and by the expanding wartime presence of North Americans on the isthmus, students emerged in the 1940s to lead an increasingly vitriolic nationalist crusade against elite–United States complicity.

This increasingly well-defined, cohesive, and sometimes militant movement challenged Panama's politicians, who relied increasingly on the National Police to contain worker unrest and middle-class agitation. First, since independence the police had provided a means of supporting civilian presidents. However, the Roosevelt administration's adaptation of the good neighbor policy coincided loosely with the nationalists' rise to power in Panama City, and the result was a series of institutional reforms by successive administrations in the thirties that fueled the transformation of the police into a well-defined, powerful military unit. This transformation crystallized initially during the 1940 presidential campaign when, for the first time, a native armed force largely dictated the outcome of a political transition through blatant police intimidation.

Second, beginning with the election of 1908, armed bands of partisan supporters figured prominently in Panama's political contests. Presidents in the thirties elevated this practice to a type of executive ritual, by integrating their bands of armed constituents ("armed patriots") into the nation's police force, to check dissension there. In 1941 President Arnulfo Arias carried this tactic one step further, by creating an entirely distinct branch of the federal government, the Policía Secreta, to absorb his personal army. This, combined with his neofascist policies, further alienated Arias's opponents, who capitalized on dissent within the National Police and uneasiness in Washington to overthrow the Arias regime in the nation's first police-sponsored revolt.

Finally, because Ricardo Adolfo de la Guardia and Enrique Jiménez were appointed rather than elected to office, their interim administrations faced a growing opposition front of unprecedented dimensions. This group consisted of students, socialists, communists, Arnulfistas, and eventually much of the rest of the nation, including thousands of women. Moreover, unlike most of Panama's previous presidents, de la Guardia and Jiménez lacked "armed patriots" to champion their causes, and never having been elected, neither president had great influence over the nation's electoral board. Unlike many of the chief executives who served during the first decades of the republic, de la Guardia and Jiménez both lacked substantive bases of popular support.

To secure their presidencies under such tenuous circumstances, both men cooperated with Washington in its plans to defend the canal during and after the war. In return for this collaboration, the Truman administration increased military assistance to Panama, and this reciprocity linked the governments of both countries in an effort to subdue Panama's expanding and increasingly militant opposition front.

As 1947 ended, the country's political system confronted a significant challenge that ultimately proved to be a defining event in Panama's history: could an unpopular interim administration so dependent on foreign support and military backing blatantly legislate against a massive opposition front that cut across social and ideological boundaries? Was the opposition sufficiently organized and united to thwart administrative efforts to collaborate with Washington? In December 1947, the debate over renegotiation of the 1942 base treaty climaxed in a showdown between the Jiménez regime and this massive opposition. Two weeks of violence, more than four dozen casualties, and the ultimate failure of President Jiménez to renegotiate the 1942 accord underscored the elite's inability to dictate national affairs as it had in the past. Ironically, in the months after the December 1947 clash, the opposition front dissipated, and in the resulting vacuum, the police emerged with a dominant voice in the nation's political sphere.

5

The Filós-Hines Debacle of December 1947 and Civilian-Police Relations

PANAMA'S FORMATIVE YEARS AS A REPUBLIC INCLUDED A NUMBER OF watershed events that helped give shape and substance to the new nation. The establishment by the United States of the massive canal enclave from 1904 to 1914 gave rise to numerous labor associations and civic action groups that organized to protect and improve the working and living conditions of Panama's workers, particularly those affiliated with the waterway. Then in the twenties and thirties, financial difficulties triggered first by the end of World War I and then by the Depression precipitated the establishment of various political parties and civic action groups that gave voice to Panama's expanding middle class. Finally, when President Harmodio Arias founded the National University, in 1935, he established the ideological bases for a powerful nationalist crusade that in future decades would come to dominate intellectual and political life on the isthmus.[1]

During the first decades of the twentieth century, these milestones shaped life along the canal, an entrepôt of world commerce known to Panamanians as "el corazón del mundo" (the heart of the world). Pivotal events such as these have occasionally caused disruption and unrest, obliging civilian authorities to rely on the police when matters got out of hand.[2]

Over the years these "states of exception" fueled a gradual shift in Panama's delicate balance of power.[3] Several decades of crisis resolution gave the nation's police increasingly sophisticated military capabilities and experienced leadership. This transition engendered exceptional unity and a general esprit de corps among its police officers; it also sparked a new group identity, a sense of professional camaraderie among officers enlisted in what Professor Mario Esteban Carranza describes as their "messianic vocation."[4]

Panama's National Police completed its decades-long transformation into a powerful military unit with its own identity in December 1947, as a result of the turmoil provoked by negotiations for the Filós-Hines Treaty. That debate, a clash of unprecedented proportions, pitted a massive, unified nationalist front against an elite regime intent on legislating blatantly against the popular will. As in times past, Panama's president called on the National

Police to subdue political opposition and maintain order. However, unlike previous "states of exception," in this crisis the police failed to stifle opposition to the treaty, and in a situation reminiscent of the 1926 Kellogg-Alfaro debate, the impressive nationalist front forced Panama's leaders to reconsider their positions with regard to the base accord. In the end, the base dilemma evolved into a bonafide crisis in hegemony, wherein Panama's formal power structure failed in its efforts to enact an unpopular treaty. Meanwhile the powerful nationalist opposition front divided into myriad factions following its successful antigovernment campaign. Thus ended the largest, most diverse, united, and focused political crusade in contemporary Panamanian history.

The extent of the conflicts that developed (or redeveloped) among opponents of the base accord became most apparent in 1948, during yet another clash between police and nationalists. This time the opposing forces clashed over an unpopular agreement between the two countries regarding commercial air traffic. The brevity of the confrontation and the nature of its outcome underscored the extent to which the opposition front had splintered following the Filós-Hines confrontation. In the 1948 episode, nationalists backed down when the police invoked a state of siege that lasted for three months. Activists' inability to mount a formidable opposition to the 1948 accord accentuated the profound fissures that continued to divide Panama's myriad civic and political action groups in the late forties and early fifties. More significantly, without any focused opposition, and with the elite Jiménez regime roundly humiliated in 1947 in its efforts to legislate against the popular will, the National Police emerged as the only group with any semblance of focus, cohesion, and organization. Ironically then, while the police force failed in its effort to stem the nationalist tide against the base treaty, it emerged as the most powerful political actor on the isthmus in the wake of the debate.

Events in Panama from 1949 to 1952 accentuated the fact that the police now occupied the top levels of Panama's political hierarchy, with a realm of control now extending to the presidency of the republic. While the National Police still formally fell under the auspices of the minister of justice, the Filós-Hines debate had finally tipped the scales of informal power in the clear favor of the police.[5]

Scholarship has tended to treat the rejection of the base treaty as an ephemeral victory for the masses and has suggested that Panamanians committed a significant economic blunder when they insisted that the United States abandon its expanded wartime presence.[6] For example, in his seminal work *The Remón Era*, Larry L. Pippin argues that the rejection of the Filós-Hines pact and the subsequent withdrawal of American troops triggered a marked economic decline on the isthmus. This hypothesis posits that by ousting the North Americans from these temporary sites, Panama lost large amounts of capital that would have aided it significantly in its postwar recovery. It also implicitly defends the American position and blames the Panamanians for their presumed shortsightedness. The facts argue against both of these suggestions.[7]

The Context of the Filós-Hines Debate

On May 18, 1942, the governments of the United States and Panama signed the Defense Site Agreement. The culmination of nearly two years of negotiations between the two nations, this pact granted the United States the right to temporarily occupy 134 defense sites throughout the republic of Panama in addition to those permanent United States installations located within the Canal Zone. The outbreak of war had placed a strategic premium on the security of the canal, and these additional bases provided for that defense (see appendix D for a list of bases included in the 1942 agreement).

Soon the number of United States military personnel stationed in Panama soared to sixty-seven thousand, as Washington augmented canal defenses and capitalized on Panama's strategic location to ferry personnel and materials to the Pacific and European fronts.[8] Commenting on the Panamanian contribution to the United States' war effort, one American official noted in 1943 that "concerning the defense of the Western Hemisphere, Panama is the most important country in the world."[9]

Like similar wartime treaties Washington had entered into with several other Latin American governments, the 1942 base agreement between Panama and the United States hinged on the principle of international protocol that prohibited the occupation of one country by another without the host nation's consent. Article I of the 1942 accord called for the United States military to evacuate the temporary sites in Panama one year after "a definitive treaty of peace" ended the war.

However, as the conflict unfolded, American commitment to international protocol gradually ebbed. Technological advances in weaponry, particularly rocket propulsion and missile systems, precipitated a change in the United States' plans to defend itself and its interests following the end of hostilities. This new blueprint called for the prolonged occupation of certain of the bases provided for in the 1942 accord.[10]

This change in plans touched off a series of protests in Panama. Nationalists pointed to the Japanese surrender in September 1945 as the "definitive treaty of peace" called for in the accord. Citing this interpretation, those Panamanians who opposed prolonging the expanded American presence called for the North Americans to evacuate the bases one year after that surrender—by September 1946. Despite widespread opposition in Panama, however, envoys from the two nations completed a deal on December 10, 1947, to prolong the 1942 Defense Sites Agreement. That day Panamanian Foreign Minister Francisco A. Filós and U.S. Ambassador Frank Hines signed the Filós-Hines Treaty, a pact that granted Washington permission to retain troops at thirteen sites American officials considered critical to the defense of the canal.

Anti-Americanism and opposition to the Jiménez presidency had existed long before the two governments signed the Filós-Hines Treaty. In fact anti-Americanism had served as a viable political tactic on the isthmus since the midnineteenth century. Thus when it became apparent in 1946 that officials in both countries planned to extend the 1942 accord despite popular disagreement, a rapidly expanding opposition front framed its antitreaty protest in scathing anti-American terms. As time passed, this popular protest focused increasingly on Panama's president for his collaboration in the treaty.

More than any other event in the history of the Panamanian republic, the renegotiation of the 1942 base accord provided a common thread that linked opposition to an unpopular government with anti-Americanism. The result was a confrontation between the pro-American Jiménez administration and its opponents that redefined political rivalry in Panama. The Filós-Hines debate transcended the immediate issue of military bases, however. At stake was whether a Panamanian president could blatantly legislate against public opinion. Opponents of the treaty dealt the elite Jiménez administration a stunning upset by forcing Panama's legislators to reject the pact after two weeks of heated deliberations.

In 1939 Hitler's invasion of Poland had triggered a crisis in international commerce. Fearing an escalation of the European conflict, industrialized nations concentrated on military concerns at the expense of peacetime production, and world trade declined rapidly. Following Poland's capitulation, many of the region's commercial markets closed or declined significantly, and the European continent entered a period of marked economic constriction.[11]

In Latin America this wartime fiscal realignment on the part of the world's industrial powers triggered a drop in the region's imports and exports throughout much of the war. Beginning in 1943, however, Britain and the United States, largely cut off from Southeast Asian sources, began importing heavily from Latin America. This increased demand triggered higher prices for many Latin American products, particularly its tropical goods. Consequently, well before the end of the conflict, several Latin American republics had recovered sufficient economic strength to service their debts and to reverse their balance-of-payment problems.[12]

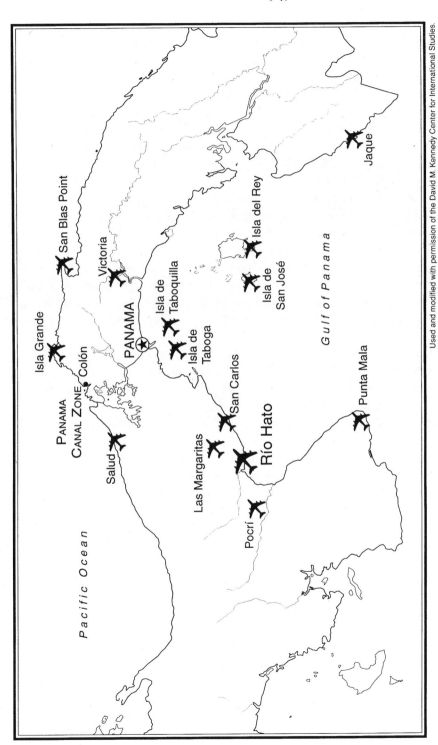

Map 1. Military Bases Included in the 1947 Filós-Hines Treaty.

Used and modified with permission of the David M. Kennedy Center for International Studies.

Unlike the economies of Latin American republics that were able to capitalize on expanded wartime markets in England and the United States, Panama's service-sector economic system was based on the transportation of foreign commerce between the Atlantic and Pacific Oceans. When world trade began to plummet in late 1939, Panama's economy deteriorated in proportion to the decline. As the war progressed, the rising number of United States naval vessels using the canal soon surpassed the dwindling number of merchant vessels making the transit, and aggregate usage plummeted from 5,903 in 1939 to 1,562 in 1944.[13]

This decrease of nearly 75 percent in canal traffic had a profound effect on Panama's economy. Available data suggest a high correlation between import and export taxes generated by commercial canal traffic and the federal government's total disposable revenue.[14] Military ships did not engage in commercial activities, particularly the import, export, or storage of manufactured goods and raw materials, and they consequently generated little revenue for Panama's government and its merchants. The sudden drop in tax revenue caused by this decline dealt a severe blow to federal coffers as well as to local merchants.[15]

The high correlation between levels of world commerce and Panama's economy meant that shifts in world trade caused corresponding changes in Panamanian society and politics. For example the wartime drop in commercial activity that began in late 1939 affected the demographic profiles of Panama City and Colón, the canal's two terminal cities. There three decades of frequently intense (if cyclical) rural-urban migration had created overcrowded conditions among the nation's urban poor; combined with the fact that more people were living longer, the result was progressively worse living conditions among residents of the nation's arrabal.

In both Panama City and Colón, rural-urban migration slowed to a trickle during the war, as people migrated elsewhere hoping to escape the increased hardships of urban living. As a consequence the populations of Panama's interior provinces of Coclé, Herrera, and Los Santos each rose sharply. Meanwhile declining birthrates in Panama City during the war reflect the increasingly difficult living conditions that existed there. During the economic hard times caused by the war, couples postponed getting married and having children—clear indications of economic distress.

When the war ended, in August 1945, life had become particularly difficult in the lower-class neighborhoods of Panama City and Colón. Unrest caused by persistent overcrowding and the loss of jobs resulted in increased criminality and police activity. Following the war officials arrested thousands of persons in Panama City and Colón for resisting authority, defacing public property, vagrancy, disrespect, slander, and a host of other charges.

Occurring mostly among young men of high school and college age, these arrests underscored the volatile character of Panamanian society in the 1940s. Confrontations between police and students also accentuated the more visible role of the National Police in the nation's affairs.[16]

Besides offering a useful means for gauging levels of unrest in Panamanian society after the war and the government's response to that discord, police data also point to two changes in postwar Panamanian society—changes that affected political activism in the late forties. First, the number of women arrested in Panama City and Colón rose dramatically in 1947, signaling increasing levels of political activity among Panamanian women. Panama's 1946 constitution had granted women the right to vote in presidential and legislative elections, and the combination of the approaching presidential election of 1948 and the base issue drew thousands of women to the nationalist antibase movement as it unfolded during the final months of 1947. The focus and momentum the women's movement received from these two hotly debated issues enabled it to play a decisive role in the rejection of the base accord.

Second, in 1946–47 the city of Colón experienced a disproportionate increase in the number of persons arrested for illegal immigration and public indecency. As the point of entry for West Indian employees of the canal company, officials were targeting the city's large Black population. While it is conceivable that criminality there increased after the war, these arrests probably reflect the Jiménez government's willingness to use race and ethnicity to discriminate against and control Colón's predominantly Black population. Certainly they accentuated the growing rift between the government and the nation's large urban Black population. As a result Blacks—both Hispanic and West Indian—overwhelmingly lent their voices to the opposition coalition.[17]

This significant increase in criminal activity in urban Panama; the age, race, and gender specifics of the charges leveled; and the subsequent return to normalcy following the Filós-Hines debate suggest one of two things: either the Jiménez administration attempted to intimidate its opponents in Panama City and Colón with carefully orchestrated (and racially and ethnically motivated) police repression, or criminal activity increased dramatically from 1945 to 1947, for unknown reasons. In either case available police records trace the increasing friction between the administration and its opponents in Panama's two largest cities.

This surge in arrests marks only one facet of the social and political unrest in Panama during and after the war. As officials in Washington and Panama City negotiated the Filós-Hines Treaty despite widespread popular opposition, student groups and political parties began consolidating their efforts to force rejection of the treaty. With Arnulfo Arias in and out of jail or in exile, this coalition of students and radical Liberal party leaders became the standard bearers for all Panamanians who opposed the base treaty specifically or the Jiménez administration generally.

The Gringo Factor

World War II had a significant effect on United States foreign policy. From 1939 to 1945 President Roosevelt relied increasingly on his senior military advisors for assistance in charting the nation's diplomatic course, and military concerns regularly outweighed diplomatic considerations in Washington's blueprint of wartime diplomacy and in its postwar plans.[18]

Nowhere in the Americas was the United States military's diplomatic influence during the war felt more keenly than in Panama.[19] The attention the canal commanded among Pentagon officials, combined with the military's increasingly powerful voice in United States' diplomatic affairs, placed tremendous pressure on Panamanian officials to comply with Washington in its military objectives regarding the defense of the canal and the security of the hemisphere. Meanwhile American soldiers continued to occupy the bases in question, and the Jiménez administration's willingness to proceed with the renegotiation process despite increasing opposition intensified the hostility Panamanian nationalists felt toward the government, which they denounced as a traitor to Panama's national interests.

Three weeks after Hitler crossed the Polish border in 1939, representatives from all the American republics met in Panama to decide how best to defend themselves from Axis aggression. At this meeting, the first of several such conferences that took place during the war, the United States sponsored a resolution calling for the creation of a "security belt" around the whole of the Americas, to provide for the collective defense of the two continents.[20]

This plan centered loosely on a system of reciprocal assistance between the Roosevelt administration and the other participating American republics. On December 29, 1940, for example, President Roosevelt declared the United States the world's "great arsenal for democracy," and the next month his administration initiated the Lend-Lease Program. The Roosevelt administration used this initiative to give weapons and other supplies to Washington's allies, which included every nation in Latin America except Panama and Argentina—two countries with purportedly fascist regimes. For their part, all Latin American republics with the exception of Argentina and Chile severed relations with the Axis powers at Washington's prompting. Several republics, including Mexico, Guatemala, Ecuador, Panama, Peru, Brazil, and Cuba, granted the United States permission to occupy sites within

their national boundaries to establish antisubmarine patrols or air ferry re-
lay points.[21]

This contribution by the Latin American republics proved decisive. While
Washington steadfastly refused to integrate more than token Latin American detachments into the Allied military cause, air bases in Latin America
facilitated a pivotal Allied victory in North Africa in 1942, by providing for
the rapid transportation to the front of personnel and war materials. Moreover, in Brazil, the Vargas regime's willingness to allow United States marines to occupy airstrips at Belem, Recife, and Natal protected the strategic
Brazilian coast from Axis aggression.[22]

As the war progressed, Germany's military application of jet propulsion,
the advent of nuclear and bacteriological weapons, and the logistical problems inherent in multiple theaters of operations shifted Washington's military strategy from one of hemispheric defense based on an inter-American
"security belt" to a plan of world security intended to protect the United
States and its interests in an era of new weapons systems. This strategic shift
in Washington's military focus had immediate implications for Roosevelt's
policy regarding the Latin American republics. State Department officials
had long recognized the diplomatic risks involved in maintaining a military
presence in these countries against the popular will, and the Roosevelt administration wanted to avoid unnecessarily aggravating anti-Americanism
in the region. Consequently, when the Allied victory in North Africa in
1942 convinced Pentagon officials that the Axis threat to Latin America had
dissipated, President Roosevelt used his January 7, 1943, State of the Union
address to declare that the war no longer posed a threat to the region. The
United States then began abandoning the temporary military sites it had
been granted by various Latin American governments at the onset of the
war. This withdrawal began immediately, starting with a small naval instal-
lation at Puerto Barrios, Guatemala.[23]

President Roosevelt's decision to begin evacuating temporary sites elsewhere in Latin America while holding on steadfastly to bases on the isthmus
marked a watershed in Panama's relations with the United States. While the
other countries had allocated a handful of sites for occupation by North
American troops, Washington had coerced Panama into granting 134 temporary sites throughout the republic, in addition to those installations located within the Canal Zone. The United States government did not evacuate
its temporary Panamanian sites following the 1942 victory in North Africa.
On the contrary, in an age when technology rendered coastal defense systems useless, military strategists in Washington developed a new kind of
plan to defend the United States and its interests from long-range attacks,
and Panama played a pivotal role in that plan. Thus, while abandoning bases

elsewhere, the United States resolved to retain its "temporary" sites in Panama for up to ninety-nine years (see appendix E for a list of bases the United States sought to retain in conjunction with this new defense strategy).[24]

In a letter to the Joint Chiefs of Staff, written ten days after the war ended, the office of the commanding general of the Army Air Force explained its postwar objectives—objectives that had clear implications for Panama: "We must be in a position to deliver damaging counter-blows, possibly within a matter of 24 hours, to any source of influence controlling aggression against us and, at the same time, we must have adequate forward bases for warning and interception of initial enemy assaults."[25]

Although this document is dated September 1945, the strategy of a national defense based on "adequate forward bases" actually began taking shape in 1943. That is when the Joint Chiefs of Staff (JCS) presented President Roosevelt with its proposal for worldwide order following the war. This plan, known as Broadview and referred to in government circles as JCS 570/2, received approval from President Roosevelt on January 7, 1944. Broadview reflected the strategic transition in American foreign policy from a regionally based defense mechanism to an international one. It depended on thirty-three key defense sites that the JCS deemed necessary for the defense of the United States and the Western Hemisphere in times of peace. In an age before rocket-launched nuclear weapons, Pentagon officials argued that the only way to defend the canal and other strategically crucial areas against nuclear strikes was to interdict launch aircraft as they approached their targets. Accordingly these bases would form "a United States strategic frontier," from which American forces could counter hostile acts with immediate airborne retaliation.[26]

General George C. Marshall, Chief of Staff of the United States Army, insisted that the sites identified in JCS 570/2 (and its successor, 570/3) be ranked according to their relative importance to the defense of the United States, ranging from those considered essential primary base areas to those nonessential secondary base areas that might prove useful if the necessary concessions could be easily obtained from the respective governments.

In response to General Marshall's mandate, the JCS included the Panama Canal as one of its primary base areas, "those areas strategically located and adequately developed, that would comprise the foundation of the base system that was essential to the security of the United States, its possessions, the Western Hemisphere, and the Philippines."[27]

This classification had little diplomatic significance, however. The 1936 Hull-Alfaro Treaty between Panama and the United States had reaffirmed Washington's jurisdiction over the Canal Zone. No additional agreement was needed to secure JCS objectives within the Zone.

On the other hand, the United States' temporary bases in Panama posed a significant diplomatic obstacle. Unlike temporary bases elsewhere in Latin America, most of which had been abandoned for largely diplomatic reasons toward the end of the war, the JCS considered the canal a "strategic essentiality" that merited a "special relationship between the United States and the Republic of Panama."[28]

"Special relationship" was Washington's way of saying it did not intend to evacuate its temporary Panama bases. Although the JCS considered these peripheral bases less pivotal to the "tactical defense of the Panama Canal" than the permanent United States installations located within the confines of the Canal Zone, they nevertheless considered them "necessary to protect primary bases and to allow access to them."[29] A September 1945 report by the Joint Staff Planners and the Joint Strategic Survey Committee clarified the strategic significance military officials attached to these secondary base areas in Panama. The JCS contended that they were necessary to "provide for securing vital U.S. installations against effective attacks by any potential enemy, including attacks with new weapons."[30] According to the report,

> This [plan] requires forces and installations disposed in an outer perimeter of bases from which to reconnoiter and survey possible enemy actions, to intercept his attacking forces, to deny him use of such bases, and to launch counteractions which alone can reach a decision satisfactory to us. These peripheral bases will be part of an integrated system, made up of a group of well-developed primary bases, and a group of connecting secondary bases to provide an unbroken series of essential stepping stones to the primary and peripheral bases in order to obtain security in depth, protection to lines of communication and logistical support of operations.[31]

The Pentagon's plan to continue occupying Panamanian "stepping stones" was formulated well before the war's end; the report also identifies reasons for those intentions. Unlike the importance of similar bases elsewhere in the region, the military value of the temporary sites in Panama overshadowed the diplomatic concerns inherent in violating an international treaty.

By adopting this approach to postwar defense, military officials in Washington placed United States interests directly at odds with the stated position of the Panamanian government, which called for the unequivocal withdrawal of United States troops from the temporary sites by September of 1946. Ironically in 1946 Washington had criticized the Soviet Union for its continued occupation of bases in Azerbaijan despite demands for their evacuation by local officials.[32] Moreover, further complicating the unpopular American position was Egypt's demand, argued before the United Nations on July 8, 1946, that British troops evacuate territory surrounding the

Suez Canal. Egyptian parallels to Panama, combined with Washington's diplomatic hypocrisy on the Azerbaijan issue, badly undermined any veneer of legality the United States might have used to justify its actions to the government and people of Panama.[33]

State Department officials secretly acknowledged the "unanimous popular opposition" that existed in Panama to renegotiation of the 1942 accord. They waited until August 30—one day before the one-year anniversary of the cessation of hostilities and one day before the evacuation deadline Panama had established with Article I of the Defense Site Agreement—to formally petition the Jiménez administration for an extension of the treaty. Less than one month later, officials in Washington attempted to restore a hint of legality to their noncompliance by declaring that "no definitive treaty of peace [had] been signed," thereby implicitly denying the expiration of the 1942 accord between Washington and Panama.[34]

On December 31, 1946, President Harry Truman reaffirmed this position. That day, in a move calculated to justify Washington's position, the State Department forwarded the following statement from President Truman to the Jiménez administration:

> Although a state of war still exists, it is at this time possible to declare, and I find it to be in the public interest to declare, that hostilities have terminated . . . It should be noted that this proclamation does not terminate the states of emergency declared by President Roosevelt on September 8, 1939, and May 27, 1941. Nor does today's action have the effect of terminating the state of war itself. It terminates merely the period of hostilities.[35]

Many other countries had granted similar military privileges to the United States under the guise of hemispheric defense, and Washington had readily abandoned those military sites "upon cessation of hostilities"—or before. However, the State Department opted for a second interpretation of the war's end regarding Panama, one that permitted a continuation of the expanded United States presence there. This diplomatic duplicity on Washington's part, combined with President Jiménez's efforts to prolong the expanded American presence in Panama (Jiménez admitted to Murray Wise of the State Department in January 1947 that he and other Panamanian merchants wanted the United States to continue occupying the bases for economic reasons), set the Panamanian government increasingly at odds with most of its citizens.

The renegotiation of the 1942 base accord created neither anti-Americanism nor opposition to the Jiménez administration; they had long been significant components of Panamanian politics and society. However, when the war ended, it became increasingly apparent that the governments of the United States and Panama intended to prolong the 1942 accord despite widespread opposition. The base issue became a patriotic rallying point for Panamanians who were opposed both to their nation's status quo and to United States imperialism.

Escalating the Confrontation

Opposition to the Filós-Hines Treaty occurred in three distinct phases. Initially political parties and student groups joined forces to compel the United States to honor the agreement to abandon the bases in question, as outlined in Article I of the 1942 accord; this first period was markedly nationalistic and anti-American. When Minister Filós and Ambassador Hines signed the treaty on December 10, a second period of protest began, one that marked a rapid expansion of the opposition front. This second phase remained primarily a nationalistic one, but those who signed the accord also showed an extraordinary disregard for public sentiment, and distrust of the government mounted during the days following the signing. Finally, following a particularly violent attack on protestors by the National Police on December 12, opposition to the Jiménez administration's use of brute force to stifle protest spread throughout the country. While demonstrators continued to frame their activities in anti-American rhetoric, this third phase is most significant, because it specifically pitted the administration against its political opponents.

The decisive final days of this dispute, December 12–22, marked a critical juncture in Panamanian politics, because opponents of the Filós-Hines Treaty ultimately forced the National Assembly to reject the pact. By successfully checking the elite's domination of the nation's legislative and diplomatic processes, protestors demonstrated the inability of a civilian government in Panama to legislate against popular will. The rejection of the treaty also highlighted changes that had occurred in the Panamanian polity since the twenties and thirties, when opponents of the status quo repeatedly succumbed to elite domination. Ironically this popular "victory" also sealed the political ascendancy of the National Police, the archnemesis of Panama's popular movements.

Initial opposition to the renegotiation of the 1942 accord began as the war ended, when it became apparent that the governments of both countries intended to prolong the previous agreement. Political parties and student groups united to establish a broad-based opposition coalition. Invoking Article I of the 1942 accord, leaders from both groups contended that the war had ended aboard the American battleship *Missouri* in September 1945.

These groups used the Panamanian press to portray the continued American presence in acerbic, patriotic terms, arguing that any continuation of the 1942 accord beyond September 1946 violated Panamanian sovereignty as outlined in the 1936 Hull-Alfaro Treaty. Consequently the debate over the base treaty evolved initially into a nationalist-versus-pro-American dialectic that helped the opposition cast negotiations for an extension of the 1942 accord in a patriotic light, with Panama as the victim of United States imperialism.

On May 9, 1947, Eloy G. Benedetti, Secretary General of the Frente Patriótico de la Juventud, wrote to Foreign Minister Ricardo J. Alfaro to express his organization's position on the pending treaty. Speaking for hundreds of Panamanian students, Benedetti argued that continued North American presence on the bases in question violated Panamanian territorial sovereignty. He called on Alfaro and other Panamanian officials to reject Washington's request for an extension of the treaty.[36]

Soon other groups joined the students in their opposition to the pending legislation. Shortly after Benedetti wrote to Alfaro, Cristóbal L. Segundo, then president of the Partido del Pueblo (Panama's small Communist party), sent a similar message to Alfaro that officially expressed his party's opposition to the treaty, urging the minister to "defend at all costs [Panama's] territorial integrity and national sovereignty." Rodrigo Molina A., general secretary of the Federación de Estudiantes de Panamá, added his group's voice to those organizations expressing their opposition to the treaty. Molina informed Minister Alfaro that the federation "emphatically denie[d]" the government's position. Molina and his fellow students refused to accept Alfaro's attempt to justify the treaty in terms of national and hemispheric interests.[37]

This new opposition front resembled in many ways the one that had formed in the midthirties to oppose the administration of President Harmodio Arias. However, unlike Arias, President Enrique Jiménez lacked a significant popular following to help counter the opposition. Moreover Panama's relationship with the international community following World War II differed considerably from that of the thirties, when the United States had played a less visible role in Panama's internal affairs. Now, given the increased strategic value American military officials assigned to the Panama Canal because of the war, diplomatic procedures frequently yielded to military initiatives in Washington's interactions with the Panamanian government. American policy makers simply ignored the social, economic, and political implications of their obstinacy.

Washington's indifference to Isthmian problems underscored Panama's singular predicament. Forced to strike an uneasy balance between the exigencies of popular opinion and Washington's unyielding demands, the Jiménez administration sought publicly to promote national interests without at the same time alienating officials in Washington. This explains, for example, why Jiménez secretly proposed a symbolic return of the bases in question. However, the Panamanian government failed miserably in its efforts to appease opponents of the treaty, and as negotiations between the two countries progressed, so too did opposition to the proposed accord.

The first phase of resistance to the new treaty culminated with its signing on December 10, 1947. The agreement signed that day represented a significant change from the one originally proposed by State Department officials before the war's end. Unlike the State Department, the War Department in fact recognized the breadth of opposition to the treaty that existed in Panama. Military planners secretly acknowledged the logic of Panamanian objections, while conceding that defense of the canal could be adequately assured from within the Zone. This position conflicted with the State Department's obstinacy regarding the 1942 agreement, based as it was on the concept of hemispheric defense. Officials at the Pentagon also pointed out that "on the basis of current estimates, it appears unlikely that either funds or troops would be available to man or develop the sites even if rights to them are acquired."[38] Furthermore the Joint Chiefs of Staff concluded that there was "little likelihood of attack on the canal within the foreseeable future—ten years."[39]

In response to the military's position on the base issue, the State Department reduced its demands from more than 32,000 hectares (seventy-five defense sites) to approximately 10,500 hectares (thirteen sites) (Appendix E). Despite this drastic cutback, the request for thirteen sites outside the Canal Zone still exceeded what military planners deemed necessary. It is important to note that in the postwar Truman administration, the State Department had regained its peacetime preeminence in diplomatic affairs, and its officials intended the United States to retain its expanded wartime presence on the isthmus. As a consequence, negotiations between Panama and the United States were shaped by the State Department's unwillingness to alter its position regarding the role of the canal in conjunction with JCS 570/2.[40]

The only obstacle that stood between the signing of the treaty and its implementation as a binding international agreement was legislative approval, which the Panamanian National Assembly undertook immediately. This triggered a flurry of activity among the opposition front, as students and political activists expanded their use of the press as a medium to express their disagreement to the pending bases accord. Using *El Panamá América*, the nation's second largest Spanish newspaper, as their primary tool of attack, opponents of the treaty orchestrated antibase rallies and other political gatherings to generate interest in, and support for, their cause (see appendix F for Panama's four largest newspapers' day-by-day accounts of the Filós-Hines debate).

As Panama's National Assembly took up the matter of ratification, several of Panama's leading politicians found themselves torn between their own partisan and economic interests and the indisputable widespread opposition to the treaty, as portrayed in the national press. Years later President Jiménez would describe Panama's political climate in December 1947 as one of "strong political tension," particularly in Panama City.[41]

Many members of the Jiménez administration owned businesses or properties that had benefited economically from the expanded North American presence. Some of these individuals expressed concern over the economic repercussions of rejecting the pact. For example President Jiménez, himself a businessman who shared investments in the nation's beef industry with Police Chief José Remón, had considerable personal interest in prolonging the expanded American presence. Panama supplied large quantities of beef to help meet the demands generated by the extra American military personnel stationed there, and both the president and Remón stood to lose much business if the United States withdrew its additional troops.

Many of those opposed to the treaty saw through the divided loyalties of their elected officials as the ratification process began. They used the press to criticize "those members of the government who are interested in approving the treaty," arguing that probase legislators engendered a "false sense of fear regarding economic repercussions" in an attempt to protect their own economic interests.[42] For the opposition, the signing of the accord on December 12 constituted the consummation of a business agreement that ran contrary to national interests. David Acosta, a student leader who helped organize and direct the protest, later wrote that students opposed the Filós-Hines Treaty because they felt it reflected the business ambitions of politicians "whose only concern was to defend their economic interests . . . thereby diminishing Panama's territorial integrity and national sovereignty."[43]

The Confrontation Escalates

On December 12 the conflict between those Panamanians who opposed the treaty and those who favored it reached crisis proportions. Panamanian law required any groups planning public assemblies to notify the appropriate mayor's office concerning their intentions. After Minister Filós and Ambassador Hines signed the treaty on December 10, the Mayor of Panama City, Mauricio Díaz, began receiving notes from the leaders of various groups. These notices expressed their intentions to carry out peaceful public demonstrations to protest the treaty.

On the morning of December 12, Díaz notified Police Chief Remón that various groups had "expressed their intention to organize protest marches this afternoon." Mayor Díaz's fateful communication illustrates the power the police now exercised in civilian politics in Panama. Díaz wrote: "As you can imagine, Mr. Commander, and I *ask you to take whatever measures necessary in this regard*, it is the firm intention of this office NOT to permit . . . meetings or public demonstrations that might interfere with . . . public order." [emphasis added][44]

Beyond identifying Remón and his force as the government's political moderator, this note had two significant results. First, by telling the police commander to use "whatever measures necessary" to prevent these public demonstrations, Díaz gave official license to Remón to use violence to prevent public displays of opposition to the Filós-Hines agreement. Second, by outlawing public demonstrations, Díaz further antagonized an opposition movement whose efforts had failed to stop the signing of the unpopular accord two days earlier. The mayor's attempt to circumvent the constitutionally guaranteed privilege of public gathering reinforced the opposition's distrust of the administration and its negative perception of the status quo. Gradually the Filós-Hines debate was becoming a showdown between the Jiménez administration and those Panamanians opposed to the treaty. For the time being, the police represented the middle ground between the two sides.

In response to the mayor's partial suspension of the nation's civil rights, student leaders at the National Institute rallied to plan exactly the type of demonstration Díaz had attempted to outlaw. More than one hundred students gathered in support of the opposition cause. Within hours after the mayor's decree, these youths took to the streets of the capital to protest the base treaty and to challenge the government's provocative edict. Hundreds more joined them as they made their way from the National Institute to the National Assembly, setting the stage for one of the largest, most violent, and most significant political confrontations in Panamanian history.

As the group made its way to historic Santa Ana Plaza, its numbers reached into the thousands. Many protestors carried placards that read "Down with Yankee Imperialism," and "Not One More Inch of Panamanian Territory." After encountering token police resistance along the route, the group approached the plaza, the historic park in downtown Panama City that Panamanians generally consider "la cuna de nuestra independencia" (the cradle of our independence). There police and protestors fought it out, and Remón's men put on an unprecedented display of police brutality. In her award-winning novel *El señor de las lluvias y el viento*, Rosa María Britton described the scene that unfolded when Remón's men arrived at the plaza. Bystanders fled for shelter as foot soldiers and mounted police beat the students with

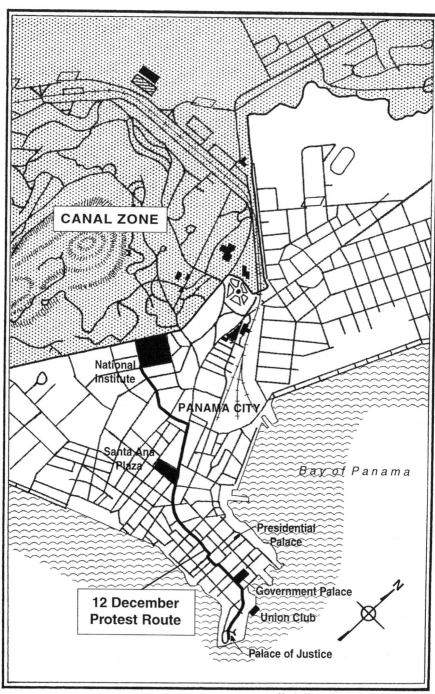

Map 2. Route of Student Protest on 12 December 1947, Panama City, Panama.

clubs, shot at them, and used tear gas to disperse them. Ultimately Remón and his men wounded sixty demonstrators. During the tense days that followed, these victims became the rallying point for antiadministration ardor in Panama.[45]

The Jiménez administration attempted to frame the December 12 actions of the National Police within the broader context of hemispheric defense. Government officials couched their explanations of the day's events in Cold War rhetoric. According to Police Chief Remón, for example,

> Among the demonstrators, I learned from members of the forces, were well-known agitators undoubtedly obeying orders from Moscow. They urged youth to overturn cars before Cecilia Theater, to erect barricades on the streets, and to climb to the balcony of the house in which the Communist Party is housed whence they exhorted students. These individuals are, among others: Deputy José A. Brower [Socialist party], his alternate Gilberto Bazán Villalaz, and Dr. Celso Solano [then general secretary of Panama's Communist party], Communist proprietor who carried the Soviet flag.[46]

President Jiménez joined Remón in blaming the December 12 riots on communist agitation, and by doing so he paraded before the nation his administration's indifference to popular sentiment. Jiménez convinced Washington that the protestors received their orders from Moscow, but as shown by the immediate and widespread response to the events of December 12, the government failed to justify its actions to the Panamanian people.

The confrontation between pro- and antibase factions in Panama resembled the 1926 and 1932 renters' strikes, when opponents of the government organized to protest policies they found objectionable. However, on December 12, 1947, the violent attack on demonstrators by the National Police produced unexpected, unprecedented results. While the police eventually succeeded in dispersing the crowd that had gathered in Santa Ana Plaza, the encounter received extensive coverage in each of Panama's major newspapers. This press coverage triggered a massive, nationwide outpouring of popular support for the opposition cause. The National Police had inadvertently accomplished in a few hours what opposition leaders had been attempting to do since late 1946—their actions united large numbers of people into a protest movement capable of checking the Jiménez administration's disregard of public opinion.

On December 13 thousands of Panamanians, shocked by the events of December 12, joined the opposition movement. That morning Mayor Díaz received a wave of letters from groups adding their names to those intending to march against the treaty.[47] These groups included "an organizing committee for the Panamanian Woman," the Communist party, and the

Panamanian Youth Congress. That same day student groups carried out sizable demonstrations in Panama City's Santa Ana Plaza and De Lesseps Park in Colón. On December 15 the much strengthened opposition carried out a nationwide walkout to protest the treaty, bringing the nation to a near standstill. Public schools throughout the republic would remain closed until after the National Assembly's rejection of the treaty on December 22.[48]

With the persistent impetus provided by student groups and civic and political organizations, circumstances began to favor the opposition movement. This shift in momentum became most apparent on December 16, when more than ten thousand women added their voices to the mounting protest by marching to the National Assembly as a group to protest ratification of the Filós-Hines Treaty. Also that same day, the Second Student Conference convened at Panama City's National Institute, and student leaders from throughout the isthmus gathered to consolidate their opposition efforts.[49]

The escalating size, continuing intensity, and persistence of the opposition movement surprised government officials in both Panama City and Washington. By December 20 opinion within the Assembly favored rejection of the treaty, due to the extraordinary show of public opposition and the apparent threat of violent reprisal. These two factors ultimately superseded any other motives legislators might have entertained. Moreover, during the final days of deliberation, demonstrators stabbed an American soldier in Colón. American military commanders responded by declaring Panama City and Colón off-limits to all United States military personnel. Their subsequent absence left pro-American assemblymen feeling particularly vulnerable to physical harm. The president of Panama's National Assembly anxiously announced that "10,000 boys with knives" waited outside to harm the legislators if they approved the treaty.[50]

By the time Panama's legislature was prepared to vote on the treaty, the opposition front had brought the nation to its knees. Most schools and businesses were closed; civic groups, labor organizations, and professional clubs had joined the opposition; and immediately prior to the vote, workers from throughout the nation threatened a general strike if the Filós-Hines pact were ratified. Panamanian officials had encountered the most well-organized, effective opposition front in the nation's history, and the government was losing ground.

Without the presence of the canal and its enhanced strategic value, urban warfare similar to earlier battles between partisan "armed patriots" might well have erupted. With the increased strength of the police and the unprecedented viability of the opposition movement, the violence of such a confrontation could have exceeded anything in Panamanian history, including the bloody Thousand Days' War.

However, responding to the overwhelming opposition to the treaty and to their own fears of violent consequences, many assemblymen who had pledged their support for the treaty undermined the administration by reversing their positions.[51] The activists won: at 9:50 P.M. on December 22, 1947, eleven deputies presented the following motion to Panama's National Assembly:

> The agreement signed in this city on the 10th instant by the representatives of the Governments of the Republic of Panama and the United States of America is hereby rejected, because the said agreement is not inspired in the principle of the juridical equality of the contracting states nor does it adhere to the norms of international law and the spirit of the inter-American system of defense.[52]

A roll call vote then resulted in a unanimous 51 to 0 rejection of the treaty.

The end of the Filós-Hines debate closed an extended period of political confrontation and violence unprecedented in Panama's forty-four-year history. Within one month the United States evacuated all its temporary Panamanian bases, in compliance with the Assembly's decision. The walkouts and strikes that had partially paralyzed Isthmian life for more than a week also ended. Workers, teachers, and students returned to their places of employment and study, and the immediate threat of further violence dissipated overnight. More significantly, only a shell remained of what had been the largest opposition movement in Panamanian history, and its rapid dispersion showed just how tenuous the alliances had been and how much activists had accomplished in assembling a front that had effectively checked the government's compliance with a foreign power.

While the short-term problems were resolved immediately, what long-term implications did the rejection of the Filós-Hines accord have for Panama? Scholars in both Panama and the United States have portrayed the treaty's rejection as a short-lived victory for the opposition, one that ultimately triggered economic difficulties that implicitly gave rise to the dictatorship of José Remón. In his definitive work on José Remón, for example, Larry L. Pippin writes, "The financial consequences of the treaty rejection hastened a post-war economic recession. . . . Increased political instability was a corollary to a stagnant economy."[53] More recently Michael Conniff has noted that "the Panamanian economy became sluggish in the postwar years due to a sharp drop in expenditures in the Canal Zone. The rejection of the bases agreement brought on a recession, with high levels of unemployment and fiscal distress."[54] According to this interpretation, radical Panamanian nationalism subordinated opportunities for progress to superficial nationalist ideals, and Panama made a serious mistake by forgoing valuable revenue.

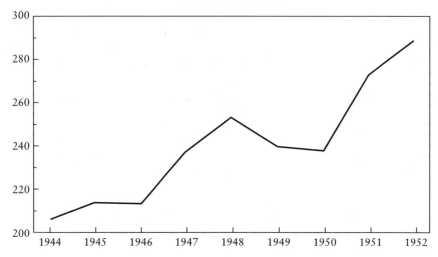

Figure 20
Panama's National Income, 1944–1952
(in millions of U.S. dollars)

Source: República de Panamá, *Contraloría General de la República Dirección de Estadística y Censo*, 1944–1952, p. 74

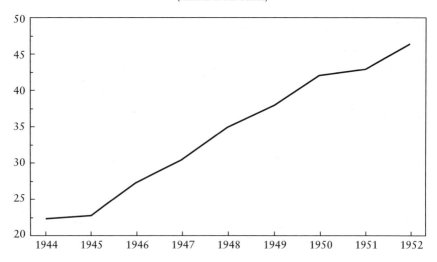

Figure 21
Exports of Goods and Services from Panama, 1944–1952*
(millions of U.S. dollars)

*excluding exports to Canal Zone

Source: República de Panamá, *The National Income and National Accounts of the Republic of Panama*, 1944–1952, p. 72

Unquestionably rationing of foodstuffs and other key products occurred in Panama following the war, just as it did in the United States and elsewhere. Furthermore that Panama's exports to the Canal Zone dropped off following the treaty's rejection is beyond doubt. Yet the current study clearly makes untenable the suggestion, posited by Pippin and others, that the treaty's rejection "hastened a post-war economic recession" and consequently "increased political instability." Rather, economic data from the period suggest that Panama's economy actually improved between 1947 and 1951, with increases in key sectors of the economy, including imports (with a slight decline in 1947), exports, income from properties and enterprises, corporate taxes, and wages, boosting Panama's overall national income for the period (see figures 20 and 21).[55] In 1948, when in accordance with Pippin's hypothesis one might expect to find the most fiscal devastation, Panama experienced marked increases in the influx of foreign investment, the amount of corporate and household taxes collected, loans extended, private consumption, and gross domestic product. These data clearly indicate that opponents of the treaty correctly perceived the nature of the pact and the motives of their politicians.

Conclusions

The end of World War II proved to be a decisive event in Panama. Thousands of laborers who had fled the Canal Zone and surrounding areas during the war began returning to Panama City and Colón. Rising crime rates, marked demographic shifts, increased competition for jobs, and social and political agitation generally greeted them upon their return (see appendix G). Meanwhile, since its inception in 1935, Panama's National University encouraged its students to sustain a state of "constant rebelliousness" to "preserve the Panamanian nationality" in the face of increasing North American imperialism.[56] Linked with thousands of high school students throughout the republic by myriad student associations and a number of teachers' unions, university students led a mounting opposition campaign even during the war against the expanded North American presence in Panama. This protest grew in size and sophistication throughout the last two years of the war, reaching its peak in 1946, when American officials refused to evacuate the additional bases they had received in a 1942 agreement.

Events surrounding the Filós-Hines negotiations provided a point of convergence that temporarily united workers, students, and much of the rest of Panama in a heated, decisive debate with their political leaders. By signing the accord on December 10, 1947, despite widespread protests, President Jiménez demonstrated his disregard for the people of Panama, and his cavalier attitude provoked considerable nationalist furor beyond that which had existed previously. Leaders of the antitreaty coalition responded by stepping up their protest, including accelerating their elaborate press campaign, in the hopes of forcing the National Assembly to veto the pact. However, these increased efforts would undoubtedly have failed without the events of December 12, 1947. That day there was a startling display of brutality, when police headed off a massive antibase rally, as participants gathered in Panama City's historic Santa Ana Plaza. First Commander José Remón unleashed his troops to use clubs, guns, and the mounted cavalry to disperse the demonstrators.

This one particularly violent confrontation shifted the emphasis of the protest from anti-American nationalism to an open struggle between the government and its opponents. This change in focus distinguished opposition to the Filós-Hines Treaty from similar earlier movements that had ended in failure. In 1932, for example, a combination of government manipulation and United States intervention had eclipsed protests aimed at reversing particularly unpopular government decisions. However, the increasing politicization of women and workers in the twenties, thirties, and forties greatly expanded both the depth and breadth of political activism in Panama. Moreover the establishment of the National University in October 1935 extended opposition to the treaty into the nation's interior, though grassroots rural student organizations. The university also provided the basis for an increasingly coherent nationalist platform.

Under these circumstances, negotiations for the Filós-Hines Treaty resulted in the convergence of a large number of politically active persons with leaders who were capable of assimilating them into a unified front. With his ability to manipulate the nation's legislative processes checked by this convergence, President Jiménez completed his term in office propped up by the National Police. Ironically then, the Filós-Hines debate completed the police's political ascension. Previously the National Police had been the institutional embodiment of elite political aspirations; after December 1947, however, the National Police assumed its position atop Panama's political hierarchy, a fact reaffirmed repeatedly in the late 1940s and early 1950s, when First Commander José Remón appointed and removed presidents at will.

Conclusion

IN THEIR 1980 WORK ON PRAETORIAN STATES, POLITICAL SCIENTISTS AMOS Perlmutter and Valerie Plave Bennett noted significant parallels between civil-military relations in ancient Rome and current conditions in Latin America, the Middle East, Africa, and Asia—regions that "have experienced a *perpetuum mobile* of coups, military governments, counter coups, civilian regimes, and further coups . . . [phenomena] usually referred to under the rubric of "praetorian states."[1] The authors continue:

> The concept of praetorianism was developed with reference to the history of the praetorian guards of ancient Rome. The declining days of Rome saw a progressive assumption of political power by the soldiery. By the third century the imperial office had become a prize for the contending ambitions of the legions, which made and unmade emperors in order to secure special donatives and privileges for themselves. Although all the legions participated with varying fortunes in the profitable struggle for political power, the praetorian guards became notorious as the most strikingly successful. Established from the time of Augustus as the sole military force within the city of Rome, their proximity to the capital frequently enabled them to play a dominating role in imperial politics. Their most celebrated exploit was the murder of Pertinax and the sale of the empire at public auction to Didius Julianus.[2]

As in ancient Rome, competing forces divided Panamanian society and politics throughout its formative first decades as a republic. And this sociopolitical fragmentation also shaped civil-military relations in Panama, elevating the police force to political prominence as successive regimes used it to govern Panama's increasingly ungovernable polity. By the late 1940s, all that remained to complete the decades-long transition to a praetorian-style political arbitrator was a crisis of sufficient magnitude to force a decisive confrontation between civilian and police officials on the Isthmus.

As we have seen, this decisive showdown occurred in December 1947. At that time the historic Filós-Hines debacle temporarily provided the unifying motivation for an unprecedented coalition of forces that had for decades been competing with one another. For several days, opposition to the base treaty caused a "state of exception" in Panama that coupled the interests and agendas of labor, middle-class activists, and various blocs within the nation's politically dominant urban elite. The convergence of these groups, many of which had previously gone to great lengths to oppose one another, defied the Jiménez regime's ability to enact an unpopular treaty, and the resulting confrontation elevated the National Police to the role of unilateral political arbiter.

First, and most notably, by the midforties Panama's middle class had come to wield considerable social and political leverage.[3] Under the energetic tutelage and encouragement of figures such as Octavio Méndez Pereira, the middle class had evolved sufficiently by the end of World War II to provide a nucleus of leadership capable of assimilating large segments of a diverse society into a surprisingly unified, focused opposition front. Students had participated in the nation's political process since the earliest years of the republic. However, as Panamanian author Jorge Conte-Porras notes in *La rebelión de las esfinges*, student movements throughout the republic remained relatively isolated, disjointed, and ineffective until the 1930s, when the establishment of the National University provided a hub for intellectual activity on the isthmus.[4] With the impetus it received from the university, coupled with the nationalist inertia generated by the war, Panama's student movement played a decisive role in successfully opposing the renegotiation of the 1942 base treaty.

Second, from 1903 to 1947 Panama's urban labor force grew quite rapidly. As historian Michael Conniff has noted with particular regard to Canal Zone workers during this period, natural increase and ongoing recruitment and immigration resulted in the disproportionate growth of Panama's urban labor force when compared to the remainder of its population.[5] This demographic expansion, focused as it was mainly in geographic pockets near the Canal Zone, fueled worker unionization and agitation. Alejandro Portes posits that worker organization in Latin America in the early and midtwentieth century provided fodder for middle-class idealists, who attempted to exploit discontent among the poor to achieve their own activist agendas. Portes's hypothesis certainly applies to Panama in the twenties, thirties, and forties, when unionization and other kinds of collective popular action provided the nation's middle-class nationalists with a manageable reservoir of dissidence from which to draw.

Finally, along with Panama's middle class and its workers, the National Police comprise the third group whose evolution and development contributed decisively to the events of December 1947 and beyond. Formally, the power to enact laws and to administer government affairs rested with the president, as outlined in the constitution. However, as numerous scholars have pointed out in their work on the erosion of political order, formal authority "tells only part of the story of power."[6] In reality the momentary convergence of interests (Carranza's "states of exception") that occurred in December 1947 represented an unprecedented political consensus that shifted Panama's balance of power so that the police came to dominate politics and government in general after December 1947.

Panama completed its transition from formal governance to informal praetorian rule—and, occasionally, informal tyranny—with the Filós-Hines conflict. By causing the unprecedented convergence of previously opposed forces, this debate in turn triggered an equally unprecedented response from the police. First Commander José Remón and his men coupled two weeks of blatant, intermittent brutality with a relentless political witch-hunt reminiscent of the Palmer Raids in the United States. Moreover, as witnessed by the much-publicized resignation of Jiménez's foreign minister, severe internal divisions jeopardized the Jiménez administration's ability to govern from that point on.

These fissures effectively ended the government's ability to rule, and with the nation's government paralyzed by internal dissension, for the first time the police dominated the state's decision-making apparatus. The extent of this subtle shift in Panama's balance of power became increasingly evident in the months and years following the December 1947 crisis. First, the police maintained a state of siege a few months after the Filós-Hines incident, when the Panamanian and United States governments reached an unpopular agreement regarding commercial air traffic in Panama. The police openly bullied opponents of the accord throughout the entire negotiating process and completely thwarted attempts to oppose the pact, actually killing two protestors and injuring several dozen others in the process. Then, from 1949 to 1951, First Commander Remón appointed and removed presidents seemingly without regard for the unconstitutionality of his actions; he actually appointed and then removed three different presidents within a five-day period in November 1949. Ironically, then, the police's "defeat" in the Filós-Hines standoff actually launched the dictatorship of First Commander José Remón, unleashing police power that had been developing below the surface of Panama's government for decades and establishing a clear precedent for Panama's more recent police-dominated regimes.

Epilogue

EVENTS FOLLOWING THE DECEMBER 1947 REJECTION OF THE FILÓS-HINES Treaty made it clear that the National Police no longer played a subservient role in Panamanian politics. Having successfully challenged elite hegemony and American imperialism, the opposition lost its organizing impetus and simply dissipated. The subsequent decline in organized activity among activist groups gave the police the upper hand in Panamanian politics after December 1947. Under these circumstances, the police made it possible for the embattled Jiménez administration to complete its term in office. Then, having dictated the outcome of the 1948 presidential election, First Commander José Remón governed the nation from his office at the Cuartel Central in Panama City. He appointed presidents and removed them at will, naming five men to that post during the period from 1948 to 1952. During one particularly unsettled week in 1949, three men served as president within a five-day span. This chaos culminated with Remón's own successful bid for the presidency in 1952.[1]

What distinguished the period 1948–52 from similarly unsettled episodes earlier in the republic's history? Did the tumult following the Filós-Hines debate establish a precedent for Panama's subsequent military governments? Soon after Panama's legislature vetoed the Filós-Hines agreement, a series of events secured police dominance of the police-elite coalition that had been developing over several decades. Combined, these factors fostered First Commander José Remón's election to the presidency in 1952. They also established a pattern of military political ascendancy for Panama's more recent military regimes.

After the treaty debate had been resolved, the first indication that the police now governed the Isthmus occurred during the 1948 presidential campaign. In Panama's first election in eight years, the urban elite chose Domingo Díaz to replace Jiménez. Díaz's opponent was former president Arnulfo Arias Madrid, candidate of the newly formed Partido Revolucionario Auténtico (PRA—Authentic Revolutionary party). Several armed clashes between the two camps failed to produce any decided advantage, and Arias and his followers devised a plan to overthrow the Jiménez administration and gain control of the police, destroying the foundation of the Díaz campaign. Upon discovering the plot, President Jiménez responded by suspending certain constitutional rights, including the freedom of speech and the right of assembly.

Up to this point, the police had not intervened in the campaign. However, when pro-Arias conspirators developed support within the Jiménez administration, the police came forward in support of the president and of the Díaz campaign. This backing handed the election to Díaz. The 1948 presidential election marked the second time in less than a decade that the police had squelched Arnulfo Arias's political aspirations.

The second indication that Panama's police now controlled its politically dominant alliance with the urban elite arose in mid-1949. Before his untimely death in August 1949, president-elect Díaz negotiated an unpopular treaty with the United States regarding commercial air traffic in Panama.[2] In protests preceding the April 13 signing of the accord, police and protestors squared off, and two deaths and dozens of injuries resulted. However, in the absence of a coherent opposition such as the one that opposed the Filós-Hines agreement, the police prevailed. With their support, President Díaz suspended constitutional rights and declared a state of siege on April 25. Maintained by the police, the state of siege remained in effect until July 29, 1949.

President Díaz's death in August 1949 provided a third display of the police's control of Panama's government. Díaz's first vice president, Daniel Chanis, became interim president on July 28, when the nation's aging chief executive became too ill to perform his duties. A rift developed between Chanis and First Commander Remón over the latter's questionable monopoly of Panama City's lucrative livestock-slaughtering industry. In November Chanis attempted to dismiss Remón for an apparent conflict of interests, accusing the police chief of misusing his position for his own financial gain. As one American official noted at the time, this disagreement resulted from "an attempt by President Chanis, at the instigation of Harmodio Arias, a prominent politician and cattle raiser, to break up an illegal slaughtering monopoly in which Colonel Remón, Chief of Police, is a principle figure."[3]

However, Remón's men rallied around him. On November 20, 1949, the police surrounded the presidential palace and demanded Chanis's resignation, which the president in fact tendered. That same day Remón sought out members of the Supreme Court, who swore in the police chief's cousin, Roberto Chiari, as provisional president to complete Díaz's term.

The next day the ousted president renounced his resignation, claiming that he had resigned under duress. For students and antipolice activists, his willingness to confront the police made him the symbol of civilian rule. Strikes broke out throughout the capital, to protest police usurpation of the nation's governmental processes. Despite widespread opposition to Chanis's forced resignation, the police once again repelled the protestors, and the Chanis resignation stood. However, three days later, on November 24, the Supreme Court ruled in favor of the deposed Chanis regime. When Remón contacted his cousin at 5:30 P.M. that day, to see how the new president planned to respond to the court's verdict, Chiari stated that he intended to honor it. Remón condemned both the Supreme Court's ruling and his cousin's decision, denouncing the latter as a coward and giving him ten minutes to vacate the presidential palace.

What happened next marks one of the strangest periods in the history of the republic. Commander Remón, recognizing the growing popular unrest sparked by this extraconstitutional game of political musical chairs, first appointed his archnemesis, Arnulfo Arias, interim president of the republic. Remón hoped to capitalize on Arias's widespread popular appeal to counter much of the opposition to his usurpation of political power. The police chief then reconvened the National Elections Board, which recounted the electoral results of the 1948 presidential election. Under the watchful eye of the first commander, the board found enough votes to declare Arias the constitutionally elected president, purportedly defeating the deceased president by the margin of 74,080 votes to 71,536 votes. One hour after the board reversed its decision, Remón rounded up twenty-four members of the National Assembly, who then convened an emergency session. The president of the assembly denounced the 1948 Díaz election as "the most ignominious fraud in the history of the republic." He then presented a resolution proclaiming Arnulfo Arias the popularly elected head of the republic.[4]

First Commander Remón had defeated efforts by two ousted presidents and the Supreme Court to oppose his manipulation of the nation's political processes. Under his command, Panama now had its third interim president in five days. Yet the Arias regime proved less than cooperative with the whims of the National Police. Arias reorganized the Secret Police he had established during his first presidency (1940–41), to counter First Commander Remón's base of support within the National Police. He then attempted to revoke the 1946 constitution, replacing it with the one he had decreed in 1941. This would have lengthened his time in office, giving him more opportunity to strengthen his grip on power.

Although the people had vigorously protested Remón's blatant manipulation of the nation's government, they now turned to him as their only recourse against the dictatorial Arias administration.[5] The police force was now the most powerful, best organized branch of government, and the people viewed Remón as the only individual capable of ousting Arias, who had already jailed hundreds of political prisoners since his appointment by the first commander.

Following an attempt by Arias to suspend the National Assembly, that body met on May 9, 1951, and impeached him.[6] The legislature then appointed first vice president Alcibíades Arosemena interim president. When Arias resisted, the police moved against him. Remón, who was positioning himself for the 1952 presidential campaign, did not himself become involved, leaving the job of ousting yet another president to his subordinates. Remón realized that Arias had the support of at least seventy thousand followers, and he believed that he needed the support of the Arnulfistas in order to create the veneer of a popular mandate in the upcoming election. He also knew that any move on his part to oust the president might trigger additional popular sympathy for Arias.[7]

On May 10, 1951, police forces led by Second Commander Bolívar Vallarino surround the presidential palace. In a violent confrontation, President Arias and his loyal palace guard resisted police efforts to remove them. After several hours of machine-gun fire and sniper activity that produced nine deaths and dozens of injuries, Arias capitulated, and the police removed him and his followers from the demolished building.[8]

With Arias out of the way and yet another of his appointees in office, Remón stepped up his preparations for the upcoming presidential campaign. He named ministers to the Arosemena cabinet, appointed malleable judges to the Supreme Court, and manipulated his political allies into key positions within the National Assembly. In this fashion the first commander assembled a combination of political faithfuls who would support his candidacy. This coalition, which ultimately included elements of the Partido National Revolucionario (National Revolutionary party), the Partido Revolucionario Auténtico (Authentic Revolutionary party), the Partido Revolucionario (Revolutionary party), the Unión Patriótica (Patriotic Union), and the Partido Liberal Doctrinario (Doctrinaire Liberal party), developed into the most decisive political bloc on the isthmus—the Coalición Patriótica Nacional (National Patriotic Coalition).

In Panama's shifting political climate after December, 1947, Remón's position as first commander of the National Police had made him the most powerful man in Panamanian politics. By aligning themselves with Remón, these five parties maneuvered themselves to be part of the anticipated windfall that would follow the commander's victory in the 1952 election. They would not be disappointed.

In addition to this attempt by many of Panama's politicians to link their fortunes with those of Remón, the United States also supported his candidacy. While State Department officials considered him a thug, they also hoped that his influence within the police would stabilize Panama's political situation. Following the June 1950 invasion of Korea, American officials stated secretly that "what is today accepted as our established policy toward Latin America (the 'Good Neighbor Policy') was originally developed in response to a situation that no longer exists."[9] The American government feared the spread of communism, and as a consequence of its concerns, it favored Remón despite his reputation as a despot. The United States government looked with favor upon his ability to manipulate the National Police: "Remón is a self-made man and is responsive to reformist pressures, but, as a former Police Chief, he is also conscious of the requirements for order and security. Internal stability during his term seems assured."[10]

Despite this disparate support base, Remón lacked a majority on the nation's Electoral Board going into the final weeks of the campaign. This would make it virtually impossible for the Coalición Patriótica to claim any sort of a popular mandate. "Remonistas" controlled seven electoral votes, opposition candidate Roberto Chiari controlled six electoral votes, and Arnulfo Arias controlled one. Throughout much of the campaign, Arias sided with the opposition Chiari bloc, thus dividing the board at seven votes apiece. However, sensing a Remón victory, Arias shifted his allegiance to the Remón camp. Arias had been banned from public office during impeachment proceedings against him in 1949. He hoped that because of his support for Remón, the Remonista majority in the new Assembly would revoke the ban. On April 9 Arias announced his support for the Remón candidacy. This gave the latter an eight to six Electoral Board advantage and, consequently, control of the pending presidential election. Remón's followers would count the vote.

Arias later backed out of his deal with the first commander and called upon his followers, including the Arnulfista delegate to the Electoral Board, to boycott the election altogether. Once again circumstances threatened Remón's control of the polling process. However, he had established a considerable following in the National Assembly, and he used that advantage to skirt this latest crisis. When Arnulfo Arias announced his boycott, pro-Remón assemblymen banned the pro-Arias member of the Electoral Board from voting. This ended the deadlock, gave Remón a seven to six advantage over Chiari, and reaffirmed his control of the nation's electoral apparatus. Most importantly, with his people firmly in control of polling, Remón led the voting by a wide margin.[11]

What significance did Remón's dictatorship and presidency hold for the Republic of Panama? As witnessed by his election in 1952, events following the pivotal Filós-Hines confrontation began a period of police control of government on the isthmus. Following Remón's assassination in 1955, his second in command, Bolívar Vallarino, assumed control of the government. Vallarino pursued a less politically dominant role than that of his martyred predecessor. A product of one of Panama's wealthiest families, he allowed the nation's small urban commercial elite to return to the political fore-front, removing the police temporarily from the fulcrum of Panama's political activities.

However, this relatively brief interlude of police quiescence ended in 1968. Following his election that year, President Arnulfo Arias challenged the police power structure when he attempted to reorganize the National Guard. This restructuring included the forced retirement of First Commander Vallarino, who commanded a significant following within the ranks of the officer corps. A few days after his election, a group of National Guard officers overthrew President Arnulfo Arias and took control of the Panamanian government, restoring the Guard to the political preeminence it had enjoyed during its heyday under Commander Remón.

For the next twenty-one years, the military dominated Isthmian politics. General Omar Torrijos Herrera, a protégé of Commander Vallarino, played a leading role in the putsch to oust Arias, and he emerged as the leader of the revolutionary junta that subsequently governed the nation for more than a decade. Following Torrijos's untimely death, Manuel Noriega, a Torrijos confidant and director of the "G2" (military intelligence) during the Torrijos regime, emerged as the new leader of the government—the new "Jefe Supremo" in Panama's military government. This period of military dictatorships, which began with Remón in the 1940s, closed only with the 1989 invasion of Panama by North American troops.

Scholars and politicians alike have portrayed the 1968 movement and Panama's subsequent governments as a clean break with the nation's political past, an unprecedented response to a crisis in representative government. Yet, as this study has indicated, the 1968 movement, together with the 1989 invasion that ended the reign of General Manuel Noriega, is only the most visible, recent manifestation of a power struggle that has gone on since before Panama's independence from Spain in 1821. During the colonial period, a pattern of government emerged on the isthmus that depended on military repression to control Panama's dynamic population. Over the next century, Isthmian government passed through various stages of development, each of which reflected the urban elite's efforts to preserve its economic, social, and political status. The police force, which played an integral role in protecting the status quo throughout the colonial and early republican period, achieved political preeminence of its own in the 1940s. At that time the events outlined above initiated a succession of military governments that endured, with brief interludes, until December 1989.

﹟

Appendix A

Demographic Trends in San Felipe and Santa Ana, 1884–1893

Period	Pop	BR	DR	Mort	GRR/NRR	Life Ex
San Felipe						
1884–88	4,822	36	38	30%	1.39/0.63	29.4
1889–93	4,124	48	13	11%	3.26/2.52	55.4
Santa Ana						
1884–88	11,047	60	66	45%	2.20/0.63	18.0
1889–93	9,549	64	28	21%	4.40/2.57	38.9

Source: Fernando Aparicio, "Panama: Society and Politics, 1885–1895," MA thesis, University of Miami (1991), 62.

(Key: Pop = population; BR = Birth Rate per thousand persons; DR = Death Rate per thousand persons; Mort = Mortality in the first year of life; GRR/NRR = Gross and Net Reproduction Ratios per thousand persons; Life Ex = Life Expectancy. Note: Santa Ana's 1891 death rate and the broadly varying life expectancy figures for both communities suggest possible underregistration of mortality data by the priests.)

❦

Appendix B

DEMOGRAPHIC TRENDS IN PANAMA CITY AND COLÓN, 1916–1945

Colón

Period	Pop	BR	DR	MIGR	GRR/NRR	Life Ex
1916–20:	35,012	23	14	53.4	1.37/0.97	49.5
1921–25:	34,865	24	15	−10.1	1.38/0.97	48.6
1926–30:	30,790	30	16	−36.8	1.71/1.20	49.0
1931–35	38,665	31	14	31.3	1.83/1.39	54.1
1936–40:	46,774	34	13	20.0	2.19/1.74	57.5
1941–45:	51,581	30	12	00.0	2.20/1.81	60.2

Panama City

Period	Pop	BR	DR	MIGR	GRR/NRR	Life Ex
1916–20:	61,704	37	22	22.5	2.20/1.32	40.1
1921–25:	69,519	36	21	9.2	2.20/1.36	41.6
1926–30:	77,556	33	16	6.2	2.03/1.41	48.2
1931–35:	97,519	32	14	29.4	2.00/1.50	53.1
1936–40:	118,450	35	13	19.1	2.26/1.77	56.6
1941–45:	131,973	32	11	00.0	2.08/1.70	59.3

Source: Data taken from República de Panamá, Contraloría General de la República, Dirección de Estadística y Censo, *Estadística Panameña* 6(6) (June 1947):1–4, and processed by *Populate*.

(Key: Pop = estimated population; BR = birth rate per thousand persons; DR = death rate per thousand persons; MIGR = migration rate per thousand persons; GRR/NRR = gross and net reproduction ratios; and Life Ex = estimated life expectancy).

Appendix C

To the Panamanian Nation*

MOVED BY THE PUREST SENTIMENT OF PATRIOTISM AND DESIROUS OF HAVING the country return to a regime of constitution and law and reestablish the effectivity of republican institutions the present regenerative movement commands the respect and the support of all the citizens of the country. In taking this action we have not been moved by any desire for personal profit or the least trait of ambition. The republic has been governed by rulers who have not respected civic rights, who have made a farce of and scorned the franchise and who have placed the country on the border of disaster and have compromised it politically, economically, and morally. It is impossible that a situation such as this should last any longer. In circumstances such as the present, citizens who love their country have no other recourse but to take action in the manner in which we have done. This determined gesture of the Panamanian citizenry must be maintained within the greatest order and the greatest composure. We hasten to repudiate any gesture or action revealing intentions other than those herein stated which are the very soul of this regenerative movement. It is impossible that the Panamanian people should continue to be a victim of exploitation and of the outrages which have characterized the action of the regime existing in the country up to the present. It is our aspiration to conduct the nation through new paths having as a base an absolutely republican government which will guarantee life and property and by a shield for the defense of those rights which are inherent in the citizens of the republic. We stand guarantors before the world and we shall respect the rights and prerogatives of the citizens up to the present ignored, and we shall give the country a just and equitable election law which will assure the absolute liberty of suffrage.

We declare that we will recognize all engagements acquired by the governments of the country and that we shall respect all obligations of an inter-

*State Department translation

national character which the Panamanian nation may have with other nations of the world. To our fellow citizens we shall recommend the greatest calm and composure. In an attitude characterized by order, disinterestedness and patriotism shall depend the success of this valiant gesture of our noble people anxious for guarantees and liberty [*sic*].

PANAMA, JANUARY 2ND, 1931

Jeptha B. Duncan	Dr. Aurelio A. Dutari
Samuel Lewis	J. M. Quiros y. Q.
Harmodio Arias	Juan Navarro D.
Fernando Guardia	Victor Florencio Goytía
Narciso Garay	Gilberto Brin
Julio J. Fábrega	Hombero Ayala P.
Domingo Díaz	S. P. Sosa
A. Francisco Arias Paredes	Ramón Arosemena
Raul Espinosa	Tomás Jacome
Damaso A. Cevera	Ramón Arias F.
Enrique A. Jiménez	Ramón Mora
Juan Antonio Jiménez	Arnulfo Arias
Generoso de Obaldía	J. D. Crespo
Manuel Quintero V.	Ricaurte Rivera S.
José de la Cruz Herrera	Enrique de la Guardia
Alejandro Tápia E.	José Dolores Guardia
Tomás Herrera	Manuel J. Díaz
Harmodio Arosemena Forte	Carlos A. Guardia
Gregorio Miro D.	Jaen Horacio Velarde
Fabian Velarde	Carlos W. Muller

Source: Record Group 59, Department of State, Legation of the United States of America to Panama, 819.00/Revolutions/41, National Archives, Washington, DC.

Appendix D

Site No.	Designation	Purpose	Original Occupation	Final Abandonment
1	Armuelles	AWS	14 July 41	26 Sept. 47
2	David	Airbase	5 Apr. 41	30 Oct. 47
3	Las Lajas	E.L.F.	9 Apr. 41	30 June 46
4	Coiba Island	AWS	5 Aug. 41	26 Sept. 47
5	La Mesa	E.L.F.	7 Apr. 41	30 June 46
6	Aguadulce	XAD	9 Apr. 41	19 Sept. 47
7	Pocri	XAD	7 Apr. 41	14 Jan. 48
8	Cape Mala	AWS	12 May 41	12 Jan. 48
9	Limon	AWS	7 Apr. 42	15 Oct. 44
10	Penonome	XAD	17 Jan. 42	31 Oct. 43
11	Anton	XAD	5 Feb. 42	31 May 44
12	Rio Hato	Airbase	1 Jan. 43	16 Feb. 48
13	Chame	XAD	16 Apr. 41	19 Sept. 47
14	Chame Point	Bombing Range	17 Jan. 42	31 Dec. 43
15	Bona Island	AWS	Not occupied	15 May 44
16	Chorrera	XAD	3 Apr. 41	30 Sept. 46
17	Taboga Island	AWS &HD	6 May 41	14 Jan. 48
18	Taboguilla Island	HD	6 May 41	14 Jan. 48
19	La Joya	XAD	7 Jan. 42	31 July 47
20	Pinas Bay (Jaque Point)	AWS	15 Apr. 41	12 Jan. 48
21	Jaque	XAD	12 Apr. 41	12 Jan. 48
22	Pinogana	AWS	11 Aug. 41	15 Oct. 47
23	Obaldia	AWS	8 July 41	13 Sept. 43
24	San Blas	AWS	8 Dec. 41	12 Jan. 48
25	Mandinga	XAD	20 Jan. 42	19 Sept. 47
26	Casa Larga	XAD	15 Jan. 42	30 Sept. 46
27	Almirante	AWS	25 Apr. 41	30 Apr. 46
28	Chepo	AWS	13 Apr. 42	15 Nov. 43

Site No.	Designation	Purpose	Original Occupation	Final Abandonment
29	Cocle del Norte	AWS	13 Mar. 42	26 Sept. 47
30	Divisa	AWS	24 June 42	26 Sept. 47
31	Pacora	AWS	25 Mar. 42	31 Dec. 43
32	Rey Island	AWS &XAD	1 Apr. 42	10 Jan. 48
33	Guias River	AWS	18 Mar. 42	1 Sept. 46
34	Taboga Island	Navy MTB Base	19 May 42	21 Mar. 46
35	Portogandi	AWS	19 Feb. 42	31 Dec. 43
36	Pacora-Victoria	AWS	29 May 42	14 Jan. 48
37	Cativa	S/L #174	15 Feb. 42	30 Sept. 46
38	Rio Salina	S/L #135	15 June 41	31 July 44
39	Rio Arriero	S/L #145	25 Apr. 41	30 Sept. 46
40	Quebrado Chunga	S/L #127	1 May 41	31 July 44
41	Rio Arriero	S/L #137	27 May 41	30 Sept. 46
42	Limon Road	S/L #154	20 May 41	31 July 44
43	Rio Harina	S/L #126	30 Apr. 42	30 Sept. 46
44	Nuevo Chagres	S/L #155	20 May 42	30 Sept. 46
45	Southwest Lagarto	S/L #165	15 Jan. 42	31 July 44
46	Loma Rancho	S/L #177	10 Apr. 42	30 Sept. 46
47	Cerro Ullama	S/L #167	15 Feb. 42	31 July 44
48	Yerba Verde	S/L #157	15 Aug. 41	30 Sept. 46
49	Escobal	S/L #169	24 Oct. 41	31 July 44
50	Quebrada Larga	S/L #156	15 July 41	30 Sept. 46
51	Rio Jobo	S/L #166	15 July 41	30 Sept. 46
52	Cerro Santa Rita	S/L #164	25 Mar. 42	31 July 44
53	Puerto Real	S/L #184	15 Oct. 41	30 Sept. 46
54	Rio Viejo	S/L #194	22 July 41	31 July 44
55	Rio Paulina-Rio Medio	S/L #125	7 Mar. 42	31 July 44
56	Taboga Island	S/L #269	19 Aug. 40	14 Jan. 48
57	Melones Island	S/L #297	24 Apr. 41	1 Sept. 46
58	Vique Point	S/L #267	2 May 42	30 Sept. 46
59	Rio Chilibre-Quebrada Ancha	S/L #234	28 Mar. 42	30 Sept. 46
60	New Arraijan	S/L #263	11 Apr. 42	30 Sept. 46
61	La Tinajita	S/L #236	20 May 42	30 Sept. 46
62	Santa Rita	S/L #246	15 Oct. 41	31 July 44
63	Rancho Vique	S/L #235	24 Mar. 42	30 Sept. 46
64	Cerro Penoncito	S/L #224	1 Apr. 42	30 Sept. 46
65	Parque Lefevre	S/L #268	29 Apr. 41	30 Sept. 46
66	Paja	S/L #243	1 Dec. 40	30 Sept. 46
67	Taboguilla Island	S/L #269	Not occupied	14 Jan. 48
68	Rio Aguacate	S/L #255	19 Apr. 41	31 July 44
69	Rio Abajo	S/L #258	24 May 41	31 July 44

Site No.	Designation	Purpose	Original Occupation	Final Abandonment
70	Pueblo Nuevo	S/L #238	25 May 41	31 July 44
71	Nuevo San Francisco	S/L #248	Not occupied	31 Dec. 43
72	Vaquita Point	S/L #275	15 Apr. 42	30 Sept. 46
73	Puerto Padre	S/L #245	31 Mar. 42	30 Sept. 46
74	San Jose - (Rio Bernandina)	S/L #265	12 Jan. 42	31 July 44
75	NE Puerto Padre	S/L #273	12 Feb. 42	30 Sept. 46
76	Paja	S/L #253	4 May 42	30 Sept. 46
77	Rio Chilibre - (Casa Larga Rd.)	S/L #264	1 Apr. 42	30 Sept. 46
78	Quebrada Federico	S/L #254	Not occupied	31 Jan. 44
79	Laguna	S/L #256	13 May 42	30 Sept. 46
80	Cerro Viento	S/L #276	23 May 42	30 Sept. 46
81	San Anton	S/L #266	8 Jan. 42	10 Sept. 44
82	Cerro Ventana	S/L #226	15 July 42	31 July 44
83	Rio Agua Sucia	S/L #176	29 July 42	31 July 44
84	Anachacuna	AWS	19 June 42	31 Apr. 46
85	Taboga Island	Navy De-gassing Range	14 Oct. 42	21 Mar. 46
86	Juan Diaz, No. 1	AWS	16 Aug. 42	1 Sept. 46
87	San Jose	AWS	6 Apr. 42	31 Oct. 43
88	El Real	E.L.F.	1 Sept. 41	30 June 46
89	Gatuncillo Bridge	Const. Camp	8 Aug. 42	31 May 44
90	Juan Diaz, No. 2	AWS	23 Sept. 42	1 Sept. 46
91	Urava Island	S/L	Not occupied	1 Sept. 46
92	Chepillo Island	O.P.	10 Oct. 42	15 Oct. 45
93	Santiago	AWS	16 Nov. 42	31 Aug. 44
94	Aligandi	AWS	16 Oct. 42	15 Oct. 47
95	Dolega	AWS	25 Nov. 42	26 Sept. 47
96	Isla Grande	AWS	7 Oct. 42	12 Jan. 48
97	Valiente Point	AWS	15 Dec. 42	26 Sept. 47
98	Rio Agua Sucia	S/L #240	1 Dec. 42	31 July 44
99	Santa Rosa	S/L #252	Not occupied	31 Dec. 43
100	Lagarterito Inlet	S/L #110	11 Dec. 42	31 July 44
101	Rio Duque	S/L #120	11 Dec. 42	1 Sept. 46
102	Rio Pescado	S/L #210	16 Apr. 43	31 July 44
103	Pito	XAD	15 June 42	19 Sept. 47
104	Aguadulce	Dock & Pipeline	1 Jan. 43	19 Sept. 47
105	Redios Point	Navy Sta.	2 Apr. 43	12 June 43
106	Boquete	Ground Observer Station	27 June 43	31 Dec. 43

Site No.	Designation	Purpose	Original Occupation	Final Abandonment
107	Chorrera	Inf. Camp	18 May 43	19 Sept. 47
108	Pacora	Inf. Camp	18 May 43	31 July 47
109	Chorrera	Gunnery Range	Not occupied	31 Dec. 43
110	Santa Maria	AWS	15 Sept. 43	26 Sept. 47
111	Tole Junction	Maint. Camp	15 Apr. 43	30 Oct. 47
112	Vacamonte Point	O.P. 20	15 Jan. 44	15 Oct. 45
113	La Playa	O.P. 21	15 Jan. 44	30 Apr. 45
114	Puerto de la Zona	O.P. 23	15 Jan. 44	15 Oct. 45
115	Prieta Point	O.P. 24	15 Jan. 44	31 May 44
116	San Carlos	O.P. 25	15 Jan. 44	30 Apr. 44
117	La Capitana	O.P. 101	15 Jan. 44	30 Apr. 44
118	Boca del Pacora	O.P. 104	15 Jan. 44	30 Apr. 45
119	Rio Pina	O.P. 219	15 Jan. 44	30 Apr. 45
120	Camp Salinas	O.P. 220	15 Jan. 44	30 Apr. 44
121	Nuevo Chagres	O.P. 221	15 Jan. 44	30 Apr. 45
122	Cano Saddle	O.P. 223	15 Jan. 44	15 Oct. 45
123	Maria Chiquita	O.P. 224	15 Jan. 44	31 Aug. 45
124	South Cerro Viento	S/L	28 Mar. 44	30 Sept. 46
125	San Jose Island	CWS	6 Mar. 44	28 Jan. 48
126	New Cape Mala	AWS	16 Oct. 44	12 Jan. 48
127	Las Margaritas	D.F. Sta.	18 Jan. 44	10 Jan. 48
128	Pedregal	Dock & Pipeline	11 Dec. 41	30 Oct. 47
129	Chambers-Nuevo Chagres	D.F. Sta.	9 Mar. 44	1 Nov. 44
130	Rio Jamaca	AWS	Not occupied	30 June 46
131	La Campaña	Inf. Camp	6 Aug. 42	30 June 45
132	Prieta Point	Mach. Gun Range	6 Jan. 45	31 July 46
133	San Carlos	Gunnery	Not occupied	11 Feb. 46
134	Old Panama	O.P. 108	8 Dec. 41	15 Oct. 45

Source: General Crittenberger's 1948 report, titled "Negotiations between the Republic of Panama and the United States of America for a Defense Site Agreement, 1946–1947," Record Group 319, Army General and Special Staffs, Plans and Operations Divisions, Decimal File, 1946–1948, 686., Case 1, National Archives, Washington, DC.

❧

Appendix E

1. *Rio Hato* (defense site #12)—in order of preference:
   (a) Long term rights (50–99 years).
   (b) 15 year rights with option of renewal for 15 years.

2. *Taboga Island* (defense sites #17 & #56)—short term (10 years) with
   option of renewal (#17 includes part of AWS station)

3. *San Jose Island*—in order of preference:
   (a) Purchase of entire island if reasonable sale price can be obtained.
   (b) 10 year rights with option of renewal at sites. Boundaries of sites desired
   to be delineated by War Department representative for negotiations.

4. *Taboguilla Island* (defense site #10)—short term rights (10 years) with
   option of renewal.

5. *Salud*—short term (10 years) training rights.

6. *San Carlos*—(old defense site #133)—short term (10 years) training rights.

7. *Rey Island* (defense site #32)—AWS station, DF station and service air
   strip—short term right (10 years) with option of renewal.

8. *Jaque* (defense sites #20 and #21)—AWS station and service air strip—
   short term (10 years) with option of renewal.

9. *Pocri* (defense site #7)—DF station, service air strip and aerial gunnery
   range—short term rights (10 years) with option of renewal.

10. *Cape Mala* (defense site #8 and #126)—AWS station—short term rights
    (10 years) with option of renewal.

11. *San Blas Point* (defense site #24)—AWS station—short term rights (10
    years) with option of renewal.

12. *Isla Grande* (defense site #96)—AWS station—short term rights (10
    years) with option of renewal.

13. *Victoria* (defense site #36)—DF station—short term rights (10 years) with
    option of renewal.

14. *Las Margaritas* (defense site #127)—DF station—short term rights (10
    years) with option of renewal.

15. *Panama National Airport*—the right of transit and technical stop of U.S. military aircraft; the right of emergency operation in the event U.S. considers the Canal is threatened; occupancy in the latter case subject to consultation between the two governments after emergency occupation is accomplished.

Source: General Crittenberger's 1948 report, titled "Negotiations Between the Republic of Panama and the United States of America for a Defense Site Agreement, 1946–1947," Record Group 319, Army General and Special Staffs, Plans and Operations Divisions, Decimal File, 1946–1948, 686., Case 1, National Archives, Washington, DC.

*See appendix D for additional site information.

§

Appendix F

Events of December 1947 as Portrayed by the Panamanian Press

December 6: President Jiménez announces that Panama has secured "important advantages in the agreement on defense sites" (*Panama American*, Dec. 6, p. 1); Panama's Foreign Ministry announces that "an agreement on the bases" has been reached (*Panama American*, Dec. 8, p. 1).

December 7: *The Panama American* announces that U.S. and Panamanian officials agree that American forces should occupy Rio Hato base for "at least" ten years (*Panama American*, Dec. 7, p. 1); U.S. State Department in Washington reaffirms Panamanian Foreign Ministry's announcement of December 6 by announcing that an agreement has been reached by the two countries regarding the bases (*Panama American*, Dec. 8, p. 1).

December 8: Foreign Minister Ricardo J. Alfaro returns to Panama from Washington amid rumors that he would resign and similar rumors warning of a "cabinet crisis" due to the base agreement (*Panama American*, Dec. 8, p. 1).

December 9: While the *Estrella de Panamá* announces that the American Congress may not have to approve the treaty (see p. 1), President Jiménez announces at a press conference that the treaty would be signed the following day, Dec. 10, 1947 (*Panama American*, Dec. 9, p. 1); Panamanian Foreign Minister Ricardo J. Alfaro resigns to protest the signing of the treaty (*Panama Star and Herald*, Dec. 10, p. 1).

December 10: The Filós-Hines Treaty is signed at 12:31 P.M. in the office of Panama's Foreign Minister (*Panama American*, Dec. 10, p. 1; *Panama Star and Herald*, Dec 10., p. 1; *Panama América*, Dec. 10, p. 1; and *Estrella de Panamá*, Dec. 10, p. 1); Alfaro's letter of resignation is reproduced in the *Star and Herald*, p. 8; President Jiménez's office issues Decree no. 239, requesting the National Assembly to convene Friday, Dec. 12; Florencio Arosemena Forte is appointed foreign minister, replacing Ricardo Alfaro (*Panama American*, Dec. 10, p. 1); students at the National Institute call for a "mournful strike" in opposition to the treaty; these same students decide to participate in a "student parade and demonstration" scheduled for Friday, Dec. 12 (ibid.); the Frente Patriótico de la Juventud writes a letter of support to Ricardo Alfaro, applauding his opposition to the "injustices" contained in the treaty (*Panamá América*, Dec. 10, p. 1.); the Federation of Panamanian

Students declares a "state of alert" for all "federated associations" in Panama (ibid.); La Asociación de Profesores de la República de Panamá calls an extraordinary session, to be held at the Instituto Nacional, to discuss their stance vis-à-vis the bases (ibid.); socialist members of the National Assembly "attack" the treaty during an evening session (*Panamá América*, Dec. 11, p. 1); three students, members of Frente Patriótico de la Juventud, are arrested in the capital, "possibly" at the request of Francisco Filós (ibid.); the Asociación Cívica Independiente expresses its official support for Ricardo Alfaro's resignation/opposition (ibid.).

December 11: Students in a Santiago school walk out in protest to the treaty (*Panamá América*, Dec. 11, p. 1); the State Department in Washington announces that the fourteen sites included in the Filós-Hines pact are part of the U.S.'s new "Master Plan" for hemispheric defense (*Panama Star and Herald*, Dec. 11, p. 1; Dec. 12, p. 1).

December 12: Panama's National Assembly convenes to begin considering the treaty for ratification (see all four newspapers for coverage); Panama City Mayor Mauricio Díaz outlaws student gatherings in the capital (see all four newspapers); Francisco Filós goes personally to the Universidad Nacional to arrest law student Secundino Torres; Panama's education minister, Max Arosemena, "bitterly opposes" this move (*Panamá América*, Dec. 12, p. 1; *Panama American*, Dec. 12, p. 1); students in Panama City protest the pact (ibid.); Ricardo Alfaro claims that the United States "forced" Panama into the treaty (*Panama American*, Dec. 12, p. 1); morning—Colonel Remón says "police and students are friends" (ibid.); afternoon—sixty persons are injured as student and social groups clash with National Police in Panama City; among these students is Sebastián Tapia, who becomes the symbol of anti-government/antiimperialist forces (*Panama American*, Dec. 13, p. 1); Arnulfo Arias's Authentic Revolutionary Party and the Socialist Party both "strongly protest" the government's suspension of civil rights; the parties also blame the government for the violence which occurred that afternoon (*Panama American*, Dec. 13, p. 1); National Assembly condemns Mayor Díaz's ban on public gatherings, and the *Panama American* reports that the mayor might be "charged by the Supreme Court with abuse of authority" (in English and Spanish, December 13, p. 1).

December 13: The Partido Nacional Revolucionario blames Filós for the violence of the 12th (*Panamá América*, Dec. 13, p. 1); PNR officials ask Jiménez to "intervene" to stop the violence—i.e., repudiate the treaty; the Panamanian Socialist Party publishes an official letter of protest in *Panamá América* ibid.); the Magisterio Panameño Unido, Asociación Nacional de Profesores, Federación Sindical de Trabajadores, Profesores de la Universidad, Vanguardia Coclesana, Joven Veraguas, Círculo de Santa Ana, and the Frente Patriótico de la Juventud attend a peaceful protest rally in Santa Ana Plaza, in the afternoon (ibid.; *Panama Star and Herald*, Dec. 14, p. 1); no police present—3,000 attend (*Panama American*, Dec. 14, pp. 1, 3); Colón high school students hold a protest in De Lesseps Park (*Panama Star and Herald*); students protest at Colegio Abel Bravo in Colón (ibid.); a decree from the mayor prevents a student protest in Aguadulce, but a formal protest is sent to the Asamblea

Nacional (ibid.); the Asociación Federada de Estudiantes Normalistas holds a "monstruoso" meeting in Santiago to protest the bases (*Panamá América*, Dec. 15, p. 1); the *Estrella de Panamá* declares that "the serene action taken by the police avoided grave consequences" (*Estrella de Panamá*, Dec. 13, p. 1); seemingly going back on his friendly declaration the day before, Remón blames "known agitators" and communists for the violence of the 12th (ibid.); lauds police violence (*Panama Star and Herald*, Dec. 13, p. 1).

December 15: Panama City schools declare a general strike in protest of the treaty (*Panama American*, Dec. 15, p. 1); morning—Mauricio Díaz resigns as mayor of Panama City (ibid.);afternoon—Díaz withdraws his resignation (*Panama American*, Dec. 16, p. 1); in reply to a telegram received from former Colón governor Victor Navas, Jiménez defends his government's position vis-à-vis the treaty in addition to the violence used to suppress the students (ibid.); opposition rally in the Parque de Colón (*Panamá América*, Dec. 15, p. 1); students at Colegio Abel Bravo (Colón) walk out in protest (ibid.); students and professors throughout Panama declare a walkout in protest of the treaty.

December 16: In the *Panama American*, Socialist Party Deputy José A. Brower denies Remón's charges that he received orders from Moscow to incite violence on the 12th (*Panama American*, Dec. 16, p. 1); the Panamanian Teachers' Union joins the students in their strike; the union, with a membership of 5,000, includes almost every teacher in the republic (*Panama American*, Dec. 16, p. 1); 10,000 university women march on the National Assembly (*Panama Star and Herald*, Dec. 16, p. 1); elementary teachers in Colón send a resolution to the Assembly in Panama City, asking them to reject the treaty by contending that "no imminent threat of war" exists (*Panamá América*, Dec. 16, p. 1).

December 17: Panamanian civic groups that opposed the treaty explain their reasons to the National Assembly (*Panama American*, Dec. 16, p. 1; *Panama Star and Herald*, Dec. 16, p. 1; *Panamá América,* Dec. 16, p.1); Panama's Popular Union Party officially opposes Filós-Hines agreement (*Panamá América*, Dec. 17, p. 1); student leaders extend their strike indefinitely, contingent on the outcome of the treaty debate (ibid.);Panamanian Minister of Education Max Arosemena resigns his post after failing to postpone the large protest by university women (ibid.); the Panamanian Federation of Students contends that there is no threat of war that would justify the continued American presence; they then demand that the Assembly reject the treaty (*Panama American*, Dec. 17, p. 1); the Liberal and National Agrarian Parties publish their official opposition to the treaty in *Panamá América* (see Dec. 17, p. 1); the general strike of Panamanian teachers and students "extends throughout the entire republic" (ibid.); the David Lion's Club expresses its official opposition to the treaty (ibid.); in a radio address to the Panamanian people, President Enrique Jiménez "most sincerely recommends" the ratification of the Filós-Hines Treaty (*Panama American*, December 18, p. 1; *Panama Star and Herald*, Dec. 18, p. 1).

December 18: Republic of Panama is declared off-limits to American servicemen stationed there, and they are confined to Canal Zone bases (*Panama*

American, Dec. 18, p. 1); the United States Navy completes its "loyalty check" of all personnel stationed in the Canal Zone (ibid.); former President Harmodio Arias and former Foreign Minister Ricardo J. Alfaro advise the National Assembly that "a threat of aggression exists in the world today," and encourage the assemblymen to ratify the treaty because "Communism faces Democracy" (ibid.); the Atalaya Youth Defense Society publishes its official condemnation of the National Guard's violent suppression of the popular will (*Panamá América*, Dec. 18, p. 2).

December 19: The legislative committee charged with considering the Filós-Hines Treaty enters into secret sessions (*Panamá América*, Dec. 19, p. 1).

December 20: The Panamanian Youth Congress denies that ousting North American soldiers will affect the nation's economy (*Panamá América*, Dec. 20, p. 1); 2,000 people in the northern Panamanian city of David march in protest against the treaty (ibid.); a large crowd protests the treaty in the city of Aguadulce (ibid., p. 5).

December 21: The committee studying the treaty calls for former Presidents Harmodio Arias, Arnulfo Arias, Ricardo J. Alfaro, and Ricardo Adolfo de la Guardia to testify in connection with the base treaty (*Panama American*, Dec. 21, p. 1).

December 22: A massive, day-long student demonstration occurs outside the National Assembly as assemblymen consider the treaty (*Panama American*, Dec. 22, p. 1); newly appointed foreign minister, Florencio Arosemena, resigns his post to protest ratification of the treaty (ibid.); at 9:50 P.M. the National Assembly rejects the Filós-Hines Treaty (*Panamá América*, Dec. 23, p. 1; *Panama Star and Herald*, Dec. 23, p. 1; *Panama American*, Dec. 23, p. 1).

Appendix G

ARRESTS IN PANAMA CITY AND COLÓN, 1946–1951
(RANDOM SAMPLE)
(A = PANAMA CITY, B = COLÓN)

Crime		1946	1947	1948	1949	1950	1951
resisting authority:							
	A:	25	87	70	50	44	51
	B:	58	63	28	35	37	14
disrespect for public officials:							
	A:	1225	1124	1030	725	903	862
	B:	425	281	265	171	191	214
defacing public property:							
	A:	19	251	15	32	289	171
	B:	0	49	0	0	0	0
carrying/using arms:							
	A:	16	50	63	55	16	33
	B:	37	26	37	27	28	10
illegal immigration:							
	A:	66	61	50	31	12	12
	B:	0	122	99	82	29	18
curfew violation:							
	A:	85	251	121	48	172	29
	B:	84	63	3	8	8	3
vagrancy:							
	A:	492	585	482	642	1096	967
	B:	324	139	134	282	330	388
illegal games:							
	A:	33	43	7	23	17	4
	B:	33	78	18	53	44	105
disrespect (general):							
	A:	1081	1164	735	562	536	471
	B:	395	272	225	303	298	306

slander:

A:	156	243	258	141	113	112
B:	10	16	19	23	17	17

fighting/scandal:

A:	1438	1135	866	706	1151	630
B:	851	1005	810	625	637	511

Source: República de Panamá, Contraloría General de la República, Dirección de Estadística y Censo, *Estadística Panameña*, 11(8–9) (August–September 1952):48–61.

Notes

Preface

1. On geographic determinism as a flawed historiographical methodology, see, for example, Celestino Andrés Araúz, Carlos Manuel Gasteazoro, and Armando Pinzón, *La historia de Panamá en sus textos*, vol. 1 (Panama City, 1980), 5–6.

As political scientist Bruce C. Porter noted recently, various factors have contributed to the formation and evolution of the modern state, including economic production, the international community, collective rational choice, geographic and cultural factors, and internal political dynamics. While exploring these factors collectively as a force in state formation, this book will focus specifically on the role of the police in the realm of domestic politics and governance. I do this not to propose some sort of reductionist explanation of government on the isthmus; rather, I take this approach to establish a framework within which to understand the function of the police—arguably a dominant function—in recent Panamanian society, and politics and, implicitly, diplomacy. See Bruce D. Porter, *War and the Rise of the State: The Military Founda-* tions of Modern Politics (New York, 1994), 8–9.

2. In his book *Panamanian Militarism: A Historical Interpretation*, Carlos Guevara Mann recently called several of these institutionalist scholars "military apologists." Name-calling aside, institutional analyses of Panama's military are many, varied, and frequently excellent. This literature includes Steve Ropp, *Panamanian Politics: From Guarded Nation to National Guard* (Stanford, 1982); Richard Millett, "The Political Process: Resistance to Change," in *Occasional Paper No. 13: Report on Panama: Findings of the Study Group on United States–Panamanian Relations* (Baltimore, 1987); George Priestly, *Military Government and Popular Participation in Panama: The Torrijos Regime, 1968–1975* (Boulder, 1986); and Renato Pereira, *Panamá: Fuerzas armadas y política* (Panama City, 1979). More recently a number of social scientists have expanded on the institutionalist motif, including Margaret Scranton, "Consolidation after Imposition: Panama's 1992 Referendum," *Journal of Interamerican Studies and World Affairs* 35 (fall 1993):65–102; William Furlong, "Panama: The Difficult

Transition towards Democracy," *Journal of Interamerican Studies and World Affairs* 35 (fall 1993):19–64; and Marco Gandásegui, "The Military Regimes of Panama," *Journal of Interamerican Studies and World Affairs* 35 (fall 1993):1–17. These three articles comprised part of an issue devoted entirely to post-invasion Panama, and each of the authors refers to Panama's "era of military regimes" as an event that began in October 1968 and ended in December 1989 (see especially the Gandásegui piece, 1993:1).

Presented in 1987 at Johns Hopkins University, at a gathering of academicians and politicians met to discuss Panama-U.S. relations, Millett's article laments the historiographical tendency to portray Panama's police as an ephemeral rather than integral component of Panamanian society. It then challenges scholars who study Panama to take care to incorporate Panama's police more fully into Isthmian society generally. This book is, to some extent, my response to Professor Millett's perceptive invitation.

3. Andrew Zimbalist and John Weeks, *Panama at the Crossroads: Economic Development and Political Change in the Twentieth Century* (Berkeley, 1991), 10.

4. George Priestly, "Panama: Obstacles to Democracy and Sovereignty," *Radical History Review* 48 (1990):89.

Introduction

1. In January of 1964, a tragic clash between Panamanian youth and

American soldiers stationed in the old Canal Zone resulted in the deaths of twenty-four Panamanians. This triggered a new round of heated negotiations between the two nations that culminated in the Torrijos-Carter pact, more than a decade later.

Some of the best works on Torrijos's accomplishments include Sharon Phillips Collazos's fine recent study, *Labor and Politics in Panama: The Torrijos Years* (Boulder, 1991); Humberto E. Ricord, "El código de 1972: Cambio radical en la legislación laboral Panameña," *Revista Jurídica Panameña* 2 (1974):140–54; and Torrijos's own compiled works, *Torrijos* (Argentina, 1986). See also Gilberto Boutin I., *Del régimen jurídico internacional de los acuerdos Torrijos-Carter de 1977* (Panama City, 1987).

2. Throughout this book I use the term *police* to refer both to the National Guard and Panama's Defense Forces. José Remón renamed the police the National Guard in 1952. Then in 1983 Manuel Noriega christened the guard the Panamanian Defense Forces (PDF), and it was the PDF that haplessly engaged United States troops during Operation Just Cause (Panamanians refer to this as "jus caos"—just chaos).

3. Ambler Moss, Dean of the University of Miami's Graduate School of International Studies and former U.S. Ambassador to Panama, described for me the many hours he passed with Torrijos at Coclecito. Moss, who negotiated much of the Torrijos-Carter Treaty, recalled the lively evenings spent swinging in a hammock opposite Torrijos, relaxing

and discussing various issues. Moss reported that during more formal meetings, the general would occasionally communicate with him by passing handwritten notes. Despite his provincial manner, however (or perhaps because of it), Ambassador Moss noted that Vargas Llosa and other distinguished writers and scholars took every opportunity to be with Torrijos and interact with him.

For a selection of Moss's own views on Panama and its canal, see Ambler H. Moss, Jr., "The Panama Treaties: How an Era Ended," *Latin American Research Review* 21 (1986):171–78. In this review essay, Moss evaluates a number of the best books regarding Torrijos and the canal. Author Shirley Christian referred to Moss's unique association with the Panamanian strongman in her Pulitzer Prize–winning account of the Nicaraguan revolution, *Revolution in the Family* (New York, 1986).

While Torrijos's supporters are many, many Panamanians also opposed his policies and disliked him intensely. Naturally many of Panama's elite despised the general and opposed him at every turn. However, many farmers lost land to his reforms, and they too intensely disliked Torrijos. For example several families currently residing in the community of Veranillo Viejo have kept the notices they received from the Torrijos government in the 1970s, notifying them that they would lose all or part of their rural land—notices they claim forced them to move to the city in search of work and sustenance.

4. See, for example, José de Jesús Martínez (more commonly known as "Chuchú"), *Mi General Torrijos* (Mexico City, 1988). This is a powerful, personal tribute to the general, by one of his closest friends and greatest admirers. Despite the warmth and accuracy of this fitting homage, however, it does little to place Torrijos's regime in any type of historical context, leaving the reader to ponder the causes, significance, and consequences of the Torrijos government. See also Graham Greene, *Getting to Know the General: The Story of an Involvement* (New York, 1984).

To get a sense of the depth and breadth of *Torrijismo* and what his association meant to other people, see the dozens of moving tributes published in his honor at the time of his death—including powerful pieces by Gabriel García Márquez and Mario Vargas Llosa. These eulogies comprise a striking commemorative publication, *Torrijos: Figura-tiempo-faena* (Panama City, 1981).

5. These volumes include, among others, R. M. Koster and Guillermo Sánchez, *In the Time of the Tyrants: Panama, 1968–1990* (New York, 1990); John Dinges, *Our Man in Panama: How General Noriega Used the United States and Made Millions in Drugs and Arms* (New York, 1990); and, perhaps most shortsightedly, Lawrence S. Eagleburger, *The Case against Panama's Noriega* (Washington, 1989).

While these books all shed additional light on the Noriega dictatorship (the *Noriegato*), they appeared within months of the invasion. While each lends valuable additional insight and many personal anecdotes, they lack incisive conclusions based on

extended archival research. Consequently each falls short of correctly
placing the Noriegato in context. In
each instance, Noriega and Torrijos—
and more generally Panama's recent
problems—appear falsely as historical
aberrations in a country seemingly
otherwise unacquainted with police-
dominated government.

6. For a distinction between
military regimes that "rule" and those
that "arbitrate," see Perlmutter, *The
Military and Politics in Modern
Times,* pp. 102–14.

7. Mario Esteban Carranza, *Fuerzas
armadas y estado de excepción en
América Latina* (Mexico City, 1978).
Carranza's work fails to fully consider
circumstances underlying these "states
of exception," but the second edition
of political scientist Morris Janowitz's
book *Military Institutions and Coercion in Developing Nations* (Chicago,
1977) does delineate them. Janowitz
contends that paramilitary organizations, particularly in developing nations, frequently fill the void created
there when government officials fail to
achieve administrative consensus
sufficient to govern the nation.

8. George Priestly, *Military Government and Popular Participation in
Panama: The Torrijos Regime, 1968–
1975* (Boulder, 1986), 2–5. Priestly's
more recent work, most notably his
1990 article in the *Radical History
Review,* goes well beyond the early
institutional and geographic deter-
minist scholarship, challenging
scholars like myself to explain Panama's military in its social, economic,
political, and historical contexts. See
prologue for further discussion of
these historiographical trends.

9. Samuel P. Huntington, *Political
Order in Changing Societies* (New
Haven, 1968), 194–97. See also
professor Huntington's pioneering
work, *The Soldier and the State: The
Theory of Politics and Civil-Military
Relations* (New York, 1964), particu-
larly pp. 80–94.

10. Amos Perlmutter and Valerie
Plave Bennett, *The Political Influence
of the Military: A Comparative
Reader* (New Haven, 1980), 199. See
also Frederick Watkins's discussion
of praetorianism in his *Encyclopedia
of the Social Sciences.*

For a more recent examination of
what happens when political order
breaks down, see Joel S. Migdal,
"Strong States, Weak States: Power
and Accommodation," in Samuel P.
Huntington and Myron Weiner, eds.,
Understanding Political Development
(Boston, 1987), 413–15. See also
Amos Perlmutter, *The Military and
Politics in Modern Times: On Profes-
sionals, Praetorians, and Revolution-
ary Soldiers* (New Haven, 1977);
Perlmutter, "The Praetorian State and
the Praetorian Army: Toward a
Taxonomy of Civil-Military Relations
in Developing Polities," *Comparative
Politics* 1 (1969):382–404; Carolyn
P. Boyd, *Praetorian Politics in Liberal
Spain* (Chapel Hill, 1979); Hermann
Oehling, *La función política del
ejército* (Madrid, 1967); Samuel E.
Finer, *The Man on Horseback: The
Role of the Military in Politics* 2d ed.
(Boulder, 1988); Alfred Stepan, *The
Military in Politics: Changing Pat-
terns in Brazil,* 2d ed. (Princeton,
1989); and Jorge Vigón Suarodíaz,
Milicia y política (Madrid, 1947).

11. Perlmutter, "Arafat's Police

State," *Foreign Affairs* (July/August 1994):9. On these competing agendas see Janowitz, *Military Institutions*.

12. For a discussion of formal power versus informal power, see Samuel Huntington, *The Soldier and the State*, 85–87. Throughout this book I use Huntington's definition of power. Drawing from Machiavelli and Aristotle, Professor Huntington defines the concept as "the capacity to control the behavior of other people" (ibid.).

A number of other classical treatises exist on the character and use of power, including Harold D. Lasswell's work, *Politics: Who Gets What, When, How?* (New York, 1936); Bertrand de Jouvenel, *On Power* (New York, 1949); and F. L. Neumann, "Approaches to the Study of Political Power," *Political Science Quarterly* (June 1950):161–80. Though dated, each of these analyses is central in the study of power.

For a constitutional delineation of political powers and privileges in post-independence Panama, as outlined in its February 13, 1904, constitution, see the International Bureau of the American Republics (José Ignacio Rodríguez, chief ed. and trans.), *American Constitutions: A Compilation of the Political Constitutions of the Independent Nations of the New World*, vol. 1 (Washington, DC, 1906), 392–422.

13. For a distinction between military regimes that "rule" and those that "arbitrate," see Perlmutter, *The Military and Politics in Modern Times*, 102–14.

14. Ibid., 103. See also Perl-

mutter's recent article, "Arafat's Police State."

15. Walter LaFeber, *The Panama Canal: The Crisis in Historical Perspective* (New York, 1978), 106–7. While I have relied on the first edition of this excellent book, the second edition deals similarly with the 1948 election. The most substantive distinction between the two editions is the latter's coverage of the post-Torrijos years. In both its editions, Professor LaFeber's book remains one of the classic treatments of the canal enclave—a required text for any student of either American diplomatic or Panamanian history.

16. John Major, *Prize Possession: The United States and the Panama Canal, 1903–1979* (Cambridge, 1993), 324.

17. This convention rerouted international commercial traffic from Albrook Air Force Base in the Canal Zone to Panama's new airport, Tocumen International. However, several groups that had opposed the Filós-Hines accord resented Washington's role in Panamanian commercial issues, and they remained suspicious of North American motives. In a series of letters to First Commander Remón in 1949, Panama City Mayor Alberto Navarro identified those groups who intended to protest the commercial agreement. See Navarro to Remón, in "Copias a comandancia, año 1949." This is a clothbound collection of documents held in Panama's National Archives.

18. Bruce D. Porter, *War and the Rise of the State: The Military Foundations of Modern Politics* (New York, 1994), 300.

19. Huntington, *The Soldier and the State*. For a more recent discussion of social fragmentation and its effects on civilian government, see Amos Perlmutter, "Arafat's Police State."

20. On liberalism in nineteenth-century Colombia, see for example David Bushnell, *The Making of Modern Colombia: A Nation in Spite of Itself* (Berkeley, 1993); Carlos Villalba Bustillo, *Los liberales en el poder: Del apogeo revolucionario a la decadencia clientelista* (Bogotá, 1982); Mario Laserna, *Bolívar, un euroamericano frente a la ilustración y otros ensayos de interpretación de la historia indo-iberoamericano* (Bogotá, 1986); and Francisco Romero Otero, *Las ideas liberales y la educación en Santander, 1819–1919: La cultura de la tolerancia y la de la intolerancia* (Bogotá, 1992). More generally, see Edward C. Banfield, ed., *Civility and Citizenship in Liberal Democratic Societies* (New York, 1992).

Regarding more recent liberal trends in Colombia, see Diana Gómez Duque, *Una guerra irregular entre dos ideologías: un enfoque liberal* (Bogotá, 1991); Helen Delper's classic treatise, *Red against Blue: The Liberal Party in Colombian Politics, 1863–1899* (University, AL, 1981); and the Partido Liberal Colombiano, *Encuentros y foros del liberalismo* (Bogotá, 1988).

21. Huntington, *The Soldier and the State*, 86.

22. See for example Jorge Conte-Porras, *Arnulfo Arias Madrid* (Panama City, 1980), 68–70; and Isidro A. Beluche Mora, *Acción Comunal: Surgimiento y estructuración del nacionalismo panameño* (Panama City, 1981), 12–15.

23. Jorge Conte-Porras, *La rebelión de las esfinges: Historia del movimiento estudiantil panameño* (Panama City, 1978), pp. 187–188.

24. Carranza, *Fuerzas armadas y estado de excepción*, 27.

25. Ibid.

Chapter 1

1. Morris Janowitz, *Military Institutions and Coercion in Developing Nations* (Chicago, 1977), Preface and Part I, "Paramilitary Forces in Developing Nations."

2. Many of the urban elite who signed the 1821 declaration had been members of Panama City's last two colonial *cabildos* (town councils). See Alfredo Figueroa Navarro, *Dominio y sociedad en el Panamá colombiano, 1821–1903*, 3d ed. (Panama City, 1982), 131–65.

3. Celestino Andrés Araúz, *La independencia de Panamá en 1821* (Panama City, 1980), 96–99; and Michael L. Conniff, *Panama and the United States: The Forced Alliance* (Athens, GA, 1992), 9–11.

4. See David Bushnell's prologue in Charles Bergquist, *Coffee and Conflict in Colombia, 1886–1910* (Durham, NC, 1986), xvii–xviii. Bushnell calls Colombia's centralist-federalist struggle "the most enduring and, at least in outward appearances, most clear-cut of the conventional Liberal versus Conservative party struggles that dominated the [nineteenth-century] political landscape"; Ernesto J. Castillero R., *Raices de la independencia de Panamá* (Panama City, 1978), 19–32; and John Lynch,

*The Spanish American Revolutions,
1808–1826,* 2d ed. (New York,
1986), 247–51.

5. On electoral fraud in nineteenth
century Colombia, see Helen Delper,
*Red against Blue: The Liberal Party in
Colombian Politics, 1863–1899* (University, AL, 1981), 116–17, 188–89.

6. Humberto E. Ricord, *Panamá
en la Guerra de los Mil Días* (Panama
City, 1989), 19–42.

7. See Castillero R., *Raices de la
independencia,* for a summary of
these independence campaigns.

8. Andrew Zimbalist and John
Weeks, *Panama at the Crossroads:
Economic Development and Political
Change in the Twentieth Century*
(Berkeley, 1991). Zimbalist and
Weeks argue that "after formal
independence the direct hold of the
ruling commercial class over the
laboring population grew, if anything, weaker" (p. 10). They base this
argument on the fact that the elite
"only effectively controlled the
masses through the police power of
the state itself" (p. 9). Yet throughout
the nineteenth century, elites in
Panama City derived their standing
from their ability to rely on foreign
troops to intervene when needed.
Consequently independence does not
represent a deterioration of elite
hegemony; rather, it accentuates the
continuation of a pattern of political
domination that existed throughout
the nineteenth century—and before.
After 1903 the United States provided Panama's small, politically
dominant urban merchant elite a
greater sense of "legitimacy" than
Colombia had ever offered.

9. On royal officials in Panama,
see Mark A. Burkholder and Dewitt
S. Chandler, *From Impotence to
Authority: The Spanish American
Crown and the American Audiencias,
1687–1808* Columbia, MO, 1977),
appendixes 5, 7, and 9. Burkholder
and Chandler establish that Panama's
colonial *audiencias* (royal courts of
justice) were staffed primarily by
peninsulares (persons born in Spain)
and that no native-born Panamanians
served as justices. For a more general
discussion of late colonial government in Spanish America, see E. Bradford Burns, *The Poverty of Progress:
Latin America in the Nineteenth
Century* (Berkeley, 1980), 18–34.

10. Alfredo Castillero Calvo, "El
movimiento de 1830," *Tareas* 5
(August–December 1961):14–17.

11. In the 1850s Blacks living in
the *extramuro* constituted 80 percent
of the population of Panama City.
See Tomás Sosa, "Breve reseña de la
evolución demográfica de la ciudad
de Panamá," *Anuario de Estudios
Centroamericanos* 7 (1981):117–26.

12. Ibid, 40–43; Simón Bolívar,
"Discurso introductorio a la constitu-
ción de Bolívia (1826)," in José Luis
Romero and Luis Alberto Romero,
comps., *Pensamiento conservador,
1815–1898* (Caracas, 1978), 3–16;
and David Bushnell, *The Santander
Regime in Gran Colombia* (Westport,
CT, 1970), 332–37. See also Herbert
S. Klein, *Bolivia: The Evolution of a
Multi-Ethnic Society* (New York,
1982), 105–7. Klein notes that Sucre
"even tried to undertake a serious
reform in the relationships between
the Indian masses and the Spanish-
speaking state, in favor of the former."

13. Recalling the Espinar-led

movement at midcentury, conservative Governor José de Obaldía called Espinar's movement a "revolución de castas"—a caste war. In his rebuttal to Obaldía's charges, first published in 1937, Espinar argued that the governor "must have recently undergone a profound organic alteration of the brain," and argued that Obaldía was something less than a man. See José Domingo Espinar, "Resumen histórico que hace el general José Domingo Espinar . . . ," *Boletín de la Academia Panameña de la Historia* 14 (July 1937):265. For further information on Espinar's organization of Panama's urban masses in 1830, see Jorge Conte-Porras and Enoch Castillero Calvo, *Santa Ana* (Panama City, 1984), 21–23.

14. On forced labor systems as a means of controlling the masses, see Hector Pérez Brignoli, *A Brief History of Central America* (Berkeley, 1989), 98–100; and Zimbalist and Weeks, *Panama at the Crossroads*, 1–9.

15. Figueroa Navarro, *Dominio y sociedad*, 84–96, 145; and Castillero R., *Raíces de la independencia*, 51–89.

16. Espinar, "Resúmen histórico," 266–67; and Figueroa Navarro, *Dominio y sociedad*, 99.

17. In 1853 officials in Bogotá approved legislation that gave the vote to all married adult males. While many states in the Colombian federal system soon reversed this law, Panama retained it, and all adult Panamanian males over the age of twenty-one continued to enjoy the right to vote until Núñez's Regeneration passed restrictive legislation in 1888 to disenfranchise Black residents of the northern coastal region. See Eric A. Nordlinger, "Political Development:

Times Sequences and Rates of Change," *World Politics* 20 (April 1968):494–520. Nordlinger argues that Colombian liberals erred in introducing universal suffrage so rapidly, and he blames this error for much of Colombia's political upheaval during the federalist experiment. See also Delper, *Red against Blue*, 192, n.4.

18. Some scholars in Panama take issue with the concept of what political scientist Steve Ropp refers to as "geographic determinism"—the idea that Panama's location and geography have determined its development as a republic. See for example Celestino Andrés Araúz, Carlos Manuel Gasteazoro, and Armando Muñóz Pinzón, *La historia de Panamá en sus textos: 1501–1903*, vol. 1 (Panama City, 1980), 5–6; and Steve Ropp, *Panamanian Politics: From Guarded Nation to National Guard* (Berkeley, 1982), 11, n.2.

19. Dexter Perkins, *A History of the Monroe Doctrine* (Boston, 1955), 29–32; Lester D. Langley, *America in the Americas: The United States in the Western Hemisphere* (Athens, GA, 1989), 40–48; and Samuel Flagg Bemis, *Latin American Policy of the United States* (New York, 1943), 103–12.

20. Colombia's name changed five times during the nineteenth century. Gran Colombia dissolved in 1830, when Venezuela and Ecuador went their own ways. Thereafter, Colombia's names included the *Republic of New Granada*, the *Granadine Federation*, the *United States of Colombia*, and the *Republic of Colombia*.

21. Renato Pereira, *Panamá: Fuerzas armadas y política* (Panama City, 1979), 3–6. See Francis B.

Loomis, Acting Secretary of State, "Use by the United States of Military Force in the Internal Affairs of Colombia, etc.," 58th Cong., 2nd Sess., Doc #143, 1904.

22. Justo Arosemena, *El estado federal de Panamá* (Panama City, 1974), 7–15, 31–76; Argelia Tello Burgos, *Escritos de Justo Arosemena* (Panama City, 1985); Octavio Méndez Pereira, *Justo Arosemena* (Panama City, 1919); Figueroa Navarro, *Dominio y sociedad*, 320–29; and Castillero R., *Raices de la independencia*, 145–51.

23. Tello Burgos, *Escritos de Justo Arosemena*, 262–63. This passage contains excerpts from two articles Arosemena published in the Colombian newspaper *El Neogranadino* July 15 and July 19, 1856.

24. On forced labor systems, see Pérez Brignoli, *A Brief History of Central America*, 98–100; and Zimbalist and Weeks, *Panama at the Crossroads*, 1–9.

25. Omar Jaén Suárez, *La población del Istmo de Panamá del siglo xvi al siglo xx* (Panama City, 1978), 534–36; and Ropp, *Panamanian Politics*, 7. Ropp states that "by the late nineteenth century, the economic base of the urban upper class consisted of: continued control of urban real estate, control of second-level positions in the Colombian bureaucracy, an administrative role in both the Panama Railroad Company and the French Canal Company, and subsidiary positions in commerce supplying goods to workers in the transit zone."

26. Figueroa Navarro, *Dominio y sociedad*, 259–62, 267–300.

27. On the origins of Panama's "tertiary economy," see Alfredo Castillero Calvo, *Economía terciaria y sociedad: Panamá siglos xvi y xvii* (Panama City, 1980). See also Christopher Ward's recent work, *Imperial Panama: Commerce and Conflict in Isthmian America, 1550–1800* (Albuquerque, NM, 1993), especially chapters 5 and 6.

28. Jaén Suárez, *La población del Istmo de Panamá*, 22.

29. Zimbalist and Weeks argue (*Panama at the Crossroads*, 8–9) that Panama's elite were in a more precarious situation than that of their Mesoamerican counterparts, because in Panama the elite's "resistance to reform and its fear of the potential power of the masses derived from the fact that the elite only effectively controlled the masses through the police power of the state itself."

30. Mercedes Chen Daley, "The Watermelon Riot: Cultural Encounters in Panama City, April 15, 1856," *Hispanic American Historical Review* 70 (1990):85–108.

31. Speaking at the Panama-Pacific Historical Congress in California in July of 1915, Theodore Roosevelt remarked that fifty-three "revolutions" had occurred in Panama during the period from 1853 to 1903. See H. Morse Stephens and Herbert E. Bolton, eds., *The Pacific in Perspective: Papers and Addresses Presented at the Panama-Pacific Historical Congress Held at San Francisco, Berkeley, and Palo Alto, California, July 19–23, 1915* (New York, 1917), 144.

In response to these numerous uprisings, the United States landed troops in Panama a dozen times during the last half of the nineteenth century. See Loomis, "Use by the United States of Military Force," 1904; Pereira, *Panamá*; and Conniff, *Panama and the United States*, 7–14.

32. Conte-Porras and Castillero Calvo, *Santa Ana*, 24–34; and Buenaventura Correoso, "Sucesos de Panamá (1886)," *Revista Lotería* 340–41 (July–August 1894):93–133. The position of president in the Federal State of Panama paralleled that of governor elsewhere in Latin America. In both instances an executive was ultimately responsible to a distant central government.

33. Aparicio, "Panama: Society and Politics, 1885–1895," master's thesis, University of Miami, 1991, 124–61; Delper, *Red against Blue*, 192, n. 4; and Zimbalist and Weeks, *Panama at the Crossroads*, 2–3.

34. For a discussion of the North American role in the 1885 crisis, see Daniel H. Wicks, "Dress Rehearsal: United States Intervention on the Isthmus of Panama, 1885," *Pacific Historical Review* 49 (1980):581–605.

35. For an excellent overview of these technological changes and their effects on Panama, see Jáen Suárez, *La población del Istmo de Panamá*, 307–33.

Chapter 2

1. On the genesis of Panama's service-sector-based economy, see Alfredo Castillero Calvo, *Economía terciaria y sociedad: Panamá siglos xvi y xvii* (Panama City, 1980).

2. Talcott Parsons, *The Social System* (London, 1964), 5. In his discussion of the formation and development of social systems, Parsons posits that one of the defining characteristics of any society is the constant drive by its members to optimize their economic, social, and political circumstances—an ambition Parsons labels the "optimization of gratification." Borrowing from the writings of Thomas Hobbes, Parsons states that "if men are free to pursue their own self-interest, the paths of rationality will not always lie in the direction of cooperation and exchange." See Edward C. Devereux, "Parson's Sociological Theory," in Max Black, ed., *The Social Theories of Talcot Parsons: A Critical Examination*, (Englewood Cliffs, NJ, 1961), 11. This accurately describes Panama immediately following independence (1903), when members of various social groups maneuvered themselves to capitalize on Panama's newfound independence and the anticipated windfall to be generated by the unfolding canal enclave. Even more than foreign intervention, this discord within Panamanian society shaped the emerging state and established a precedent for the viability of police brutality on the isthmus. For a definition of *state*, see Max Weber, "Politics as a Vocation," in *From Max Weber: Essays in Sociology*, ed. and trans. H. H. Gerth and C. Wright Mills (New York, 1946), 78.

3. On components of Panama's evolving middle class at the turn of the century, see Georgina Jiménez de López, "La clase media en Panamá," in Marco Gandásegui, ed., *Las clases*

sociales en Panamá: Grupos human-os, clases medias, elites y oligarquía (Panama City, 1993), 23–39.

4. Juan Antonio Susto, "De la Guerra de los Mil Días: El puente de Calidonia," *Revista Lotería* 44 (July 1959):34–50; and Humberto E. Ricord, *Panamá en la Guerra de los Mil Días* (Panama City, 1986), 93–111.

5. See Devereux, "Parson's Socio-logical Theory".

6. This social fragmentation is reminiscent of Samuel Huntington's praetorian state. According to Huntington, social classes that are badly fragmented are largely incapable of unified action. In turn-of-the-century Panama, distrust of foreigners on the one hand and a desire to capitalize on the potential of the isthmus as an emporium of world commerce on the other represented the only cohesive elements that bound diverse elements of the new state together. As the new nation took shape from 1903 to 1931, however, nationalist antipathy failed to translate into a cohesive front that could effectively challenge the status quo. Instead the pursuit of their own distinct, often conflicting agendas frequently placed activist segments of the population in direct opposition to one another, rather than providing an adhesive to bind them together in a unified front.

7. The Church of Jesus Christ of Latter-Day Saints (LDS) maintains microfilm copies of Catholic Church parish records from throughout Panama during the period in question. My analysis of these documents confirms that, with the exception of Panama City's wealthiest neighbor-hoods and the internal provinces of

Chitré and Las Tablas (where a rural elite managed large land and cattle estates), illegitimacy rates soared during the Thousand Days' War and the first years of the new republic. See for example the registros parroquiales from David (films 760741–760747), Aguadulce (films 1809803–1809804), Santa Ana (films 1091673–1091675), Las Tablas (film 1089178), and Chitré (films 1089485–1089846).

Throughout this project, I have used illegitimacy as one of several methods of quantifying and gauging societal stress, underscoring the effects of specific events (war, inde-pendence, canal construction, depres-sion, etc.) on Panama's general populace. Other analytical methods used in this study include region-by-region comparisons of gross and net reproduction ratios, life expectancy, migratory patterns, and dependency sectors—those portions of society aged fourteen and under and sixty-five and over.

8. For specific data regarding Panama's elite San Felipe neighbor-hood during this period, see particu-larly volume 18 of La Merced's registros parroquiales (film 1094128, LDS). For comment on illegitimacy as a measure of resource deprivation, see William Durham's discussion in his *Scarcity and Survival in Central America: Ecological Origins of the Soccer War* (Stanford, 1979), 9–12.

9. For a discussion of the effects these reforms had on Panama, see Nicolás Sánchez-Albornoz, *The Population of Latin America: A History* (Berkeley, 1974), 79–81.

10. For the national period, crime rates further corroborate conclusions

regarding comparative standards of living. For this earlier period, however, I base my conclusions on illegitimacy, gross and net reproduction ratios, life expectancy, and dependency ratios.

11. Jorge Conte-Porras, "Victoriano Lorenzo y la Guerra de los Mil Días como antesala de la independencia," *Boletín de la Academia de la Historia* 4 (July–September 1975):49. See also Ricord, *Panamá en la Guerra de los Mil Días*, 150–53; and Eduardo Lemaitre Román, *Panamá y su separación de Colombia* 2d ed. (Bogotá, 1972), 432–37.

For further information on the Guaymí, see Phillipe I. Bourgois, *Ethnicity at Work: Divided Labor on a Central American Banana Plantation* (Baltimore, 1989), 111–59.

12. Ricord, *Panamá en la Guerra de los Mil Días*, 245–49.

13. Bourgois, *Ethnicity at Work*, 111. The only tribes in Panama that approach the Guaymí in remoteness and poverty are the Bogotá and the Chocó. For additional comment on the Guaymí, see John R. Bort and Mary W. Helms, eds., "Panama in Transition: Local Reactions to Development Policies," *University of Missouri Monographs in Anthropology* no. 6 (Columbia, MO, 1983), 3–14.

14. See for example Conte-Porras, "Victoriano Lorenzo y la Guerra de los Mil Días," 54–55; and Ricord, *Panamá en la Guerra de los Mil Días*, 283. For a helpful, concise synopsis of the events surrounding the volatile demise of the nationalist campaign, see Michael L. Conniff, *Panama and the United States: The Forced Alliance* (Athens, GA, 1992), 60–61.

15. See Ricord, *Panamá en la Guerra de los Mil Días*, 245–49.

16. On the evolution of political coalitions in Panama following independence, see Steve Ropp, *Panamanian Politics: From Guarded Nation to National Guard* (Stanford, 1982), 19–25.

17. Walter LaFeber, *The American Age: United States Foreign Policy at Home and Abroad since 1750* (New York, 1989), 225–30. In 1850 the United States and Great Britain had signed the Clayton-Bulwer Treaty, wherein both nations agreed not to construct a canal across the Central American isthmus without first consulting with the other signee.

18. G. A. Mellander, *The United States in Panamanian Politics: The Intriguing Formative Years* Danville, IL, 1967), 10–12, 25–27; and Ropp, *Panamanian Politics*, 15.

19. Mellander, *The United States in Panamanian Politics*, 10–12, 25–27. The revolutionary junta consisted of José Augustín Arango (attorney for the railroad), Frederico Boyd, and Tomás Arias. Noticeably absent from this list was Amador, whom Mellander contends was being groomed by Panama's wealthy to serve as the nation's first president; he suggests that Amador did not serve on the junta in order to avoid the appearance of *continuismo*.

20. Manuel Amador Guerrero, "Como se inició nuestra independencia," *Épocas* (October 25, 1947):9; and Oscar Teran, *Panamá: Historia crítica del atraco yanqui mal llamado en Colombia* la pérdida de Panamá y

en Panamá nuestra independencia de Colombia (Bogotá, 1976), 428–29.

21. On the debate regarding Bunau-Varilla's role in the treaty process, see John Major, "Who Wrote the Hay-Bunau-Varilla Convention?" *Diplomatic History* 8 (Spring 1984):115–23. Major recently expanded this discussion in chapter 2 of his monograph *Prize Possession: The United States and the Panama Canal, 1903–1979* (Cambridge, 1993).

22. For coverage of these elections, see the following articles in the *New York Times*: "Elections in Panama Must be O.K.'d by Taft," May 11, 1906, p. 1; "Panama Must Make Its Election Fair," June 12, 1908, p. 5; "Troops at Panama Election," June 29, 1908, p. 1; "Want Us to Intervene: Panama Parties Would Insure Fair Play at Coming Elections," May 4, 1912, p. 4; "Guns for Panama Election," May 11, 1912, p. 2; "Wants Us to Intervene, Would Insure Fair Election, Says Former President," May 28, 1916, p. 19; and "America Assumes Control in Panama," June 29, 1918, p. 3.

23. In 1903 United States troops cemented Panama's independence from Colombia by denying Colombian troops access to Panama City; in 1904 American troops surrounded the presidential palace to protect President Amador when he disbanded the nation's military; in 1918 Washington sent soldiers to occupy the province of Chiriquí, following a particularly violent election, and the troops remained there until 1921 to protect the extensive United Fruit Company holdings in the province;

in 1921 soldiers from the Canal Zone entered the capital and turned back a large gathering of people intent on ousting Belisario Porras from the presidency during a heated border dispute with Costa Rica; and in 1925 American marines occupied Panama City and Colón to enforce President Chiari's unpopular property tax. On these military excursions see for example Carlos Cuestas Gómez's enlightening work, *Soldados Americanos en Chiriquí* (Panama City, 1990).

24. Joel S. Migdal, "Strong States, Weak States: Power and Accommodation," in Samuel P. Huntington and Myron Weiner, eds., *Understanding Political Development* (Boston, 1987); and Samuel P. Huntington, *The Soldier and the State: The Theory of Politics and Civil-Military Relations* (New York, 1964).

25. Belisario Porras, "Reflexiones canaleras o la venta del istmo," *Tareas* 5 (August–December 1961):3–11. See also Celestino Andrés Araúz, *Belisario Porras y las relaciones de Panamá con Los Estados Unidos* (Panama City, 1988). Andrés Araúz's treatment is apologetic, but his brief discussion of Porras fairly portrays him as Panama's archetypical liberal.

26. Huntington, *The Soldier and the State*, 84.

27. RG 59, Lot 55 D 216, Records of the Office of American Republic Affairs, 1918–1947, Memoranda on Panama, Box 57, "American Assistance to Panama in the Maintenance of Order," 1924, National Archives, Washington, DC (NA).

28. See *La Estrella de Panamá*, November 28, 1904, p. 1; and Mel-

lander, *The United States in Panamanian Politics*, 66–67.

29. Ibid., 66–67.

30. For an excellent, detailed study of the police during the first years of the republic, see Mayor Dimas Arturo López V., comp., *Las fuerzas armadas de la República de Panamá, período 1903 a 1973* (Panama City, 1973), 15–16, 31–32. Officials of the Torrijos government produced this extensive work in 1973 to commemorate the 1968 revolution. Since that time, it has circulated internally within the nation's armed forces as a quick reference for officials of the Torrijos, Noriega, Endara Perez Balladares governments. Its usefulness increased greatly following the 1989 invasion of Panama, when North American officials temporarily confiscated all the records of Panama's armed forces. This excellent but now rare compilation helps fill the information void created by that event.

31. For a helpful and succinct discussion of "cohesive political action" as opposed to "social classes [that] are fragmented and incapable of unified political action," see Amos Perlmutter, "Arafat's Police State," *Foreign Affairs* (July/August 1994):8–9.

32. "Jiménez Accuses the Government," *Panama Star and Herald* (May 18, 1906), p. 5. As a New York City police officer, Jiménez was a veteran of Tammany politics. He nevertheless bristled at Amador's lack of scruples. See also Teniente Coronel Rubén Darío Paredes, "La policía en Panamá," n.p., n.d.; and "Breve historia de la policía nacional y la guardia nacional," n.d., n.p. Members of the Torrijos regime produced these two works to commemorate the founding of the National Guard.

33. RG 59, Belisario Porras to Frank B. Kellogg, December 14, 1927, RG 59, Department of State, File No. 819.00/1398, p. 3, NA. Porras refers to a letter wherein Roosevelt warned the Amador administration against using the police to "refuse a large number of people the opportunity of casting their votes."

34. "Dr. Porras Declared Alien: Liberal Leader Forfeits Citizenship," *The Panama Star and Herald* (November 20, 1905), p. 1.

35. George F. Roberts, *Investigación económica de la República de Panamá* (Panama City, 1932), 25–28, 324–30.

36. Alfredo Figueroa Navarro, *Dominio y sociedad en el Panamá Colombiano, 1821–1903* (Panama City, 1982), 174–75. The Chiari family of Panama City provides a prime example of this type of monopolistic investment. After immigrating from Italy, the Chiaris invested heavily in the sugar and beef industries, particularly slaughtering. Using their considerable political contacts, they built large fortunes around these two industries, arguably Panama's most prosperous at the time. For additional comment on the Chiari family sugar and beef empires, see also Marco Gandásegui's helpful article, "La concentración del poder económico en Panamá," in Marco Gandásegui, ed., *Las clases sociales en Panamá*, 156–58.

37. "The Party Within and the Party Without," *The Panama Star and Herald* (April 20, 1919), p. 1. This article, a commentary on the

state of Panama's political parties, argued that "two marked tendencies of public opinion in the national territory [exist], that which desires the predominance of the wealthy classes and that which has in mind the preeminence of the working classes and the poor."

38. Price to Secretary of State, April 25, 1919, RG 59, Department of State, Division of Latin American Affairs, File 819.00/819, NA. Price, American Minister to Panama, noted that the distinction between conservatives and liberals was blurring and that "parties are merely groups of men who united to a certain chieftain and remain with him as long as he proves successful and rewards their labors."

39. Taft to Amador, May 12, 1908, RG 59, Records of the Division of Latin American Affairs, 1904–1944, Box 15, Panama, "Relations with the U.S., 1904–1918," NA.

40. Note to Secretary of State, February 1, 1927, RG 59, Department of State, Division of Latin American Affairs, Legation of the United States of America, File 819.00/1334, NA. This note provides a clear summary of the role of electoral boards in Panamanian politics. As its author notes, "No citizen can vote if he cannot present his Cédula on the day of the elections."

41. James Howe, *The Kuna Gathering: Contemporary Village Politics in Panama* (Austin, TX, 1986), 17–20, 246. Howe contends that "of all the factors encouraging communal conflict among the island Kuna, the *role of outsiders* most deserves emphasis." Howe's argument applies

clearly to events of the mid-1920s, including decree no. 38. Beginning in 1923, the Porras administration positioned police on the Kuna Yala island of Narganá to suppress traditional Kuna practices. Using the police in this fashion, Porras successfully manipulated the Kuna vote. However, in 1925, the Kuna revolted, with the assistance of American activist Richard O. Marsh.

On the 1925 Kuna revolt see Oakah L. Jones, "Cuna Rebellion and Panamanian Power, 1925," *Proceedings of the Pacific Coast Council on Latin American Studies* 12 (1986):77–85; James Howe, "La lucha por la tierra en la costa de San Blas (Panamá), 1900–1930," *Mesoamérica* 29 (1995):67–76; and Francisco Herrera, "Richard O. Marsh y su intervención en la política panameña," *Revista Milenio* 1 (1995): 48–78.

42. Jorge Conte-Porras, *Requiem por la revolución* (San José, Costa Rica, 1990), 172–74. Noriega's annulment of the 1988 election underscores the fact that ballot box manipulation—*paquetazos* in all their forms—remains a viable path to public office in Panama today. I am personally acquainted with a number of law students from the National University who in 1988 helped smash ballot boxes and destroy their contents, once it became apparent that Noriega's hand-picked candidate would lose.

For a broader discussion of voting districts, voter *cédulas*, and so forth, see "Ley 28 de 1930 (de 5 de Noviembre) sobre las elecciones populares," and "Ley numero 83 (de 1° de Julio de 1941) sobre Cédula de Identidad

Personal," in República de Panamá, Ministerio de Gobierno y Justicia, *Leyes sobre elecciones populares,* Juan Antonio Susto, comp. (Panama City, 1941), 15–67. While this compilation is a later amendment of the 1904 laws, it nonetheless provides insight into Panama's electoral laws. For the text of the 1904 laws, see República de Panamá, "Título IV, Libro Primero del Código Administrativo."

43. Samuel P. Huntington has posited that when other methods of control fail, politicians resort to organizing civilian paramilitary forces to carry out their policies. When the Generation of ´31 split intos competing factions, successive presidents in the 1930s organized their own paramilitary units to eclipse opposition to their agendas, thereby reducing Panama to a fractured praetorian state. See Migdal, "Strong States, Weak States," 414.

On urban exchanges among praetorian guards in Panama, see Jorge Conte-Porras, *Arnulfo Arias Madrid* (Panama City, 1980), 187–89.

44. Weber, "Politics as a Vocation." Weber defines the term *state* as "a community that claims the monopoly of the legitimate use of force within a given territory." In Panama's case, urban landowners monopolized the use of force following independence, legitimizing it, at least in Washington's eyes, by invoking the security of the canal as justification for the forcible suppression of political opponents.

45. Blackburn to Taft, June 5, 1908, RG 185, General Correspondence of the Isthmian Canal Commission, 1905–1914, NA. To a certain

extent, La Coalición Republicana resembled in 1908 the tiny aristocracy that dominated Panama City politics during the transportation bonanzas of the 1850s and 1860s and then again in the mid-1880s, when Panama's modern "tertiary economy" took shape. For a glimpse into Panama's development as a tertiary economy, see Alfredo Castillero Calvo's useful discussion, *Economía terciaria y sociedad*).

46. Ernesto LaClau, "Towards a Theory of Populism," in *Politics and Ideology in Marxist Theory* (London, 1977), 170–72.

47. "American Assistance to Panama in the Maintenance of Order," 1924, Record Group 59, Lot 55 D 216, Records of the Office of American Republic Affairs, 1918–1947, Memoranda on Panama, Box 57, NA.

48. Ibid.

49. United States, Department of State, *Foreign Relations of the United States* 1 (Washington, DC, 1912): 1140.

50. On the 1912 election, see "Guns for Panama Election," *New York Times* (May 11, 1912), p. 2.

51. See RG 59, "American Assistance to Panama in the Maintenance of Order"; J. A. Ferguson, "Statement on Political Situation," RG 59, Division of Latin American Affairs 1904–1944: "Panama: Relations with the United States, 1904–1918," Box 15, NA; and Soler, *Panamá: Historia de una crisis* (Mexico City, 1989). See also Soler's work *El pensamiento político en los siglos xix y xx* (Panama City, 1988), 187–88. In his introduction to a section titled "El populismo

neoliberal," Soler characterizes Porras as the father of Panamanian neoliberalism, the champion of anti-imperialism in Panama.

For additional insight into Porrismo, see La Junta Política Nacional, "La opinión nacional y la candidatura presidencial de 1920 a 1924" (Panama City, 1920); and "The Liberal Program," *The Panama Star and Herald* (January 28, 1920), p. 1. In this latter declaration, Porristas proclaimed that they were determined "to encourage the immigration of sane elements into the country by means of special laws." This was particularly racist, given the liberals' later treatment of the Kuna.

52. On the 1916 disarming of Panama's police, see Isidro Beluche Mora, *Acción Comunal: Surgimiento y estructuración del nacionalismo panameño* (Panama City, 1981), 26–28.

53. Soler, *Panamá: historia de una crisis*, 38–56. Soler provides an excellent account of Panamanian politics from 1903 to 1925, including the appointment of North Americans to key administrative posts within the Panamanian government. See also Fernando Aparicio, "Significación, alcances y limitaciones de la experiencia porrista: 1912–1924," *Revista Humanidades* 3 (December 1993): 149–54.

54. For excellent coverage of the position of instructor general in Panama's National Police during this period, see López V., *Las fuerzas armadas*, 15–16, 31–32. As mentioned earlier, on May 13, 1916, the United States partially disarmed the Panama police by taking their rifles from them, following an incident

involving citizens of both countries. The police retained their revolvers, however, and continued to function as the only armed branch of Panama's government under Lamb.

55. Soler, *Panamá: Historia de una crisis*, 38–56.

56. For a useful discussion of this late nineteenth century upheaval, see Armando Muñóz Pinzón, "Conmociones sociales: Las sublevaciones campesinas de Pesé y Parita," in Rodrigo Espino and Raúl Martínez, eds., *Textos de la historia de Centroamerica y el caribe, vol. 2: Panamá* (Mexico City, 1988), 455–69. See also Alfredo Figueroa Navarro, "Tensiones sociales en el arrabal según la correspondencia consular francesa (1850–1880)," in Espino and Martínez, *Textos*, 469–78.

57. On Panama's large population of West Indian labor during the first years of the new republic, see for example Lancelot S. Lewis, *The West Indian in Panama: Black Labor in Panama, 1850–1914* (Washington, DC, 1980); and George Westerman, *Los immigrantes antillanos en Panamá* (Panama City, 1980). These two works complement nicely Michael Conniff's exhaustive work *Black Labor on a White Canal* (Pittsburgh, 1985).

On Blacks generally as a component of Isthmian society, see either the 1920 census or Roberts, *Investigación económica*, 41.

58. See for example República de Panamá, Contraloría General de la República, Dirección de Estadística y Censo, *Boletín de estadística* no. 68 (1928) (Panama City, 1929), 7–9 ("nacimientos ocurridas en la república, durante el año 1928"; and

"defunciones ocurridas en la república, durante el año 1928").

59. For a general discussion of workers in the canal zone, see Marco Gandásegui, *La lucha de clases y la Zona del Canal* (Panama City, 1975).

60. For statistics on these working-class communities, see for example República de Panamá, Contraloría General de la República, Dirección de Estadística y Censo, *Boletín de estadística* no. 68 (1928) (Panama City, 1929):7–9 ("nacimientos ocurridas en la república, durante el año 1928"; and "defunciones ocurridas en la república, durante el año 1928").

61. Just as Pedro Prestán's death had in 1885, this strike severely undermined the West Indians' ability to negotiate with White Panama. However, in 1925 the West Indian community once again achieved prominence in the nation's labor forum, when middle-class nationalists temporarily broke with their own prejudices and enlisted the support of Black workers to protest a new tax the government had levied against landlords.

62. These included the following groups: Sociedad del Gremio de Carpinteros, Sociedad Hijos de Trabajo, Sociedad Unión Obrero, Unión Obrera Panameña Latinoamericana de la Zona del Canal, Sociedad Progresista de Pescadores, Sociedad de Empleados de Comercio de Panamá, Unión Federal, Confiteros y Pasteleros, Sociedad de Beneficencia de Expendedores de Carne, Sociedad del Gremio de Sastres de Panamá, Gremio de Montadores de Construcción de Hierro y Acero, Sociedad de Socorros Mutuos, Unión Benéfica de Barberos, and the Sociedad de Tipógrafos de Panamá. Source: *El Obrero* 1 (August 6, 1921), p. 111, as cited in Gandásegui et al., *Las luchas obreras en Panamá (1850–1978)* (Panama City: Centro de Estudios Latinoamericanos, "Justo Arosemena" (CELA), 1980), p. 50.

63. See Perlmutter, "Arafat's Police State."

64. On Gompers and the PAFL, see Paul G. Buchanan, "The Impact of U.S. Labor," in Abraham F. Lowenthal, ed., *Exporting Democracy: The United States and Latin America* (Baltimore, 1991), 155–56.

65. Ibid.; and Price to Secretary of State.

66. Ropp contends that urban-rural migration following the war contributed to this economic downswing by reducing the size of the nation's urban workforce and markets. See Ropp, *From Guarded Nation to National Guard*, 21.

67. On the economic crisis that engulfed the Panamanian government in the mid and late twenties, see Roberts, *Investigación económica*, 25–28, 473–95; Pantaleón García, "La administración del Ing. Florencio H. Arosemena: Crisis y Acción Comunal," *Revista Milenio* 1 (1995):79–112; Aparicio, "Significación, alcances y limitaciones"; Patricia Pizzurno de Araúz, "Los millones de la posteridad (1904–1954)," *Revista Milenio* 1 (1995):113–32; and Jeptha B. Duncan and Octavio Méndez Pereira, "Una entrevista con el Dr. W. T. Burres," *Cuasimodo: Magazine Interamericano* 1 (June 1919):46–51.

68. See Ropp, *From Guarded Nation to National Guard*; Figueroa

Navarro, *Dominio y sociedad*; and Omar Jáen Suárez, *La población del Istmo de Panamá*. These rural middle-class activists owed their socioeconomic status to the economic growth and diversification that occurred in regions of the interior following the disastrous effects of the Bourbon Reforms in the eighteenth century. See the discussion of these families and their place in Isthmian society in chapter two, below.

69. Harmodio Arias and his younger brother, Arnulfo, are perhaps the most visible activist components of Panama's rural middle class. The Arias family owns lands in Panama's interior; Harmodio and Arnulfo went to Panama City following their education abroad, and as activists each came to play a vital role in the nation's political affairs.

70. United States minister to Panama in 1926, Roy T. Davis, incorrectly advised his superiors in Washington that *Acción Comunal* had formed in 1926 specifically to oppose the 1926 Kellogg-Alfaro Treaty. This error has influenced Panamanian historiography in the United States, such as Walter LaFeber, *The Panama Canal: The Crisis in Historical Perspective* (New York, 1978), 80, and has diminished the significant implications of popular organization prior to that treaty. However, Isidro Beluche, one of the founding members of the organization, has written a commemorative work about Acción Comunal that dispels the error and places this moderate nationalist movement in proper historical perspective—it was founded in 1923, not 1926. See Isidro A. Beluche

Mora, *Acción Comunal: Surgimiento y estructuración del nacionalismo panameño* (Panama City, 1981), 12–15.

71. Everardo E. Tomlinson H., "El contrato de arrendamiento de fincas urbanas," (thesis, University of Panama, 1959), 7, as cited in Alexander Cuevas, Everaldo Tomlinson, and Demetrio Porras, *Alcances e interpretaciones del problema inquilinario a través de la historia* (Panama City, 1975), 143.

72. George Priestly, *Military Government and Popular Participation in Panama: The Torrijos Regime, 1968–1975* (Boulder, CO, 1986), 13. Priestly asserts that United States marines "bayoneted to death many Panamanians at Santa [Ana] Plaza."

73. República de Panamá, Secretario del Estado, "Memoria que el Secretario de Estado hace en despacho de relaciones exteriores . . . "(Panama City, 1936), 11. This document is a summary of the 1926 treaty and reasons for its rejection. Translation by the author.

74. See Note to Secretary of State, February 1, 1927, RG 59, Department of State, Division of Latin American Affairs, Legation of the United States of America, File 819.00/1334, NA.

Chapter 3

1. Amos Perlmutter, "Arafat's Police State," *Foreign Affairs* (July/August 1994), 9. This chapter published previously in the *Hispanic American Historical Review* (November 1996).

2. Samuel P. Huntington, *The Soldier and the State: The Theory of Politics and Civil-Military Relations* (New York, 1964), 86.

3. On increased political participation spawned by worsening social fragmentation, see Samuel P. Huntington, *Political Order in Changing Societies* (New Haven, 1968), 194–97. See also Morris Janowitz, *Military Institutions and Coercion in the Developing Nations* (Chicago, 1977), particularly the preface and part 1, "Paramilitary Forces in the Developing Nations."

For additional information regarding Panama's political and economic elite in the late 1920s, see Ricaurte Soler, *Panamá: Nación y oligarquía, 1925–1975* (Panama City, 1976), 31–36.

4. President Arnulfo Arias took office October 1, 1940, and the next month he reappointed Captain José Remón to the police force. Some scholars have argued that Arnulfo rehired Remón to spite his older brother, former president Harmodio Arias. Regardless of motives, Remón's rehiring later dramatically altered the course of Panamanian history. See Larry L. Pippin, *The Remón Era: An Analysis of a Decade of Events in Panama, 1947–1957* (Stanford, 1964), 1–3; and Concha Peña, *José Antonio Remón Cantera: Ensayo de biografía con notas de mi cuaderno de periodista* (Panama City, 1955), 4–5. See also Major Dimas Arturo López, comp., *Las fuerzas armadas de la República de Panamá, período 1903–1973* (Panama City, 1973), 99.

5. See Huntington, *The Soldier and the State*, 84.

6. Mario Esteban Carranza, *Fuerzas armadas y estados de excepción an América Latina* (Mexico City, 1978), 68–72 and 236–37; and George Priestly, *Military Government and Popular Participation in Panama: The Torrijos Regime, 1968–1975* (Boulder, CO, 1986), 2–5.

On the progressive assumption of political power by the military, see Amos Perlmutter and Valerie Plave Bennett, *The Political Influence of the Military: A Comparative Reader* (New Haven, 1980), 199.

7. On Panama's financial circumstances in the twenties, see George F. Roberts, *Investigación económica de la República de Panamá* (Panama City, 1932), especially 25–28, 324–30.

8. Jorge Conte-Porras, *Panameños ilustres* (Panama City, 1978), 204–15.

9. Soler, *Panamá: Nación y oligarquía*, 31. These groups, especially Acción Comunal, also included significant elements of the rural middle class—most notably the Arias brothers.

10. For additional comment on Panama's political elite in the late 1920s, see Jorge Conte-Porras, *Arnulfo Arias Madrid* (Panama City, 1980), 244–46.

11. Isidro Beluche, *Acción Comunal: Surgimiento y estructuración del nacionalismo panameño* (Panama City, 1981), 37.

12. This platform appears in several different publications, including Beluche's commemorative 1981 work, *Acción Comunal*, 33–44; and Conte-Porras, *Arnulfo Arias Madrid*, 68–69. Translation by the author.

13. On crime rates in the 1920s, see República de Panamá, Contra-

loría General de la Nación, Dirección de Estadística y Censo, *Boletín de estadística*, various volumes and years. On a quarterly, semiannual, and annual basis, the Panamanian government produced a report in the *Boletín* that it labeled "Resúmen de infracciones reportadas por la Policía de la República." Each report then went on to divide crime into various classifications, including type of crime, profession and nationality of perpetrator, province where the crime occurred, and so forth. In the 1930s the government renamed the *Boletín*, calling it instead the *Estadística Panameña*.

14. Alejandro Portes, "The Politics of Urban Poverty," in Alejandro Portes and John Walton, *Urban Latin America: The Political Condition from Above and Below* (Austin, TX, 1976), 70–110.

15. Alexander Cuevas, "El movimiento inquilinario de 1925," in Alexander Cuevas, Everaldo Tomlinson, and Demetrio Porras, *Alcances e interpretaciones del problema inquilinario a través de la historia* (Panama City, 1975), 133–41.

16. República de Panamá, Secretario del Estado, "Memoria que el Secretario de Estado hace en despacho de relaciones exteriores . . ." (Panama City, 1936), 11. This document contains a summary of the 1926 treaty and the reasons for its rejection. Translation by the author.

For additional comment on the Kellogg-Alfaro negotiations, see John Major, *Prize Possession: The United States and the Panama Canal, 1903–1979* (New York, 1993), 110–15.

17. Nationalists accused the elite

Chiari and Arosemena administrations of defending capitalism at the expense of workers, of being antidemocratic, of repeated violation of Panamanian citizens' right to congregate, of dishonest use of public funds, and of destroying the institution of democracy based on popular suffrage. Conte-Porras, *Arnulfo Arias Madrid*, 82.

18. Beluche, *Acción Comunal*, 36–37.

19. Joyce to State, September 25, 1934, RG 59, State Department Decimal File 819.00-General Conditions/84, Legation of the United States to Panama, National Archives, Washington, DC (NA).

A few years after the revolt, Victor F. Goytía told his account of the revolt to Robert P. Joyce, third secretary of the American Legation to Panama. Goytía, one of the organizers of Acción Comunal, stated that Arias entered the palace "as a medical adviser and friend of the then president [*sic*] and would open the gates to the plotters." Goytía also stated that he "saw Arnulfo injecting stimulating drugs into the arms of the plotters before the uprising took place." See also the eyewitness account of Isidro A. Beluche Mora, *Acción Comunal*, especially 66–81.

20. RG 59, Department of State, Legation of the United States of America to Panama, 819.00/Revolutions/41, NA.

21. Walter LaFeber, *The Panama Canal: The Crisis in Historical Perspective* (New York, 1978), 79–83.

22. Dawson to Thurston, January 2, 1931, RG 59, Department of State, Legation of the United States of America to Panama, 819.00/Revolu-

tions/41, NA. In this flyer, revolutionaries led by Arnulfo Arias called for an end to Panama's ancien régime.

23. Davis to State, March 23, 1931, RG 59, State Department Decimal File 819.00/1552, Legation of the United States to Panama, NA.

24. Alfaro considered asking the United States for arms in 1932, but it appears that he did not do so. See Almon Wright's report, "The United States and Panama, 1933–1949," U.S. Department of State, Top Secret Research Project #499 (August 1952), 14–17.

25. On these paramilitary units, see for example "Notas Editoriales," *El Panamá América*, May 22, 1940, p. 4. This article recounts Alfaro's creation of the Reserva Nacionalista in 1932 and compares that to his armed followers in 1940, the Guardia Cívica Nacionalista (the Nationalist Civic Guard). See also Janowitz, *Military Institutions and Coercion*.

For a distinction between militaries that "arbitrate" and those that "rule," see Amos Perlmutter, *The Military and Politics in Modern Times: On Professionals, Praetorians, and Revolutionaries* (New Haven, 1977), 103.

26. For additional information regarding the 1932 presidential campaign and election, see Davis to State, July 12, 1932, RG 59, State Department Decimal File 819.00-General Conditions/84, Legation of the United States to Panama, NA; and "Political Situation in Panama," April 16, 1936, RG 59, Lot 55 D 216, Records of the Office of American Republic Affairs, 1918–1947, Memoranda on Panama, vol. 1 (January 1936–July 1939), NA.

27. Davis to State, June 17, 1932, RG 59, State Department Decimal File, 819.00 General Conditions/83, Legation of the United States to Panama, NA.

28. "President Arias Outlines Panama's Economic Program," *The Panama American* (February 8, 1933), p. 1; and "Una audiencia presidencial inolvidable," *El Panamá América* (July 14, 1933), p. 1. See also Pantaleón García, "The Good Neighbor Policy in Panama: The Alfaro-Hull Treaty," (master's thesis, University of Miami), 24–26.

29. Michael Conniff, *Black Labor on a White Canal: Panama, 1904–1981* (Pittsburgh, 1985), 80–83. On more recent developments in labor and politics on the isthmus, see Sharon Phillips Collazos, *Labor and Politics in Panama: The Torrijos Years* (Boulder, CO, 1991).

30. Coniff, *Black Labor*, 80–83.

31. On the Chiari empire, see Marco Gandásegui, ed., *Las clases sociales en Panamá: Grupos humanos, clases medias, elites y oligarquía* (Panama City, 1993), 156–58.

32. Joyce to State, September 25, 1934. While nepotism is not unique to the Arias administration, this is nonetheless significant to our understanding of Panama in the 1930s. On economic subterfuge in Panama in the 1920s, see George F. Roberts, *Investigación económica de la República de Panamá . . .* (Panama City, 1932), 327–34. For further information on the Roberts Report and the problems it identified, see Conte-Porras, *Panameños ilustres*, 173–84.

33. Mélida Ruth Sepúlveda. *Harmodio Arias Madrid: El hombre, el estadista, y el periodista* (Panama City, 1983), 183; and Ricaurte Soler, *Panamá: Historia de una crisis* (Mexico City, 1989), 42.

34. Peña, *José Antonio Remón Cantera*, 1–5.

35. Dimas Arturo López V., *Las fuerzas armadas de la República de Panamá*, 19–21, 44. Since Torrijos ordered this document's publication, each of Panama's recent governments—including those of Torrijos, Noriega, Endara, and Pérez Balladares—have relied extensively on this valuable compilation for salary information and general police and military guidelines.

36. On the changing role of the military throughout Latin America following WWI, see Lyle N. McAlister, "The Military," in John J. Johnson, ed., *Continuity and Change in Latin America* (Stanford, 1964), 136–60; and Brian Loveman and Thomas M. Davies, eds., *The Politics of Antipolitics*, 2d ed. (Lincoln, NE, 1989), 89–159. For a good general discussion of the changing role of the military in world politics, see S. F. Finer, *The Man on Horseback: The Role of the Military in Politics*, 2d ed. (Boulder, CO, 1988).

37. Jorge Conte-Porras, *Requiem por la revolución* (San José, Costa Rica, 1990), 161–70.

38. Warden Wilson to Edwin C. Wilson, September 19, 1932, RG 59, State Department Decimal File 819.51/713, United States Legation to Panama, NA.

39. Davis to State, January 22, 1932, RG 59, State Department Decimal File 819.00/Revolutions, Legation of the United States to Panama, NA. Davis reports that officials in Panama City had confiscated a few handguns that purportedly belonged to would-be counterrevolutionaries. Davis also reports here that former president Rodolfo Chiari was meeting clandestinely with members of the police force, for the purpose of mapping out a counterrevolt.

40. For data on demographic changes in Panama during the late twenties and early thirties, see for example *Estadística Panameña* 7(6)(June 1950):1–4. For economic figures for the same period, see *Estadística Panameña* 11(6)(June 1952):54, for example. See also George E. Roberts, *Investigación económica de la República de Panamá*, 474.

41. Demetrio Porras, "El movimiento inquilinario," in Cuevas, Tomlinson, and Porras, *Alcances e interpretaciones del problema inquilinario*, 169–98.

42. Marco Gandásegui et al., *Las luchas obreras en Panamá, 1850–1978* (Panama City, 1980), 46–47; Conniff, *Black Labor on a White Canal*; and Armando Muñóz Pinzón, *La huelga inquilinaria de 1932* (Panama City, 1974), 37.

43. The Panamanian government has published general data on illegitimacy in the republic. Nevertheless these records fail to provide localized information that would facilitate gauging fluctuations in standards of living by region and social class. To overcome this problem, I used parochial records to gauge illegitimacy on the local level. I obtained micro-

filmed copies of these invaluable documents through the Family History program of The Church of Jesus Christ of Latter-Day Saints (LDS). See for example the registros parroquiales from the San José parish in David (LDS films 760741–760747), the parish of San Juan Bautista in Aguadulce (films 1809803–1809804), the parish of Santa Ana in Panama City (films 1091673–1091675—this is a working-class parish), the parish of La Merced in Panama City (films 1094125 and 1094128—this is not a working-class parish), the parish of Santa Librada in Las Tablas (film 1089178), and the parish of San Juan Bautista in Chitré (films 1089485–1089846).

Only the provinces of Panamá and Chiriquí experienced significant population increases in the 1930s (see table 2). I attribute this increase to people who fled severe crop problems in Bocas del Toro, apparently going to David, and people fleeing the interior generally, ending up in the arrabal and seriously distending that already overflowing population of urban needy. Illegitimacy among the poor increased in each instance, underscoring the declining standards of living among the needy in each city. The overcrowding, unemployment, and general desperation engulfing Panama's poor during the Depression contributed significantly to the unstable climate confronting Panama's presidents in the 1930s.

44. On August 17, President Arias issued decree no. 142, which organized three hundred of Arias's supporters into the Guardia Cívica Nacional. Arrests of renters and their leaders immediately surged, as these armed reinforcements moved to squelch the rebellion. Before the formalization of their fighting status on the seventeenth, these three hundred militants, who called themselves the Asociación Reserva Nacionalista, had volunteered their services to the Arias presidency. Arias lauded their earlier display of loyalty as a demonstration of patriotism. In light of this support, Arias formalized their status on the seventeenth, by making them a part of his administration. See Muñóz Pinzón, *La huelga inquilinaria.*

45. Joyce to State, September 25, 1934. Goytía had left Acción Comunal on the evening of January 1, 1931—only hours before the coup—to express his objection to the manner in which the protest had taken shape under the leadership of Arnulfo Arias. See also Conte-Porras, *Arnulfo Arias Madrid,* 71.

46. Raul Leis, "The Cousin's Republic," *NACLA Report of the Americas* 4 (July–August 1988):26.

47. See Carlos Cuestas Gómez, *Soldados americanos en Chiriquí* (Panama City, 1990), particularly 307–24.

48. Jorge Conte-Porras, *La rebelión de las esfinges: Historia del movimiento estudiantil panameño* (Panama City, 1978), 14–18. For further discussion of students and APRA, see Steve Stein, *Populism in Peru: The Emergence of the Masses and the Politics of Social Control* (Madison, 1980), 132–46; and Ruth Berins Collier and David Collier, *Shaping the Political Arena* (Princeton, 1991), 150–53.

49. Sepúlveda, Harmodio Arias Madrid, 155. Pp. 155–59 contain the text of the speech President Harmodio Arias gave October 7, 1935, inaugurating the National University.

50. Conte-Porras, *Rebelión de las esfinges*, 17. For results of this January 1947 survey, see Mavis Biesanz and John Biesanz, *The People of Panama* (New York, 1955), 155. For additional comment on Méndez Pereira and the development of a national consciousness among Panama's youth, see Conte-Porras, *Panameños ilustres* and Patricia Pizzurno Gelos, *Harmodio Arias Madrid y la Universidad de Panamá* (Panama City: Editorial de la Lotería Nacional, 1995).

51. Wright, "The United States and Panama, 1933–1949," 14–17; and United States, Department of State, *Foreign Relations of the United States* 4 (1935):890. On Panama's financial situation in mid-1931, see Davis to State, July 14, 1931, RG 59, State Department Decimal File 819.00 General Conditions/77, Legation of the United States to Panama, NA. Davis reported that "at the present moment it is planned to dismiss 1200 men employed by the Central Roads Board who will further increase the precarious situation of the country." See also García, "La administración del Ing. Florencio H. Arosemena," 79–112.

52. República de Panamá, Secretario del Estado, "Memoria que el Secretario de Estado hace en el despacho de relaciones exteriores . . . "; and "Joint Statement," September 2, 1937, RG 59, Lot 55 D 216, Records of the Office of American Republic Affairs, 1918–1947, Memoranda on Panama, Box 54, vol. 1 (January 1936–July 1939), NA.

On economic nationalism in Latin America and the United States' response thereto, see Michael L. Krenn, *U.S. Policy toward Economic Nationalism In Latin America, 1917–1929* (Wilmington, DE, 1990), 21–37.

53. Thurston to White, March 30, 1931, RG 59, State Department Decimal File 819.00 Revolutions/48, Legation of the United States to Panama, NA.

54. See letters dated February 17, 1937, and March 9, 1937, RG 59, Lot 55 D 216, Records of the Office of American Republic Affairs, 1918–1947, Memoranda on Panama, Box 54, vol. 1 (January 1936–July 1939), NA.

55. Ibid.

56. Davis to State, June 19, 1931; and LaFeber, *The Panama Canal*, 86–88.

57. See "Political Situation in Panama," April 16, 1936, RG 59, Lot 55 D 216, Records of the Office of American Republic Affairs, Memoranda on Panama, Box 54, vol. 1 (January 1936–July 1939), NA. This document gives a ten-page overview of the 1936 election, including all parties and their candidates.

58. Conte-Porras, *Requiem por la revolución*, 172–74; and Conte-Porras, *Arnulfo Arias Madrid*, 85.

59. Humberto Ricord, "La oligarquía Panameña en el banquillo de los acusados," in Virgilio Araúz, *Cinco Ensayos* (n.p., n.d.), 8–9; and López V., *Las fuerzas armadas de la República de Panamá*, 171.

60. Law no. 25 of October 19, 1938, as cited in López V., *Las*

fuerzas armadas de la República de Panamá, 172–75.

61. Almon R. Wright, "Defense Sites Negotiations between the United States and Panama, 1936–1948," *Department of State Bulletin* 27(685) (August 11, 1952). On these concessions, see David N Farnsworth and James W. McKenney, *U.S.-Panama Relations, 1903–1978: A Study in Linkage Politics* (Boulder, CO, 1983), 26–28.

62. Bryce Wood, *The Dismantling of the Good Neighbor Policy* (Austin, TX, 1985), x.

63. Bonsal to Welles, December 10, 1942, RG 59, Lot 55 D 216, Records of the Office of American Republic Affairs, 1918–1947, Memoranda on Panama, Box 55, vol. 4 (September 1941–January 1943), NA.

64. For information regarding problems between the Arias brothers during Arnulfo's brief presidency, see the military attaché report dated December 28, 1940, RG 165, Records of the War Department General and Special Staffs, Military Intelligence Division Correspondence, 1917–1941, Report No. 5,192, File #2657-M-290, NA.

Chapter 4

1. Dawson to Thurston, January 2, 1931, RG 59, State Department Decimal File 819.00/Revolutions/32, Legation of the United States to Panama, National Archives, Washington, DC (NA). This document is particularly significant because it contains a flyer that coup leaders distributed on the morning of the revolution. Titled "To the Panamanian Nation," the flyer outlines the objectives of the insurrectionists, who proclaimed themselves "moved by the purest sentiment of patriotism."

2. Jorge Conte-Porras, *Arnulfo Arias Madrid* (Panama City, 1980), 82. For further insight into Arnulfo Arias, see Juan Manuel Pérez, "Panama: The Rise and Fall of Arnulfo Arias, 1931–1941" (Ph.D. diss., Georgetown University, 1993).

3. On the de la Guardia family's socioeconomic ties in the 1940s and 1950s, see Marco A. Gandásegui, "La concentración del poder económico en Panamá," in Marco A. Gandásegui, ed., *Las clases sociales en Panamá: Grupos humanos, clases medias, elites y oligarquía* (Panama City, 1993), particularly 176–78.

4. I do not list the 1932 tenants' strike in this list of nationalist successes because president Harmodio Arias forcibly squelched it. Unlike the 1926 tenant uprising, the 1932 protest was almost exclusively a working-class phenomenon–which undoubtedly explains why it failed.

5. For further insight into Panama's wartime fiscal situation, particularly the later years, see República de Panamá, Contraloría General de la República, Dirección de Estadística y Censo, *The National Income and National Accounts of the Republic of Panama, 1944–1952* (Panama City, 1953). Like the earlier Roberts report, this document was prepared (in English and Spanish) at the request of the Panamanian government; the compiler in this case was H. Rijken van Olst, a United Nations expert on national income statistics.

The best work on student organization and activism in Panama during this era is Jorge Conte-Porras's *La rebelión de las esfinges: Historia del movimieito estudiantil panameño* (Panama City, 1978).

6. Michael L. Conniff, *Panama and the United States: The Forced Alliance* (Athens, GA, 1991), 91.

7. See Conte-Porras, *La rebelión de las esfinges*, p. 188.

8. This standoff between the Partido Nacional Revolucionario and the Frente Popular established a precedent for temporary election coalitions that has endured since that time.

9. "El Partido Nacional Revolucionario tiene deuda de gratitud con esta provincia," *El Panamá América* (May 13, 1940), pp. 1–2. This article contains the text of the campaign speech Arias gave in the city of Santiago de Veraguas, where he had kicked off his campaign months earlier. The text is particularly significant because it concluded his campaign tour of the Panamanian countryside.

For a thorough synopsis of every newspaper published in Panama in 1940, see Major L. D. Carter, G2 (Panama) Report to War Department General Staff, October 30, 1940, RG 165, Records of the War Department General and Special Staffs, Military Intelligence Division Correspondence, 1917–1941: File no. 2657-M-290, NA. Major Carter notes correctly that Harmodio Arias used his own paper, *El Panamá América*, to support his own successful candidacy in 1932, in addition to those of Juan Demóstenes Arosemena in 1936 and Arnulfo Arias in 1940. With a circulation reported at fourteen thousand in 1940, El Panamá América was Panama's second largest Spanish language newspaper. It was a powerful medium of political expression.

10. This conflict between armed constituencies competing for political office has evolved since the 1940 election. Jorge Conte-Porras noted that "the battles between these opposing groups became urban warfare, including public exchanges of gunfire; these confrontations accentuated the organization of violence through the creation of paramilitary groups who were ready to defend victory with arms." See Jorge Conte-Porras, *Arnulfo Arias Madrid*, 188.

11. The 1940 election pitted Arnulfo Arias's Panameñista movement (a coalition that included the Partido Nacional Revolucionario, the Partido Conservador, the Partido Liberal Demócrata, and the Partido Liberal Unido) against the Chiari bloc of the Liberal party, known as the Frente Popular, which supported the Alfaro candidacy. These coalitions established a precedent for temporary election-time alliances that continues today in Panama.

12. Steve Ropp, *Panamanian Politics: From Guarded Nation to National Guard* (Stanford, 1982), 26; and Jorge Conte-Porras, *Arnulfo Arias Madrid*, 30.

13. Dispatch from Lima to State, August 8, 1941, RG 59, General Records of the Department of State, Office of American Republic Affairs, 1918–1947, Memoranda on Panama, vol. 3: January 1941–August 1941, NA.

14. The electoral board declared that Arnulfo Arias had won the election by a margin of 107,759 to 3,022. Panameñista is another name used to describe Arias and his followers. I discuss the term more fully later in this chapter.

15. República de Panamá, Ministerio de Relaciones Exteriores, "Boletín semanal de información para las embajadas, legaciones, y consulados de la república," no. 5, March 8, 1941, p. 9.

16. In his discussion of populism, political scientist Ernesto LaClau spoke of the "disaffected members of the dominant sector" who turn to the masses for popular support when the former turn against the state. These disaffected few constitute what LaClau refers to as the "raw material" of populism. See Ernesto LaClau, "Towards a Theory of Populism," in *Politics and Ideology in Marxist Theory* (London, 1977). Harmodio and Arnulfo Arias both fit LaClau's model.

17. Walter LaFeber, *The Panama Canal: The Crisis in Historical Perspective* (New York, 1978), 93. This quote comes from RG 59, "Memorandum by Military Intelligence Division," State Department Decimal File 819.00/2106, Box 3728, NA.

18. Chapin to State, June 20, 1938, RG 59, Lot 55 D 216, Records of the Office of American Republic Affairs, 1918–1947, Memoranda on Panama, Box 54, vol. 1 (January 1936–July 1939), NA.

19. Bonsal to Wells, June 15, 1941, RG 59, Lot 55 D 216, Records of the Office of American Republic Affairs, 1918–1947, Memoranda on Panama, Box 55, vol. 3 (January 1941–August 1941), NA.

20. Ibid.; and Dimas Arturo López V., comp., *Las fuerzas armadas de la República de Panamá: Período 1903 a 1973* (Panama City, 1973), 176–81. López provides a list of secret police salaries in addition to a copy of the organization's charter in its entirety.

21. See Arias's campaign comments in *El Panamá América* (May 13, 1940).

22. Wise to Daniels and Bonsal, September 29, 1941, RG 59, Lot 55 D 216, Records of the Office of American Republic Affairs, 1918–1947, Memoranda on Panama, Box 55, vol. 4 (September 1941–January 1943), NA; *Gaceta Oficial*, February 14, 1941, pp. 3–4. The latter document outlines the Arias administration's criterion for defining a "quality Panamanian" in racial and ethnic terms. These standards reaffirmed Article 23 of the 1941 constitution. See also Ricaurte Soler, *El pensamiento político en los siglos xix y xx* (Panama City, 1988), 365–77. In the course of his first inaugural address (October 1940), Arias referred to "parasitic migratory affluence" caused by a predominance of foreign merchants and the Canal Zone.

23. Ropp, *Panamanian Politics*, 21–25. See also LaClau, "Towards a Theory of Populism".

24. On the inclusion of Jews among the list of prohibited immigrants under the Arias regime, see Wise to Daniels and Bonsal, September 29, 1941, RG 59, Lot 55 D 216, Records of the Office of American Republic Affairs, 1918–1947, Memoranda on Panama, Box 55, vol. 4 (September 1941–January 1943), NA.

25. Ibid.

26. On the social security system instituted by the Arias administration in April 1941, see Act no. 23, as recorded in República de Panamá, *Gaceta Oficial* no. 8481 (Panama City, 1941), p. 1. While the de la Guardia administration revised this act in April 1943 (see *Gaceta Oficial* no. 9099, p. 1), Arias's creation of a welfare state remains as one of his most prominent political legacies—much like that of Franklin Delano Roosevelt in the United States.

27. República de Panamá, Ministerio de Relaciones Exteriores, "Boletín semanal de información para las embajadas, legaciones, y consulados de la república," no. 3 (February 22, 1941), p. 1; and no. 14 (May 10, 1941), pp. 2–3. Here the Arias administration outlined its plan to make $250,000 available to farmers and industry for the development of the Panamanian economy. This came partially in response to Arias's fledgling efforts to renegotiate Panama's foreign debt and the subsequent threat of capital shortage.

For total social security payments, by class of disability, during the period 1941–49, see República de Panamá, Contraloría General de la Nación, Dirección de Estadística y Censo, *Estadístico Panameño* 8(9) (July 1949):7.

Since 1904 Panama's official currency has been the United States dollar.

28. Soler, *El pensamiento político*; and *Gaceta Oficial* (March 18, 1941), p.1. Arias later took control of the nation's beef industry, making it illegal for Panamanian cattle growers to submit bids for domestically raised

cattle. The Arias administration took over these negotiations and then arranged a lucrative agreement with the Panamanian Railroad Commissary to sell the latter three thousand head of cattle. Francisco "Panchito" Arias worked out an agreement to supply the other six thousand cattle the Americans would need over the course of the year. See Wise to Barber and Finley, May 30, 1941, RG 59, Lot 55 D 216, Records of the Office of American Republic Affairs, 1918–1947, Memoranda on Panama, Box 55, vol. 3 (January 1941–August 1941), NA.

29. See for example Duggan to Welles, June 2, 1938, RG 59, Lot 55 D 216, Records of the Office of American Republic Affairs, 1918–1947, Memoranda on Panama, Box 54, vol. 1 (January 1936–July 1939), NA; and Memorandum from Lieutenant Ralph C. Smith, June 1941, RG 165, Records of the War Department General and Special Staffs, Military Intelligence Division Correspondence, 1917–1941, File Nos. 10110-2874 (?—last four digits are illegible), NA; and Lieutenant Colonel L. D. Carter to Assistant Chief of Staff, G2, War Department, Washington, June 23, 1941, RG 165, Records of the War Department General and Special Staffs, Military Intelligence Division Correspondence, 1917–1941: File No. 10110-2874/9 (see also 12, attached), NA. These documents pertain to Japanese, Italian, and German nationals residing in Panama. The Smith memorandum calls for the monthly development of "Anti-Security Rosters" that identify each of these nationals by name and

by their monthly activities. The Carter document is the first of dozens of such lists contained in this particular set of files.

30. See Barber to Finley and Baker, February 8, 1940, RG 59, Lot 55 D 216, Records of the Office of American Republic Affairs, 1918–1947, Memoranda on Panama, Box 54, vol. 2 (August 1939–December 1940), NA. This document, written as American policy makers prepared their petition to the Panamanian government, outlines specific contractual guidelines to be observed during negotiations, including the amount of rent to be paid.

31. General Crittenberger, "Negotiations between the Republic of Panama and the United States of America for a Defense Site Agreement, 1946–1947: Evacuation of Sites and Termination of 1942 Agreement," RG 319, Army General and Special Staffs, Plans and Operations Divisions, Decimal File, 1946–1948, 686., Case 1, NA. Prepared as a summary of all negotiations relating to the auxiliary American bases in Panama during World War II, this is the most comprehensive single document available in English on the subject of the negotiations between Panama and the United States that began in August 1940. For the best overall account available in either language, see República de Panamá, Ministro de Relaciones Exteriores, *Sitios de defensa, Tomos 1–17 (1942–1947)*. This collection of primary documentation is located in file cabinet no. 62, drawer nos. 62.1 and 62.2 of the Archivos de Relaciones Exteriores in Panama City.

32. On October 18, 1940, Hitler wrote this congratulatory note to Arias. Hitler to Arias, República de Panamá, Ministerio de la Presidencia, Archivos Nacionales, Ciudad de Panamá. This rare document, along with further communication between the two leaders, is kept in an unmarked folder in the Archives of the Presidency of the Republic. Author's translation.

33. Barber to Daniels et al., October 17, 1940, RG 59 Lot 216, Records of the Office of American Republic Affairs, 1918–1947, Box 54, vol. 2 (August 1939–December 1940), NA.

34. John A. Cooley, "The United States and the Panama Canal, 1938–1947: Policy Formulation and Implementation from Munich through the Early Years of the Cold War," (Ph.D. diss., Ohio State University, 1972), 145–46.

35. Finley to Bonsal, February 5, 1942, RG 165, Records of the War Department General and Special Staffs, Military Intelligence Division Correspondence, 1917–1941, File Nos. 10110-2874 to 10110-2962, NA.

36. República de Panamá, Ministerio de Relaciones Exteriores, "Boletín semanal de información para las embajadas, legaciones, y consulados de la república," no. 5 (March 8, 1941), pp. 1–6. This is the Arias administration's official explanation of why it had conceded Washington its petition.

37. Bonsal to Welles, June 15, 1941, RG 59, Lot 55 D 216, Records of the Office of American Republic Affairs, 1918–1947, Memoranda on Panama, Box 55, vol. 3 (January 1941–August 1941), NA.

38. Statement by Secretary of State Cordell Hull, RG 59, Lot 55 D 216, Records of the Office of American Republic Affairs, 1918–1947, Memoranda on Panama, Box 55, vol. 4 (September 1941–January 1943), NA. Article III of the 1941 constitution prohibited Panama's presidents from leaving the country without first notifying their subordinates.

39. Arias's secret police established an institutional precedent that continues in Panama today. Torrijos's DENI (Departamento Nacional de Inteligencia) and Panama's own G2 (intelligence) have frequently been used to repress political opposition, much as Arias's *Policía Secreta* was in 1940–41.

40. The National Archives in Panama City house a series of valuable documents dealing with the National Police during the 1930s, 1940s, and 1950s. Included in two loosely bound, unlabeled books and one "Memoria del Ministerio de Gobierno y Justicia" are officer lists, retirement information, and generally a decent (if poorly organized) collection of documents dealing with the evolution of the National Police/National Guard, particularly its disproportionate growth in the 1940s, when Remón used his capacity to recruit from among the nation's working class. Unfortunately, in the wake of the 1989 invasion, these few documents are all that remain accessible to inquiring scholars; consequently a thorough analysis of the officer corps has yet to be made and will not be possible until documentation confiscated in the invasion is released for public scrutiny. A cur-

sory reading of the data included therein confirms what Larry L. Pippin and others have said about Remón: it is clear that he made the police a vehicle of social mobility for a select few of the nation's poor, and this made him popular among some quarters of the nation's working class.

Further corroboration of these observations comes from an interview I conducted with Gonzalo Tapia, Asesor Personal to various of Panama's presidents dating from the forties, including the regime of Domingo Díaz Arosemena, which was overthrown by Remón in July 1949. In his capacity within the Arosemena government, Sr. Tapia was an eyewitness to the July 28, 1949, coup, wherein Remón masterminded the removal of the Arosemena regime. Sr. Tapia indicated that Remón astutely used his office to build a base of support among the poor of Panama City, often appearing at local beer gardens and indulging in a *trago* with the common folk. Interview conducted with Sr. Tapia in his office in the presidential palace, July 4, 1989.

41. Larry L. Pippin, *The Remón Era: An Analysis of a Decade of Events in Panama, 1947–1957* (Stanford, 1964), 3. De la Guardia assumed office on October 9, 1941, the day the Arias regime fell. That day, in fulfillment of his agreement with Remón, the newly appointed president made Remón second commander.

42. English to State, "Un-American Activities in Panama During the Period September–October 1941," December 11, 1941, RG 59, Lot 55 D 216, Records of the Office of

American Republic Affairs, 1918–1947, Memoranda on Panama, Box 55, vol. 4 (September 1941–January 1943), NA.

43. LaFeber, *The Panama Canal*, 97–98.

44. On Panama's cooperation with the United States on the issue of Japanese internment, see for example Wise to Walmsley et al., memorandum titled "Internment of Japanese in the Event of War between the United States and Japan," November 5, 1941, RG 59, Lot 55 D 216, Records of the Office of American Republic Affairs, 1918–1947: Memoranda on Panama, Box 55, vol. 4 (September 1941–January 1943), NA; Wise to Daniels, memorandum entitled "Main Developments in our Relations with Panama during the Past Year," November 29, 1941, ibid.; and Wise to Daniels et al., memorandum titled "Question of Requesting Panama to Deny Visas to all Native Spaniards," November 29, 1942, ibid..

45. Letter to Daniels et al., July 7, 1942, RG 59, General Records of the Department of State, Office of American Republic Affairs, 1918–1947, Memoranda on Panama, vol. 4 (September 1941–January 1943), NA. De la Guardia had no intention of calling an election or plebiscite to poll the people concerning his administration. One must therefore speculate what he meant by the "freely and frankly expressed" will of the people.

46. Wise to Bonsal, April 17, 1943, RG 59, Lot 55 D 216, Records of the Office of American Republic Affairs, 1918–1947, Memoranda on Panama, Box 56, 5 (January 1943–

May 1945), NA; Memorandum of Conversation including Enrique Jiménez, Augusto Boyd, and Laurence Duggan, Director, Office of American Republic Affairs, May 27, 1944, ibid.; Wise to Cabot and Bonsal, August 5, 1943, ibid.; and Marco Gandásegui, *La concentración del poder económico en Panamá* (Panama City, 1967), 54–67.

47. Wise to Cabot and Bonsal, May 11, 1943, RG 59, Lot 55 D 216, Records of the Office of American Republic Affairs, 1918–1947, Memoranda on Panama, Box 56, vol. 5 (January 1943–May 1945), NA.

48. On Fábrega, see López V., *Las fuerzas armadas de la República de Panamá*, 99; on de la Guardia's use of his office to distribute jobs and favors, see Wise to Cabot and Bonsal, April 17, 1943, RG 59, Lot 55 D 216, Records of the Office of American Republic Affairs, 1918–1947, Memoranda on Panama, Box 56, vol. 5 (January 1943–May 1945), NA.

49. John C. Dreier to Butler and Braden, secret memorandum titled "Panamanian Desire for a Military Establishment," November 3, 1945, RG 59, Lot 55 D 216, Records of the Office of American Republic Affairs, 1918–1947, Memoranda on Panama, Box 56, vol. 6 (June 1945–December 1947), NA.

50. In his thorough examination of Panamanian political history, John Cooley incorrectly argues that "Panama got neither guns nor launches" from the United States during this period (Cooley, "The United States and the Panama Canal," 140). However, see Wise to Wilson, Walmsley, and Wright, November 19, 1941, RG

59, Lot 55 D 216, Records of the Office of American Republic Affairs, 1918–1947, Memoranda on Panama, Box 55, vol. 4 (September 1941–January 1943), NA; and Daniels to Wilson, February 25, 1942, RG 59, Lot 55 D 216, Records of the Office of American Republic Affairs, 1918–1947, Memoranda on Panama, Box 55, vol. 3 (January 1941–August 1941) and vol. 4 (September 1941–January 1943), NA. See also McGregor to Bonsal, January 8, 1944, RG 59, Lot 55 D 216, Records of the Office of American Republic Affairs, 1918–1947, Memoranda on Panama, Box 56, vol. 5 (January 1943–May 1945), NA. With regard to Panama's request for jeeps in addition to more machine guns and submachine guns, McGregor stated here that the State Department should "avoid any of the formalities of Lend Lease procedure." Panama (during the presidency of Arnulfo Arias) and Argentina (during the administration of Juan Domingo Perón) were the only two Latin American countries that did not receive support from the Lend-Lease program.

51. Wise to Daniels and Bonsal, September 3, 1943, RG 59, General Records of the Department of State, Office of American Republic Affairs, Memoranda on Panama, Box 56, vol. 5 (January 1943–May 1945), NA.

52. Ibid.

53. Jorge Conte-Porras, *La rebelión de las esfinges*, 15–17, 37–57. The FEP's platform is found on page 42. These groups included La Vanguardia Coclesana, La Jóven Veraguas, La Federación de Sociedades Santeñas, Los Caballeros del Barú, El Círculo de Amigos de Santa Ana, La

Juventud Unida Pro-San Carlos, and La Asociación Revolucionaria de la Juventud (ARJU—the Panamanian branch of the Peruvian Aprista movement). See also p. 44.

54. On the disintegration of de la Guardia's cabinet, see Robert G. McGregor to Cabot, Bonsal, et al., February 24, 1944, RG 59, Lot 55 D 216, Records of the Office of American Republic Affairs, 1918–1947, Memoranda on Panama, Box 56, vol. 5 (January 1943–May 1945), NA.

55. Philip W. Bonsal to Stettinius, Memorandum titled "Visit of Panamanian Ambassador," February 8, 1944, RG 59, Lot 55 D 216, Records of the Office of American Republic Affairs, 1918–1947, Memoranda on Panama, Box 56, vol. 5 (January 1943–May 1945), NA.

56. McGregor to Duggan and Cabot, April 11, 1944, RG 59, Lot 55 D 216, Records of the Office of American Republic Affairs, 1918–1947, Memoranda on Panama, Box 56, vol. 5 (January 1943–May 1945), NA.

57. Ibid.

58. See República de Panamá, Contraloría General de la República, Dirección de Estadística y Censo, *National Income and National Accounts*, especially 44–85.

59. In January 1944 President Roosevelt had approved the Joint Chiefs' blueprint for a postwar world. This plan, known as JCS 570/2, called for the continued occupation of the temporary bases included in the 1942 agreement. Thus well before the war ended, American officials had no intention of complying with the treaty they had signed with the Panamanian government.

60. For an overview of opposing political blocs in Panama in 1946, see Wise to Cochran et al., "Panama—Political Blocs—Leftist Activities," July 10, 1946, RG 59, Lot 55 D 216, Records of the Office of American Republic Affairs, 1918–1947, Memoranda on Panama, Box 56, vol. 6 (June 1945–December 1947), NA.

61. For a report on crime during and after the war, see for example *Estadística Panameña* 11(8–9) (August–September 1952):48–61.

62. Dispatch to Cochran and Wise titled "*Arnulfista* Activities," November 30, 1945, RG 59, Lot 55 D 216, Records of the Office of American Republic Affairs, 1918–1947, Memoranda on Panama, Box 56, vol. (June 1945–December 1947), NA. In this report officials stated that "since the exploding of the bomb near former President de la Guardia's company there have been no other acts of terrorism in Panama."

63. Wise to Cochran et al., Memorandum titled "Panama—Arnulfo Arias," January 16, 1946, Rg 59, Lot 55 D 216, Records of the Office of American Republic Affairs, 1918–1947, Memoranda on Panama, Box 56, vol. 6 (June 1945–December 1947), NA. This document provides a brief but thorough account of the planned coup.

64. Wise to Cochran et al., Memorandum titled "Panama—Political Blocs—Leftist Activities," July 10, 1946, RG 59, Lot 55 D 216, Records of the Office of American Republic Affairs, 1918–1947, Memoranda on Panama, Box 56, vol. 6 (June 1945–December 1947), NA; Wise to Cochran et al., "Panamanian Political Situation," July 10, 1946, ibid.; and Solana to Newbegin et al., October 7, 1946, ibid.

65. *Gaceta Oficial* (December 28, 1945), p. 1. Jiménez hoped to undermine support for the Arnulfista movement by painting Arias and his followers in an anti-Semitic light following World War II.

66. Pippin, *The Remón Era*, 41–43.

67. United States, Department of State, *Foreign Relations of the United States* 9 (1946):1112–13; Solana memorandum to Wise, Newbegin, and O'Neill, October 3, 1946, RG 59, Lot 55 D 216, Records of the Office of American Republic Affairs, 1918–1947, Memoranda on Panama, Box 56, vol. 6 (June 1945–December 1947), NA; and Wise to Clayton and Briggs, September 12, 1946, ibid. In this last document, Wise reports that the Jiménez administration "has been seeking some 'symbolic' return of all bases before entering into the negotiation of a new agreement."

68. On electoral changes made by the Jiménez government in 1946, see República de Panamá, Jurado Nacional de Elecciones, "Ley 39 (de 19 de Septiembre de 1946) Sobre Elecciones Populares y Sentencias Dictadas por la Honorable Corte Suprema de Justicia en relación con esta Ley" (Panama City, n.d.).

69. Wise to Duggan, Memorandum titled "Suffrage in Panama," October 20, 1942, RG 59, Lot 55 D 216, Records of the Office of American Republic Affairs, 1918–1947, Memoranda on Panama, Box 55, vol. 4 (September 1941–January 1943), NA. Wise pointed out that, as outlined in Article 61 of the 1941 consti-

tution, "the Legislature may confer citizenship on Panamanian women over 21 years of age, with the limitations and the requisites established by law." Wise further pointed out that women "may take part only in the election of provincial councils (ayuntamientos provinciales) created by Article 173 of the 1941 constitution." He continued by stating that women "who have finished courses in secondary instruction may vote," but they were not permitted to vote in the presidential or federal legislative elections.

70. Dreier to Butler and Braden, secret memorandum titled "Panamanian Desire for a Military Establishment," November 3, 1945, RG 59, Lot 55 D 216, Records of the Office of American Republic Affairs, 1918–1947, Memoranda on Panama, Box 56, vol. 6 (June 1945–December 1947), NA.

71. Ibid.

72. Wise to Cochran et al., Memorandum titled "Panama—Political Blocs—Leftist Activities," July 10, 1946, RG 59, Lot 55 D 216, Records of the Office of American Republic Affairs, 1918–1947, Memoranda on Panama, Box 56, vol. 6 (June 1945–December 1947), NA.

73. Wise to Clayton and Briggs, Memorandum titled "Panama—Defense Sites Question," September 12, 1946, RG 59, Lot 55 D 216, Records of the Office of American Republic Affairs, 1918–1947, Memoranda on Panama, Box 56, vol. 6 (June 1945–December 1947), NA. Notice that this memorandum bears the date September 12—eleven days *after* the deadline that called for the

United States to abandon the bases in question.

74. Wise to Bennet et al., "Panama—Defense Sites," January 2, 1947, RG 59, Lot 55 D 216, Records of the Office of American Republic Affairs, 1918–1947, Memoranda on Panama, Box 56, vol. 6 (June 1945–December 1947), NA.

75. Ibid.

Chapter 5

1. On social and political assimilation see, for example, Leo Spitzer, *Lives in Between: Assimilation and Marginality in Austria, Brazil, and West Africa, 1780–1945* (Cambridge, 1989). While Spitzer's is an analysis of individuals and families, the factors he identifies that affect assimilation on the individual and family levels might well apply to groups in emerging states such as Panama, where political and social mobility form the bases of a dynamic national reality.

For a helpful, recent discussion of the effects of development and modernity on third world societies, see A. Douglas Kincaid and Alejandro Portes, eds., *Comparative National Development: Society and Economy in the New Global Order* (Chapel Hill, NC, 1994). The articles in the collection by Gary Gereffi ("Rethinking Development Theory: Technological Change and Socioeconomic Restructuring in Latin America") and Bryan R. Roberts ("Urbanization, Development, and the Household") are particularly useful in a discussion of contemporary Panama; their comments on society and modernity are valuable in a consideration of urban Panama.

2. Mario Esteban Carranza, *Fuerzas armadas y estados de excepción an América Latina* (Mexico City, 1978).

3. Samuel Huntington, *The Soldier and the State: The Theory of Politics and Civil-Military Relations* (New York, 1964), 86. Huntington defines *power* as "the capacity to control the behavior of other people."

4. Carranza, *Furezas armadas,* 27.

5. While informal authority is much more difficult to gauge, it is as real as constitutional law and, in Panama, is the only way to explain the events of 1949–52.

6. Historians in both countries tend to dismiss the rejection of the Filós-Hines Treaty as a short-lived victory for the masses, during a period generally considered by both Panamanian and American authors as a "continuation of the status quo." For example, David Acosta, a Panamanian scholar and participant in the events of December 1947, has provided a thorough first-person account of the Filós-Hines negotiations. Nevertheless, his book, *La influencia decisiva de la opinion pública en el rechazo del convenio Filós-Hines de 1947* (Panama City, 1983), fails to address the significance of these events beyond the treaty's rejection. See also George Priestly, *Military Government and Popular Participation in Panama: The Torrijos Regime, 1968–1975* (Boulder, CO, 1986); Walter LaFeber, *The Panama Canal: The Crisis in Historical Perspective* (New York, 1989); Reinato Pereira, *Panamá: Fuerzas armadas y política* (Panama City, 1978); and Ricaurte

Soler, *El pensamiento político en los siglos xix y xx* (Panama City, 1987).

7. See, for example, Larry Pippin's *The Remón Era: An Analysis of a Decade of Events in Panama, 1947–1957* (Stanford, 1964), 21. Pippin hypothesized that financial collapse in Panama following World War II derived from the rejection of the base treaty. More recently many scholars have embraced this assumption without testing it, although it neglects two significant issues. First, permitting such a collapse would have been contrary to State Department plans regarding Panama, where the fear of Communism called for economic stabilization in and around the Canal Zone. Second, Panama's economic condition in the late forties depended on world commerce, which was recovering from its depressed war status. Thus increased levels of commerce following the war meant increased canal activity, which in turn aided the Panamanian economy.

8. John Major, "Wasting Asset: The U.S. Re-Assessment of the Panama Canal, 1945–1949," *Journal of Strategic Studies* 3 (September 1980):123–46. Major provides the most thorough account to date of Washington's changing perceptions of the Panama Canal following World War II. Based heavily on primary sources, the study nevertheless relies solely on documents in English. By ignoring Panamanian documents, including communication from Panamanian officials in the United States National Archives, Major bypassed official and unofficial documentation that would have bolstered his discussion of the canal.

It is unfortunately all too common among non-Panamanian scholars, to discuss Panama's relations with the United States using only North American data.

9. Representative Charles Eaton's statement regarding Panama's significance appeared in República de Panamá, Ministerio de Relaciones Exteriores, "Boletin semanal de información para las embajadas, legaciones, y consulados de la república" I (April 10, 1943). Translation by the author. This statement by Congressman Eaton reflects a conviction that had existed in the United States since the earliest days of the canal's operation. In 1919, for example, Senator Claude A. Swanson noted that "this Canal, with the exception of our home territory, is the most valuable possession we have." See Major, "Wasting Asset," 123.

10. Colonel Max S. Johnson, Chief, Strategy Section, Operations and Plans Division, June 10, 1946, RG 319, Army General and Special Staffs, Plans and Operations Division, OPD 381, Box 96, National Archives, Washington, DC (NA). This note from Colonel Johnson calls for the Caribbean Defense Command to submit to the Operations and Plans Division "an estimate of potential enemies' capabilities and intentions with respect to the Panama Canal." Part of the shift in strategy described above, this and similar reports triggered a strategy known as Broadview, an outline to defend the canal and the rest of the Americas from advanced weapons systems.

11. Similar shifts in spending occurred during World War I, for example, when the British spent nearly 37 percent of their national income on the war. This generated less profit than peacetime production, reduced Britain's supply of circulating capital, and greatly increased its national and per capita debts. Occurring as it did on two fronts instead of one, World War II required even greater mobilization and commensurate budgetary adaptation. See Harvey E. Fisk, *The Inter-Ally Debts: An Analysis of War and Post-War Public Finance* (New York, 1924), 21; J. Laurence Laughlin, *Credit of the Nations: A Study of the European War* (New York, 1918), 282–85; and Eleann Kerr, *The Effect of Wars and Revolutions on Government Securities: Internal and External* (New York, 1917), 3–4, 16–17, and 28–29. For similar data on World War II, see note 7, above.

12. United Nations, Department of Economic and Social Affairs, Economic Commission for Latin America, *External Financing in Latin America* (New York, 1965), 23–34; and Max Winkler, *Investments of United States Capital in Latin America* (New York, 1971), 275–83.

13. República de Panamá, Contraloría General de la República, Dirección de Estadística y Censo, *Estadística Panameña* 2(6) (June 1952):54. This document charts all canal traffic by net weight, cargo tonnage, and the amount of toll collected for the period 1915–50.

14. Walter LaFeber incorrectly posits that the war "fueled hemispheric prosperity," which benefited the Panamanian economy generally. While increases in government

spending did benefit elite financiers with access to government contracts, available data suggest that the standard of living of most Panamanians actually declined during the war. See LaFeber, *The Panama Canal*, 99–100.

15. República de Panamá, Contraloría General de la República, Dirección de Estadística y Censo, *Estadística Panameña* 9(1) (January 1950):2. This document outlines Panama's national fiscal situation from 1941 to 1949, thus highlighting marked declines in government credit. On import and export taxes collected by the Panamanian government during this period, see República de Panamá, Contraloría General de la República, Dirección de Estadística y Censo, *The National Income and National Accounts of the Republic of Panama, 1944–1952* (Panama City, 1953), 75–85. This report, prepared for the Panamanian government by Dr. H. Rijken van Olst, United Nations Expert on National Income Statistics, provides valuable data and estimates regarding Panama's fiscal structure. For import and export figures, see República de Panamá, Contraloría General de la República, Dirección de Estadística y Censo, *Estadística Panameña* 7(11–12) (November–December 1948):4–6.

16. For an analysis of crime in Panama City and Colón from 1946 to 1951, including analysis by gender, nationality, and profession, see *Estadística Panameña* 11(8–9) (August–September 1952):48–61.

17. Ibid.

18. Leslie Bethell, "From the Second World War to the Cold War: 1944–1954," in Abraham F. Lowen-thal, ed., *Exporting Democracy: The United States and Latin America* (Baltimore, 1991), 41–70.

19. See statement by Representative Charles Eaton in "Boletin semanal de información" 1 (April 10, 1943).

20. For an account of inter-American relations during the war, see Laurence Duggan, *The Americas: The Search for Hemisphere Security* (New York, 1949), 82–122. Duggan served as a senior State Department official during the Roosevelt administration and attended many conferences on inter-American defense during the war. This account is therefore a valuable, though biased, first-hand synopsis of the events.

21. On United States foreign policy during the war, see for example Robert Dallek, *Franklin Delano Roosevelt and American Foreign Policy, 1932–1945* (New York, 1979); Patrick J. Hearndon, *Roosevelt Confronts Hitler: America's Entry into World War II* (Champaign, IL, 1987); Waldo Heinrichs, *Threshold of War: Franklin D. Roosevelt and American Entry into World War II* (New York, 1988); and J. Gary Clifford, "Both Ends of the Telescope: New Perspectives on FDR and American Entry into World War II," *Diplomatic History* 13 (spring 1989):213–30.

22. RG 218, Records of the Joint Chiefs of Staff, Central Decimal File, 1946–1947, Post War Military Base Requirements, 360 (12/19/47), Part 1, Bulky Package, NA. These three sites are representative of the general support Vargas gave to the United States military. In May 1947 a report produced by the Plans and Operations Division of the Army General

Staff noted regarding Brazil: "All facilities at Brazilian airports and facilities for delivery, transportation, and storage of petroleum products are available for use by U.S. military aircraft. The United States has the right to jointly occupy and maintain the airports of: Amapa, Belem (land and seaplane), Sao Luis, Fortaleza, Natal (land and seaplane), Recife, Fernando de Noronha, and Bahia (land and seaplane), all in northern Brazil."

23. On the first of these withdrawals, see United States, Department of State, *Foreign Relations of the United States* 9 (1945):156–58. For a thorough discussion of the impact of these new weapons systems, particularly the atomic bomb, on Washington's plans for the Panama Canal, see Major, "Wasting Asset." Major focuses on the two-fold dilemma Washington faced regarding the canal. First, the United States government had to decide what strategic value to assign to the canal after the war; second, Washington had to determine how the canal would fit into its blueprint for a postwar world. Renegotiation of the 1942 base accord was central to both of these issues.

24. United States, Department of State, *Foreign Relations of the United States* 5 (1943):310–12. During negotiations for the Filós-Hines Treaty following the war, Panamanian officials secretly contacted the governments of other countries that had granted Washington temporary privileges during the war in the name of hemispheric defense. When asked about the nature of their relations

with the United States, officials from these countries, including Cuba, Brazil, and Ecuador, all responded that the United States had willingly abandoned the sites "upon cessation of hostilities" (beginning soon after the Japanese surrender at Pearl Harbor). On these other evacuations, see for example Ambassador Abdiel Arias to Minister of Foreign Relations Ricardo J. Alfaro, Rio de Janeiro, April 14, 1947; República del Ecuador to Honorable Embajada de Panamá, "Memorandum," May 27, 1947; and note from Panama's Ambassador in Cuba to Minister Alfaro, July 18, 1947. These three letters and those from other American republics surveyed are located in República de Panamá, Ministro de Relaciones Exteriores, *Sitios de defensa, Tomos 1–17 (1942–1947)*. All seventeen volumes are held in Panama's Archivos de Relaciones Exteriores, file cabinet no. 62, drawer nos. 62.1 and 62.2.

25. Memorandum titled "Over-All Examination of U.S. Requirements for Military Bases and Rights: Memorandum by the Commanding General, Army Air Force," September 10, 1945, RG 218, Records of the United States Joint Chiefs of Staff, JCS 570/37, CCS 360, Box 266, NA.

26. This plan (570/2 and later 570/3) hinged on three strategic periods: enforced peace in Europe and war in the Pacific; worldwide peace enforced under the Four Power Agreement, pending establishment of a worldwide organization for collective security; and peace maintained by formally established worldwide machinery. See Joint Secretariat

Memorandum titled "Joint Chiefs of Staff: U.S. Base Requirements for Post-War Air Bases," January 10, 1944, RG 218, CCS 360, Box 264, NA.

27. JCS Joint Memorandum titled "Strategic Concept and Plan for the Employment of United States Armed Forces: Report by the Joint Staff Planners Concurred on by the Joint Strategic Survey Committee," September 19, 1945, RG 218, Records of the United States Joint Chiefs of Staff, JCS 1518, CCS 381, Box 293, p. 7, NA; and James F. Schnabel, Historical Division, Joint Chiefs of Staff, *The History of the Joint Chiefs of Staff: The Joint Chiefs of Staff and National Policy* (Washington, DC, 1979), 299–315. These primary base areas included the Philippines, the Hawaiian Islands, the Marianas Islands, the southwestern Alaska-Aleutian area, Newfoundland, Puerto Rico, the Virgin Islands, and the Azores, in addition to the Canal Zone.

28. Major, "Wasting Asset," 129.

29. JCS Joint Memorandum titled "Strategic Concept and Plan for the Employment of United States Armed Forces"; and Schnabel, *History of the Joint Chiefs of Staff*, 304–6. These secondary areas included central and western Alaska, Midway Island, Johnson Island, Wake Island, Marcus Island, Bonin-Volcano Islands, Truk Island, Kwajalein Island, Manus, American Samoa, the Galapagos Islands, the Ryukyus Islands, Canton Island, Bermuda, Iceland, Greenland, the Cape Verde Islands, Ascension Island, Guantanamo Bay (Cuba), Trinidad, and the Natal-Recife area of Brazil, in addition to the temporary airfields in the Republic of Panama.

30. Schnabel, *History of the Joint Chiefs of Staff*, 304–6.

31. Ibid.

32. When Japanese troops and white Russians withdrew from eastern Siberia, the Lenin government (USSR) united Armenia and Azerbaijan in March 1922 to form the Transcaucasian Soviet Federated Socialist Republic. Then in 1936 the new Soviet constitution made Azerbaijan, Georgia, and Armenia separate Federated Socialist Republics. This change more accurately reflected the region's ethnic diversity. Like many eastern Siberians, Azerbaijanis resented Russian imperialism, including the expanded Russian military presence, with air bases, in Azerbaijan during the Second World War.

33. On the Azerbaijan incident, see Pippin, *The Remón Era*, 20; on the Anglo-Egyptian conflict, see Major, "Wasting Asset," 136.

34. Patterson to Secretary of State James F. Byrnes, September 12, 1946, RG 319, Army General and Special Staffs, Plans and Operations Division, Decimal File 676. to 678., 1946–1948, Case 1, Box 135, NA. On State Department acknowledgment of popular opposition in Panama, see Solana memorandum, October 3, 1946, RG 59, Lot 55 D 216, Records of the Office of American Republic Affairs, 1918–1947, Memoranda on Panama, Box 56, vol. 6 (June 1945–December 1947), NA.

35. "Cessation of Hostilities of World War II: A Proclamation by the President of the United States of America," December 31, 1947. This proclamation is located in a file titled "Sitios de defensa, o, expiración del

convenio de 1942–6. Convenio de 10 de Diciembre de 1947," Archivo y Biblioteca de Relaciones Exteriores, Panama City, Panama.

36. Benedetti to Alfaro, "Sitios de defensa- o -expiración del convenio de 1942–6. Convenio de 10 de Diciembre de 1947," Archivo de Relaciones Exteriores, Panama City, Panama. This is an unbound folder. Benedetti's May 9 letter sparked a heated exchange with Alfaro that lasted several days and that clarified Alfaro's—and the administration's—position regarding the 1942 agreement.

37. Ibid.

38. Secret letter to the commanding general, Caribbean Defense Command Canal Zone, May 20, 1947, RG 319, Army General and Special Staffs, Plans and Operations Division, Decimal File 676. to 678., 1946–1948, Case 1, Box 135, NA.

39. See Bennett to Briggs et al., RG 59, Records of the Office of American Republic Affairs, 1918–1947, Memoranda on Panama, Box 56, vol. 6 (June 1945–December 1947), NA; Newbegin to Wise and Briggs, "War Department Willing to Withdraw from Bases," ibid.; and "United States Requirements for Military Rights in the Republic of Panama," May 20, 1947, RG 319, Army General and Special Staffs, Plans and Operations Division, Decimal File 676. to 678., 1946–1948, Case 1, Box 135, NA.

40. Barber to Finley and Baker, February 8, 1940, RG 59, Records of the Office of American Republic Affairs, 1918–1947, Memoranda on Panama, Box 54, vol. 2 (August

1939–December 1940), NA. In this early document it is apparent that the State Department and the military already disagreed regarding the situation in Panama.

41. Enrique A. Jiménez, *Memorias* (Panama City, 1956), 96–97.

42. "Es falso el temor de represalias económicas," *El Panamá América* (December 20, 1947), p. 1.

43. Acosta, *La influencia decisiva de la opinion pública*, 27.

44. See Díaz to Remón (Comandante Primer Jefe del Cuerpo de Policía Nacional), 12 December 1947, "Notas enviadas: sección administrativa, sección judicial, Policía Nacional y sección de extranjero del cuerpo de policía. Enero a Diciembre 1947," Archivo Nacional, Panama City. This set of documents contains a series of letters from Díaz to Remón, written between December 12, 1947, and December 20, 1947, wherein Díaz advises Remón of notification he has received from various groups, in compliance with the law, stating their intentions to congregate peacefully.

45. Interview with Dr. Rosa María Britton, Panama City, July 1989. See especially chapter 14, "Andrés." Dr. Britton won the 1984 "Ricardo Miró" award for this excellent novel.

46. *Foreign Relations of the United States* 8 (1947):943–44; "Remón Regrets Disturbances; Lauds Police," *Panama Star and Herald*, December 13, 1947; and "Declaraciones del Cmdte. José A. Remón," *La estrella de Panamá*, December 13, 1947, p. 1. According to State Department reports, the Communist Party of

Panama had approximately one thousand members in 1947. For more information on the Partido del Pueblo, see Pippin, *The Remón Era*; and Acosta, *La influencia decisiva de la opinion pública*.

47. Groups of protestors who joined the opposition cause, or stepped up their earlier efforts, after the events of December included (in no particular order) the Patriotic Youth Front, the Association of Panamanian Professors, the Federation of Panamanian Students, the Union for Collaboration of Teachers in Schools in the Capital, the National Society of Panamanian Nurses, the United Teachers of Chorillo, the Federated Association of Arts and Crafts, the Social Club of Vista Hermosa, the Assembly of Delegates of the Federation of Parents' Clubs of the Capital City, the Independent Civic Association, Veraguas Youth, the Panamanian Teachers' Union (five thousand members—nearly every teacher in the republic), the National Revolutionary Party, the Authentic Revolutionary Party, the Socialist Party, the Liberal Party, a group of ten thousand women marchers, the National Agrarian Party, the Popular Union, the Renovator Party, University Women, the Communist Party, the Professors of Physical Education (Panama City), the Youth Society of Atalaya, the Parent-Teacher Association of the National Institute, the International Assembly of Panamanian Youth, the student body of the Escuela Panamá, and the Union of Panamanian Theater Operators. See Appendix F.

For further comment on these groups, see Acosta, *La influencia decisiva de la opinion pública*, 30–31.

48. Díaz to Remón, (Comandante Primer Jefe del Cuerpo de Policía Nacional), 12 December 1947, "Notas enviadas: sección administrativa, sección judicial, Policía Nacional y sección de extranjero del cuerpo de policía [*sic*]. Enero a Diciembre 1947," Archivo Nacional, Panama City

49. Regarding student activities, see "Students Hold Quiet Meeting against Bases," and "Colon Students Hold Protest Rally in Park," *Panama Star and Herald*, December 14, 1947, p. 1; "Paro General Decretan Estudiantes y Profesores," *El Panamá América*, December 15, 1947, p. 1; "Panama Schools on Strike; Five Teachers Are Jailed," *Panama American*, December 15, 1947, p. 1; "El Paro Es Completo en las Escuelas del Gobierno y Privadas," *Panamá América*, December 16, 1947, p. 1; and "El Paro Se Extiende A Toda La República," *El Panamá América*, December 17, 1947, p. 1.

For coverage of the women's march of December 16, see "10,000 Women Protest against Bases," *Panama Star and Herald*, December 17, 1947, p. 1; and "En Forma Solemne Pidió Ayer La Mujer Panameña Rechazo Del Pacto," *El Panamá América*, December 17, 1947, p. 1.

50. "Knives and Bases," *Time* (December 29, 1947), 26. Assembly President Harmodio Arosemena Forte is quoted as saying, "Nobody will vote for the bases when they can look out the window and see 10,000 boys sharpening their knives." On the evening of December 19, Arosemena had attended an antitreaty rally in Panama City, where he pledged

himself to vote against the treaty. It is therefore conceivable that his statement regarding "10,000 boys with knives" intentionally exaggerated the situation to sway opinion within the assembly. See "Es falso el temor de represalias económicas," *El Panamá América* (December 20, 1947), p. 1.

51. See *Foreign Relations of the United States* 8 (1947):944–45; and Jorge Conte-Porras, *La rebelión de las esfinges: Historia del movimieito estudiantil panameño* (Panama City, 1978), 54–55. Officials in both countries had previously thought that they had sufficient support in the National Assembly to pass the legislation. However, as noted in the *Foreign Relations* document, "several deputies from the province of Colón stated privately that, while they promised Jiménez their vote, they did not promise to allow themselves to be shot at."

52. "Por Unanimidad se Pronunció la Cámara," *El Panamá América*, December 23, 1947, p. 1; "U.S. Official Says 'No' Vote 'Most Unfortunate,'" *Panama American*, December 23, 1947, p. 1.

53. Pippin, *The Remón Era*, 21.

54. Conniff, *Panama and the United States: The Forced Alliance* (Athens, GA, 1992), 102–3. Here Conniff cites Remón and the 1952 report by Almon Wright, "The United States and Panama, 1933–1949," U.S. Department of State, Top Secret Research Report 499 (August 1952). Pippin referred to earlier works by John Biesanz and Richard G. Massock citing rising unemployment, market shrinkage, and declining imports triggered by the war's end. Similarly Wright notes rationing of certain foodstuffs following the war, but he fails to deal specifically with other issues broached by Pippin and his sources.

55. See República de Panamá, Contraloría General de la República, Dirección de Estadística y Censo, *The National Income and National Accounts of the Republic of Panama*, 75–85. See note 15, above, for further sources on Panama's fiscal situation during this period.

56. Conte-Porras, *La rebelión de las esfinges*, 17; and Mavis Biesanz and John Biesanz, *The People of Panama* (New York, 1955), 155. For the text of Harmodio Arias's dedicatory speech, offered at the dedication of the National University on October 7, 1935, see Mélida Ruth Sepúlveda, *Harmodio Arias Madrid: El hombre, el estadista, y el periodista* (Panama City, 1983), 155–59. For further insight into student activities during this period, see Conte-Porras, *Panameños ilustres* (Panama City, 1978), 204–15.

Conclusion

1. Amos Perlmutter and Valerie Plave Bennett, *The Political Influence of the Military: A Comparative Reader* (New Haven, 1980), 199–200.

2. Ibid.

3. As elsewhere in the text, the meaning of *power* here is Samuel P. Huntington's definition: "the capacity to control [or affect] the behavior of other people." See Huntington, *The Soldier and the State: The Theory*

of *Politics and Civil-Military Relations* (New York, 1964).

4. Conte-Porras, *La rebelión de las esfinges: Historia del movimiento estudiantil panameño* (Panama City, 1978).

5. Michael Conniff, *Black Labor on a White Canal: Panama, 1904–1981* (Pittsburgh, 1985).

6. Huntington, *The Soldier and the State*.

Epilogue

1. These men included Domingo Díaz Arosemena (October 1, 1948–July 28, 1949), Daniel Chanis (July 28, 1948–November 20, 1949), Roberto F. Chiari Remón (November 20, 1949–November 24, 1949), Arnulfo Arias Madrid (November 25, 1949–May 10, 1951), and Alcibíades Arosemena (May 10, 1951–October 1, 1952). To understand how these individuals fit into Panama's sociopolitical structure, see Marco Antonio Gandásegui, *La concentración del poder económico en Panamá* (Panama City, 1967), 43–68.

2. This commercial convention rerouted international commercial traffic from Albrook Air Force Base in the Canal Zone to Panama's new airport, Tocumen International. However, several groups that had opposed the Filós-Hines accord resented Washington's role in Panamanian commercial issues, and they remained suspicious of North American motives. In a series of 1949 letters to First Commander Remón, Panama City Mayor Alberto Navarro identified those groups intending to

protest the commercial agreement. See Navarro to Remón, in "Copias a comandancia, año 1949." This is a clothbound collection of documents held in the National Archives in Panama City.

3. Barber to Miller, November 29, 1949, RG 59, Lot 53 D 26, Records of Assistant Secretary of State Edward G. Miller, National Archives, Washington, DC (NA).

4. See *El Panamá América*, November 25, 1949, p. 1.

5. On the afternoon of May 9, 1951, Murray Wise, American Chargé d'Affaires in Panama, reported that "a large and most impressive anti-Arias manifestation was staged before the *Comandancia* last night; purpose was to get Remón to move against Arias. Remón refused. . . . This morning a completely effective nation-wide strike was called." See Wise to Miller, May 9, 1951, RG 59, Lot 53 D 26, Records of Assistant Secretary of State Edward G. Miller, NA.

6. Pippin, *The Remón Era: An Analysis of a Decade of Events in Panama, 1947–1957* (Stanford, 1964), 73.

7. Commenting on Remón's ongoing predicament vis-à-vis the Arnulfistas, one official of the Central Intelligence Agency made the following observation in January of 1952: "Remón, as President, could expect the continuing, implacable opposition of the Patriotic Front [Arnulfistas] and the Communists. If he had come to power by the use of force those elements would claim justification for their charge of militarism against him and would probably receive greater popu-

lar sympathy for their continued opposition than would otherwise be the case. Remón could probably control the situation, however, so long as he had the support of the National Police." See United States, Central Intelligence Agency, "Special Estimate: Probable Political Developments in the Republic of Panama through Mid-1952" (SE-21: January 24, 1952), 2.

8. See Commander Remón's account of these events in "Informe presentado por el Coronel José Antonio Remón Cantera, Comandante Primer Jefe del Cuerpo de Policía Nacional . . ." (Panama City, 1951).

9. Halle to Miller, memorandum titled "Development of U.S. Latin American Policy in Terms of U.S. World Objectives," October 26, 1950,

RG 218, Records of the United States Joint Chiefs of Staff, NND867203, Box 1, Tab 1, National Archives, Washington, DC (NA).

10. United States, Central Intelligence Agency, "National Intelligence Estimate Number 80-54: The Caribbean Republics" (August 24, 1954), p. 6. Submitted by the director of the Central Intelligence Agency, this report was a collaborative effort between various civilian and military branches of the United States intelligence community.

11. See "Major Deal Reached by RP Parties," *Panama Star and Herald*, April 10, 1952, p. 1; and República de Panamá, Contraloría General de la República, *Estadística electoral: Elecciones populares de 1948 y 1952* (Panama City, 1956).

☙

Bibliography

Unpublished Primary Sources

Iglesia Católica. Registros Parroqiales. LDS Church microfilmed copies of original documents. Parishes consulted for this study include the parish of San José in David (films 760741–760747), the parish of San Juan Bautista in Aguadulce (films 1809803–1809804), the parish of Santa Ana in Panama City (films 1091673–1091675), the parish of La Merced in Panama City (films 1994125 and 1094128), the parish of Santa Librada in Las Tablas (film 1089178), and the parish of San Juan Bautista in Chitré (films 1089485–1089486). Special thanks to my research assistant, Kirk Hawkins, for his assistance with these documents.

República de Panamá. Ministro de Gobierno y Justicia. Policía Nacional. Documents from various years. This collection is held in Panama's National Archives in Panama City. It is indexed in a book entitled "Inventario de los documentos del Período Republicano: 1903–." See especially pages 38–39 of the index, entries 311–21. See also the folder labeled "Notas enviadas: sección administrativa, sección judicial, Policía Nacional y sección extranjero del cuerpo de policía: Enero a Diciembre 1947." This is an especially important collection, because many police records were confiscated during the 1989 invasion and are not available for public scrutiny. Neither invading forces nor looters violated the National Archives.

República de Panamá. Ministerio de la Presidencia. Correspondence between Adolf Hitler and Arnulfo Arias. These documents are kept in an unmarked manila folder in the National Archives in Panama City.

República de Panamá. Ministerio de Relaciones Exteriores. "Sitios de defensa, Tomos 1–17: 1942–1947." This is the single most complete, accessible collection of documents in existence on the subject of the base controversy during the period 1940–47. It is located in file cabinet no. 62, drawer nos. 62.1 and 62.2 in the Archives of Foreign Relations in Panama City.

United States. Central Intelligence Agency. "National Intelligence Estimate Number 80-54: The Caribbean Republics" (August 24, 1954).

———. "Report on Panama." In *CIA Research Reports: Latin America, 1946-1947.* Microform. Richter Library collection, University of Miami, Coral Gables, FL.

———. "Special Estimate: Probable Political Developments in the Republic of Panama through Mid-1952" (SE-21: January 24, 1952).

United States. Department of the Army. Record Group 319. Army General and Special Staffs. Plans and Operations Divisions. Decimal File 1946–1948. Various files. National Archives, Washington, DC.

United States. Department of State. Record Group 59. Records of the Office of American Republic Affairs. Various files. National Archives, Washington, DC.

———. Record Group 59. General Records of the Department of State. Office of American Republic Affairs, 1918–1947. Vols. 1–3. Various files. National Archives, Washington, DC.

———. Record Group 59. Records of the Division of Latin American Affairs: Legation of the United States of America. Various files. National Archives, Washington, DC.

———. Record Group 59. Records of the Division of Latin American Affairs. Various files. Includes numerous boxes under the subheading of "Memoranda on Panama." National Archives, Washington, DC.

United States. Joint Chiefs of Staff. Record Group 218. Records of the United States Joint Chiefs of Staff. Central Decimal File, 1946–1947. Post War Military Base Requirements. Various files. National Archives, Washington, DC.

———. Record Group 218. Records of the United States Joint Chiefs of Staff. Various boxes and files. National Archives, Washington, DC.

United States. Panama Canal Commission. Record Group 185. General Correspondence of the Isthmian Canal Commission. Various years. National Archives Annex, Washington, DC.

United States. War Department. Record Group 165. Records of the War Department General and Special Staffs. Military Intelligence Division Correspondence, 1917–1941. Various files. National Archives, Washington, DC.

Published Primary Documents

La Junta Política Nacional. *La opinión nacional y la candidatura presidencial de 1920 a 1924.* Panama City, Panama: Los Talleres de La Estrella de Panamá, 1924.

Pan American Union. *Bulletin of the Pan American Union* 56 (March 1923).

Remón Cantera, José Antonio. "Informe presentado por el Coronel José Antonio Remón Cantera, Comandante Primer Jefe del Cuepo de Policía Nacional a los sucesos ocurridos en la ciudad de Panamá, durante los

días 6, 7, 8, 9, y 10 de Mayo de 1951 . . ." Panama City: Editora de la
Nación, 1951.

República de Panamá. Caja de Seguridad Social. Departamento Actuarial y de
Estadística. *Diez años de labor: Síntesis estadística.* Panama City, Panama: Imprenta Nacional, 1952.

República de Panamá. Contraloría General de la República. Dirección de
Estadística y Censo. *Boletín de estadística.* Panama City, Panama. Various volumes. Held at the General Accounting Office, Panama City.

————. *Boletín estadística: Secciones agrícola y demográfica.* Panama City,
Panama: Imprenta Nacional. Various volumes. Held at the General
Accounting Office, Panama City.

————. *Censo de población 1940: Volúmenes provinciales.* Panama City,
Panama: Imprenta Nacional, 1943–44.

————. *Estadística electoral: Elecciones populares de 1948 y 1952.* Panama
City, Panama: Imprenta Nacional, 1956. Held at the General Accounting Office, Panama City.

————. *Estadística Panameña.* Panama City, Panama: Imprenta Nacional.
Various volumes. Held at the General Accounting Office, Panama City.

————. *The National Income and National Accounts of the Republic of Panama: 1944–1952.* Panama City, Panama: n.p., 1953. This report was
prepared for the government of Panama by Dr. H. Rijken van Olst,
United Nations expert on national income statistics.

República de Panamá. Jurado Nacional de Elecciones. *Ley 39 (de 19 de Septiembre de 1946) sobre elecciones populares y sentencias).* Panama City,
Panama: Imprenta Nacional, Orden 0246, 1948.

República de Panamá. Ministerio de Gobierno y Justicia. *Memoria del Ministerio de Gobierno y Justicia.* Panama City, Panama: Imprenta de la
Nación, 1945.

————. Juan Antonio Susto, comp. *Leyes sobre elecciones populares.* Panama
City, Panama: Imprenta Nacional, 1941.

República de Panamá. Ministerio de Relaciones Exteriores. "Boletín semanal
de información para las embajadas, legaciones, y consulados de la república." Panama City, Panama: Imprenta Nacional. Various editions. Held
at the Archives of Foreign Relations, Panama City, Panama.

————. *Memoria del Ministro de Relaciones Exteriores.* Panama City, Panama:
Imprenta Nacional, 1948.

República de Panamá. Policía Nacional. Comandancia. "Informe presentado
por el Coronel José Antonio Remón Cantera, Comandante Primer Jefe
del Cuerpo de Policía Nacional a la Honorable Asamblea Nacional de
Panamá en relación con los sucesos ocurridos en la ciudad de Panamá,
durante los días 6, 7, 8, 9, y 10 Mayo de 1951." Panama City, Panama:
Editora de la Nación, 1951.

República de Panamá. Secretaría de Agricultura y Obras Públicas. Dirección
General de Censo. *1930 Censo Demográfico.* Tomos I–II. Panama City,
Panama: Imprenta Nacional, 1931.

———. Departamento de Estadística. Sección Demográfica. *Boletín de estadística.* Panama City, Panama: Imprenta Nacional. Various volumes. Held at the General Accounting Office, Panama City.

———. Departamento de Estadística. Secciones Demográfica-Commercial-Economía [*sic*]. *Boletín de Estadística.* Panama City, Panama: Imprenta Nacional. Various volumes. Held at the General Accounting Office, Panama City.

República de Panamá. Secretario del Estado. "Memoria que el Secretario de Estado hace en despacho de relaciones exteriores presenta a la Asamblea Nacional en sus sesiones ordinarias de 1936." Panama City, Panama: Imprenta de la Nación, 1936. Held at the Archives of Foreign Relations, Panama.

Roberts, George. *Investigación económica de la República de Panamá.* Panama City, Panama: n. p., 1932. Roberts, Vice President of the National City Bank of New York, was commissioned by the government of Panama to review the Panamanian federal budget. This report contains his findings. It is located in the University of Florida library system, call no. 330.9862 R644i.

Schnabel, James F. *The History of the Joint Chiefs of Staff: The Joint Chiefs of Staff and National Policy.* Washington, DC: U.S. Government Printing Office, 1979.

United Nations. Department of Economic and Social Affairs. Economic Commission for Latin America. *External Financing in Latin America.* New York: n. p., 1965.

United States. Department of State. "Use by the United States of Military Force in the Internal Affairs of Colombia, etc. . . " 58th Cong., 2d. Sess., Doc. no. 143 (1904).

———. *Foreign Relations of the United States.* Various years.

United States. Senate. Joint Congressional Committee on Inaugural Ceremonies. *Inaugural Addresses of the Presidents of the United States from Washington (1789) to Bush (1989).* Bicentennial Edition. 101st Cong., 1st Sess., Senate Doc. No. 101–10. Washington, DC: U.S. Government Printing Office, 1989.

Published Secondary Sources: Monographs

Acosta, David. *La influencia decisiva de la opinión pública en el rechazo del convenio Filós-Hines de 1947* 3d ed. Panama City, Panama: Impresora de la Nación, 1983.

Aguilar, Luis E., ed. *Marxism in Latin America.* New York, New York: Alfred A. Knopf, 1968.

Alfaro, Ricardo J. *Medio siglo de relaciones entre Panamá y los Estados Unidos.* Panama City, Panama: Imprenta Nacional, 1953.

———. *Historia documentada de las negociaciones para la celebración del tratado de 1926*. Panama City, Panama: Editorial Universitaria, 1982.

Araúz, Celestino Andrés. *Belisario Porras y las relaciones de Panamá con Los Estados Unidos*. Panama City, Panama: Imprenta Universitaria, 1988.

———. *La independencia de Panamá en 1821*. Panama City, Panama: n.p., n.d.

———. *Panamá y sus relaciones internacionales*. 2 vols. Panama City, Panama: Editorial Universitaria, 1994.

Araúz, Celestino Andrés, Carlos Manuel Gasteazoro, and Armando Muñóz Pinzón. *La historia de Panamá en sus textos*. Vol. 1. Panama City, Panama, 1980.

Araúz, Celestino Andrés, and Patricia Pizzurno Gelós. *El Panamá columbiano, 1821–1903*. Panama City, Panama: Litho Editorial Chen, 1993.

Araúz, Virgilio. *Cinco ensayos*. n.p., n.d.

Arosemena, Justo. *El estado federal de Panamá*. Panama City, Panama: Editorial Universitaria, 1974.

Banfield, Edward C., ed. *Civility and Citizenship in Liberal Democratic Societies*. New York: Paragon House, 1992.

Bell, Abraham. *El movimiento estudiantil de 1958*. Panama City, Panama: n.p., 1992.

Beluche Mora, Isidro A.. *Acción Comunal: Surgimiento y estructuración del nacionalismo panameño*. Panama City, Panama: Editorial Condor, 1981.

Bemis, Samuel Flagg. *Latin American Policy of the United States*. New York: Harcourt Brace, 1943.

Benedetti, Adolfo Alberto. *Arnulfo Arias: El caudillo*. Panama City, Panama: Editora Humanidad, 1963.

Bergquist, Charles. *Coffee and Conflict in Colombia, 1886–1910*. Durham, NC: Duke University Press, 1984.

———. *Labor and the Course of American Democracy: U.S. History in Latin American Perspective*. New York: W.W. Norton, 1997.

Biesanz, Mavis, and John Biesanz. *The People of Panama*. New York: Columbia University Press, 1955.

Bolton, Herbert Eugene, and E. Morse Stephens, eds. *The Pacific in Perspective: Papers and Addresses Presented at the Panama-Pacific Historical Conference Held at San Francisco, Berkeley, and Palo Alto, California, July 19–23, 1915*. New York: Macmillan, 1917.

Borah, Woodrow, and Sherburne Cook. *Essays in Population History*. 3 vols. Berkeley: University of California Press, 1971–79.

Bourgeois, Phillipe I. *Ethnicity at Work: Divided Labor on a Central American Banana Plantation*. Baltimore, MD: Johns Hopkins University Press, 1989.

Boutín I., Gilberto. *Del régimen jurídico internacional de los Acuerdos Torrijos-Carter de 1977*. Panama City, Panama: Lotería Nacional de Beneficencia, 1987.

Boyd, Carolyn P. *Praetorian Politics in Liberal Spain*. Chapel Hill, NC: University of North Carolina Press, 1979.

Britton, Rosa María. *El señor de las lluvias y el viento*. San José, Costa Rica: Litografía y Imprenta LIL, S.A., 1983.

Bulmer-Thomas, Victor. *The Political Economy of Central America Since 1920*. New York: University Press, 1987.

Burkholder, Mark A., and Dewitt S.Chandler. *From Impotence to Authority: The Spanish American Crown and the American Audiencias, 1687–1808*. Columbia: University of Missouri Press, 1977.

Burns, Edward Bradford. *The Poverty of Progress: Latin America in the Nineteenth Century*. Berkeley: University of California Press, 1980.

Bushnell, David. *The Santander Regime in Gran Colombia*. Westport, CT: Greenwood Press, 1954.

———. *The Making of Modern Colombia: A Nation in Spite of Itself*. Berkeley: University of California Press, 1993.

Carranza, Mario Esteban. *Fuerzas armadas y estado de excepción en América Latina*. Mexico City: Siglo Veintiuno Editores, 1978.

Castillero Calvo, Alfredo. *Conquista, evangelización y resistencia: ¿Triunfo o fracaso de la política indigenista?* Panama City, Panama: Editorial Mariano Arosemena, 1995.

——— *Economía terciaria y sociedad: Panamá siglos xvi y xvii*. Panama City, Panama: La Nación, 1980.

———. *Los negros y mulatos libres en la historia social panameña*. Panama City, Panama: Impresora Panamá, 1969.

Castillero R., Ernesto J. *Raices de la independencia de Panamá*. Panama City, Panama: Impresora de la Nación, 1978.

———. *La causa inmediata de la emancipación de Panamá*. Panama City, Panama: Imprenta Nacional, 1933.

Christian, Shirley. *Revolution in the Family*. New York: Vintage Books, 1986.

Collier, Ruth Berins, and David Collier. *Shaping the Political Arena: Critical Junctures, the Labor Movement, and Regime Dynamics in Latin America*. Princeton, NJ: Princeton University Press, 1991.

Conniff, Michael. *Panama and the United States: The Forced Alliance*. Athens: University of Georgia Press, 1992.

———. *Black Labor on a White Canal: Panama, 1904–1981*. Pittsburgh: University of Pittsburgh Press, 1985.

Conte-Porras, Jorge. *Requiem por la revolución*. San Jose, Costa Rica: Litografía y Imprenta LIL, S.A., 1990.

———. *Arnulfo Arias Madrid*. Panama City, Panama: Litho Impresora Panamá, 1980.

———. *La rebelión de las esfinges: Historia del movimiento estudiantil panameño*. Panama City, Panama: Litho Impresora Panamá, 1978.

Conte-Porras, Jorge, and Enoch Castillero Calvo. *Santa Ana*. Panama City, Panama: Banco Nacional de Panamá, 1984.

Cuestas Gómez, Carlos. *Soldados Americanos en Chrirquí*. Panama City, Panama: Litografía ENAN, S.A., 1990.

Cuevas, Alexander, Everaldo Tomlinson, and Demetrio Porras. *Alcances e interpretaciones del problema inquilinario a través de la historia*. Panama City, Panama: Ediciones de la Revista Tareas, 1975.

Dallek, Robert. *Franklin Delano Roosevelt and American Foreign Policy, 1932–1945*. New York: Oxford University Press, 1979.

Delper, Helen. *Red against Blue: The Liberal Party in Colombian Politics, 1863–1899*. University: University of Alabama Press, 1981.

Diez Castillo, Luis A.. *El canal de Panamá y su gente*. Panama City, Panama: Imprenta Julio Mercado Rudas, 1981.

Dinges, John. *Our Man in Panama: How General Noriega Used the United States and Made Millions in Drugs and Arms*. New York: Random House, 1990.

Duggan, Laurence. *The Americas: The Search for Hemisphere Security*. New York: Henry Holt and Company, 1949.

Durham, William H. *Scarcity and Survival in Central America: Ecological Origins of the Soccer War*. Stanford: Stanford University Press, 1979.

Eagleburger, Lawrence S. *The Case against Panama's Noriega*. Washington, DC: United States Department of State, Bureau of Public Affairs, Editorial Division, 1989.

Espino, Rodrigo, and Raúl Martínez, eds. *Textos de la historia centroamericana y el Caribe, vol. 2: Panamá*. Mexico City: Instituto de Investigaciones Dr. José María Luís Mora, 1988.

Farnsworth, David N., and James W. McKenney. *U.S.–Panama Relations, 1903–1978: A Study in Linkage Politics*. Boulder, CO: Westview Press, 1983.

Figueroa Navarro, Alfredo. *Dominio y sociedad el Panamá colombiano, 1821–1903*. 3d ed. Panama City, Panama: Editorial Universitaria, 1982.

Finer, S. E. *The Man on Horseback: The Role of the Military in Politics*. 2d ed. Boulder, CO: Westview Press, 1988.

Fisk, Harvey E. *The Inter-Ally Debts: An Analysis of War and Post-War Public Finances*. New York: Banker's Trust Company, 1924.

Fox, Robert W., and Jerrold W. Huguet. *Population and Urban Trends in Central America and Panama*. Washington, DC: Inter-American Development Bank, 1977.

Gandásegui, Marco A. *La democracia en Panamá*. Mexico City: Editorial Mestiza, S.A. de C.V., 1989.

———. *La concentración del poder económico en Panamá*. Panama City, Panama: Ediciones de la Revista Tareas, 1967.

———. *La fuerza de trabajo en el agro: Experiencia de desarrollo capitalista en Panamá*. 2d ed. Panama City, Panama: CELA, 1990.

———. *La lucha de clases y la zona del canal*. Panama City, Panama: Asociación Panameña de Sociología, 1975.

Gandásegui, Marco A., Georgina Jiménez de López, Hernán F. Porras, and Ricaurte Soler. *Las clases sociales en Panamá: Grupos humanos, clases medias, elites y oligarquía*. Panama City, Panama: Centro de Estudios Latinoamericanos "Justo Arosemena" (CELA), 1993.

Gandásegui, Marco A., Alejandro Saavedra, Andrés Achong, and Iván Quintero. *Las luchas obreras en Panamá, 1850–1978*. Panama City, Panama: Talleres Diálogo, 1980.

Goldrich, Daniel. *Radical Nationalism: The Political Orientations of Panamanian Law Students*. Michigan State University: Bureau of Social and Political Research, 1961.

Gómez Duque, Diana. *Una guerra irregular entre dos ideologías: Un enfoque liberal*. Bogotá, Colombia: Ediciones Tercer Mundo, 1991.

Greene, Graham. *Getting to Know the General: The Story of an Involvement*. New York: Simon and Schuster, 1984.

Guevara Mann, Carlos. *Panamanian Militarism: A Historical Interpretation*. Athens: Ohio University Press, 1996.

Hearndon, Patrick J. *Roosevelt Confronts Hitler: America's Entry into World War II*. Champaign: University of Illinois Press, 1987.

Heinrichs, Waldo. *Threshold of War: Franklin D. Roosevelt and American Entry into World War II*. New York: Oxford University Press, 1988.

Howe, James. *Cantos y oraciones del congreso cuna*. Panama City, Panama: Editorial Universitaria, 1979.

———. *The Kuna Gathering: Contemporary Village Politics in Panama*. Austin: University of Texas Press, 1986.

Huntington, Samuel P. *The Soldier and the State: The Theory of Politics and Civil-Military Relations*. New York: Vintage Books, 1964.

———. *Political Order in Changing Societies*. New Haven, Connecticut: Yale University press, 1968.

Huntington, Samuel P., and Clement H. Moore, eds. *Authoritarian Politics in Modern Society: The Dynamics of Established One-Party Systems*. New York: Basic Books, 1970.

Huntington, Samuel P., and Joan M. Nelson, eds. *No Easy Choice: Political Participation in Developing Countries*. Cambridge, MA: Harvard University Press, 1976.

Huntington, Samuel P., and Joseph S. Nye, Jr., eds. *Global Dilemmas*. Lanham, Maryland: University Press of America, 1985.

Huntington, Samuel P., and Myron Weiner, eds. *Understanding Political Development: An Analytical Study*. Boston: Little, Brown, and Company, 1987.

Jaén Suárez, Omar. *La población del Istmo de Panamá del siglo xvi al siglo xx*. Panama City, Panama: Impresora de la Nación, 1978.

———. *Geografía de Panamá*. Panama City, Panama: Imprenta del Banco Nacional de Panamá, 1985.

Janowitz, Morris. *Military Institutions and Coercion in Developing Nations*. Chicago: University of Chicago Press, 1977.

Janowitz, Morris, and Stephen D. Wesbrook, eds. *The Political Education of Soldiers*. Beverley Hills, CA: Sage Publishers, 1983.

Jiménez, Enrique A. *Memorias*. Panama City, Panama: Star and Herald Company, 1956.

Jurado, Jilma Noriega de. *Verdad y miseria de nuestros partidos políticos.* Panama City, Panama: n.p., n.d.

Kerr, Eleann. *The Effect of Wars and Revolutions on Government Securities: Internal and External.* New York: William Morris Imbrie & Co., 1917.

Klein, Herbert S. *Bolivia: The Evolution of a Multi-Ethnic Society.* New York: Oxford University Press, 1982.

Koster, R. M., and Guillermo Sánchez. *In the Time of the Tyrants: Panama, 1968–1990.* New York: W.W. Norton, 1990.

Krenn, Michael. *The Chains of Independence: U.S. Policy toward Central America, 1945–1954.* Armonk, NY: M.E. Sharpe, 1996.

———. *U.S. Policy toward Economic Nationalism in Latin America, 1917–1929.* Wilmington, DE: Scholarly Resource Books, 1990.

LaClau, Ernesto. *Politics and Ideology in Marxist Theory.* London: NLB, 1977.

LaFeber, Walter. *The American Age: United States Foreign Policy at Home and Abroad Since 1750.* New York: Norton Press, 1989.

———. *The Panama Canal: The Crisis in Historical Perspective.* New York, New York: Oxford University Press, 1978.

Langley, Lester. *America in the Americas: The United States in the Western Hemisphere.* Athens: University of Georgia Press, 1989.

Laserna, Mario. *Bolívar, un euro-americano frente a la ilustración y otros ensayos de interpretaci—n de la historia indoamericano.* Bogotá, Colombia: Ediciones Tercer Mundo, 1986.

Laughlin, J. Laurence. *Credit of the Nations: A Study of the European War.* New York: Charles Scribner's Sons, 1918.

Lemaitre Román, Eduardo. *Panamá y su separación de Colombia.* Bogotá, Colombia: Banco Popular, 1972; 4th ed., 1993.

Lewis, Lancelot S. *The West Indian in Panama, 1850–1914.* Washington, DC: University Press of America, 1980.

Lieuwen, Edwin L. *U.S. Policy in Latin America.* New York: Praeger Publishers, 1965.

López V., Dimas Arturo, comp. *Las fuerzas armadas de la República de Panamá, período 1903 a 1973.* Panama City, Panama: n.p., n.d.

Loveman, Brian, and Thomas M. Davies, eds. *The Politics of Antipolitics.* 2d ed. Lincoln: University of Nebraska Press, 1989.

Lynch, John. *The Spanish American Revolutions, 1808–1826* 2d ed. New York: W.W. Norton, 1986.

Major, John. *Prize Possession: The United States and the Panama Canal, 1903–1979.* Cambridge: Cambridge University Press, 1993.

Martin, Michel Louis, and Ellen Stern McCrate, eds. *The Military, Militarism, and the Polity: Essays Published in Honor of Morris Janowitz.* New York: Free Press, 1984.

Martínez, José de Jesus. *Mi General Torrijos.* Mexico City: Presencia Latinoamericana, 1988.

McCain, William D. *Los Estados Unidos y la República de Panamá.* 3d ed. Panama City, Panama: Editorial Universitaria, 1994.

Mellander, G. A.. *The United States in Panamanian Politics: The Intriguing Formative Years.* Danville, IL: Interstate Printers and Publishers., 1971.

Mena García, María del Carmen. *La sociedad de Panamá en el siglo xvi.* Seville: Artes Gráficas Padura, S.A., 1984.

———. *Temas en historia panameña.* Panama City, Panama: Editorial Universitaria, 1996.

Méndez Pereira, Octavio. *Justo Arosemena.* Panama City, Panama: Imprenta La Nación, 1919.

Muñóz, Hernando Franco. *Movimiento obrero panameño, 1914–1921.* Panama City, Panama: n.p., 1979.

Muñóz Pinzón, Armando. *La huelga inquilinaria de 1932.* Panama City, Panama: Editorial Universitaria, 1974.

Navas, Luis. *El movimiento obrero en Panamá, 1880–1914.* San José, Costa Rica: Artes Gráficas de Centroamérica, 1979.

Oehling, Hermann. *La función política del ejército.* Madrid: Instituto de Estudios Políticos, 1967.

Oller de Mulford, Juana. *Valores femeninos panameños.* Panama City, Panama: n.p., 1978.

Parsons, Talcott. *The Social System.* London: Free Press, 1964.

Partido Liberal Colombiano. *Encuentros y foros del liberalismo.* Bogotá, Colombia: Biblioteca del Pensamiento Liberal Colombiano, 1988.

Peña, Concha. *José Antonio Remón Cantera: Ensayo de biografía con notas de mi cuaderno de periodista.* Panama City, Panama: Imprenta La Nación, 1955.

Pereira, Renato. *Panamá: Fuerzas armadas y política.* Panama City, Panama: Ediciones Nueva Universidad, 1979.

Pérez Brignoli, Hector. *A Brief History of Central America.* Ricardo B. Sawrey and Susana Stettri de Sawrey, trans. Berkeley: University of California Press, 1989.

Perkins, Dexter. *A History of the Monroe Doctrine.* Boston: Little, Brown, and Company, 1955.

Perlmutter, Amos. *Egypt, The Praetorian State.* New Brunswick, NJ: Transaction Books, 1974.

———. *The Military and Politics in Modern Times: On Professional, Praetorians, and Revolutionary Soldiers.* New Haven, CT: Yale University Press, 1977.

———. *Modern Authoritarianism: A Comparative Institutional Analysis.* New Haven, CT: Yale University press, 1981.

———. *Political Roles and Military Rulers.* Totowa, NJ: F. Cass, 1981.

Perlmutter, Amos, and Valerie Plave Bennett, eds. *The Political Influence of the Military: A Comparative Reader.* New Haven, CT: Yale University Press, 1980.

Phillipps Collazos, Sharon. *Labor and Politics in Panama: The Torrijos Years.* Boulder, CO: Westview Press, 1991.

Pippin, Larry LaRae. *The Remón Era: An Analysis of a Decade of Events in Panama, 1947ñ1957.* Stanford, CA: Institute of Hispanic American and Luso-Brazilian Studies, 1964.

Pizzurno Gelós, Patricia. *Harmodio Arias Madrid y la Universidad de Panamá.* Panama City, Panama: Editorial de la Lotería Nacional, 1985.

Porras, Hernan F. *Papel histórico de los grupos humanos de Panamá.* Panama City, Panama: Litho Impresora Panamá, S.A., 1973.

Porter, Bruce D. *War and the Rise of the State: The Military Foundations of Modern Politics.* New York: The Free Press, 1994.

Portes, Alejandro, and John Walton. *Urban Latin America: The Political Condition from Above and Below.* Austin: University of Texas Press, 1976.

Priestly, George. *Military Government and Popular Participation in Panama: The Torrijos Regime, 1968–1975.* Boulder, CO: Westview Press, 1986.

Rael de González, Matilde. *Octavio Méndez Pereira: Una figura cumbre en la literatura panameña.* Panama City, Panama: Editorial Universitaria, 1987.

Ricord, Humberto. *Los clanes de la oligarquía panameña y el golpe militar de 1968.* Panama City, Panama: n.p., 1968.

———. *Noriega y Panamá: Orgía y aplastamiento de la narcodictadura.* Mexico City: Impresora Eficiencia, 1991.

———. *Panama en la Guerra de los Mil Días.* Panama City, Panama: Instituto Nacional de Cultura, 1989.

Rodríguez, José Ignacio, chief ed. and trans. *American Constitutions: A Compilation of the Political Constitutions of the Independent Nations of the New World.* Vol. 1. Washington, DC: U.S. Government Printing Office, 1906.

Romero, José Luis, and Luis Alberto Romero, comps. *Pensamiento conservador, 1815–1898.* Caracas, Venezuela: Editorial Arte, 1978.

Romero Otero, Francisco. *Las ideas liberales y la educación en Santander, 1818–1919: La cultura de la tolerancia y la de la intolerancia.* Bucaramanga, Colombia: Ediciones UIS, 1992.

Ropp, Steve. *Panamanian Politics: From Guarded Nation to National Guard.* Stanford: Stanford University Press, 1982.

Ruddle, Kenneth, and Philip Gillette, eds. *Latin American Political Statistics.* Los Angeles: University of California Press, 1972.

Samudio, David, Carlos Castro, Aníbal Pastor, Vilma Médica, and Elías A. Curundú. *Estudio socio económico y cultural de las familias que residen en la comunidad urbana de Curundú.* Panamá City, Panamá: Fundación Techo, 1993.

Sánchez-Albornoz, Nicolas. *The Population of Latin America: A History.* Trans. by W. A. R. Richardson. Berkeley: University of California Press, 1974.

Scranton, Margaret E. *The Noriega Years: U.S.–Panamanian Relations, 1981–1990.* Boulder, CO: Westview Press, 1991.

Sepúlveda, Mélida Ruth. *Harmodio Arias Madrid: El hombre, el estadista, y el periodista.* Panama City, Panama: Editorial Universitaria, 1983.

Soler, Ricaurte. *Clase y nación: problemática latinoamericana.* 2d ed. Panama City, Panama: Poligráfica S.A., 1985.

———. *Panamá: Historia de una crisis.* Mexico City: Siglo Veintiuno Editores, 1989.

———. *Panamá: Nación y oligarquía, 1925–1975.* Panama City, Panama: Ediciones de la Revista Tareas, 1976.

———. *El pensamiento político en los siglos xix y xx.* Panama City, Panama: Dutigrafía, 1988.

Souza, Ruben Darío César A. de León, Hugo A. Victor, and Carlos F. Changmarin. *Panamá 1903–1970.* Santiago, Chile: Sociedad Impresora, 1971.

Stein, Steve. *Populism in Peru: The Emergence of the Masses and the Politics of Social Control.* Madison: University of Wisconsin Press, 1980.

Stepan, Alfred. *The Military in Politics: Changing Patterns in Brazil.* Princeton: Princeton University Press, 1971.

———. *Rethinking Military Politics: Brazil and the Southern Cone.* Princeton, New Jersey: Princeton University Press, 1988.

Tello Burgos, Argelio. *Escritos de Justo Arosemena.* Panama City, Panama: Dutigrafía, 1985.

Teran, Oscar. *Panamá: Historia crítica del atraco yanqui mal llamado en Colombia la pérdida de Panamá y en Panamá nuestra independencia de Colombia.* Bogotá, Colombia: Carlos Valencia Editores, 1976.

Torrijos Herrera, Omar. *Torrijos.* Buenos Aires, Argentina: Editorial Cartago, 1986.

Vigón Suarodíaz, Jorge. *Milicia y política.* Madrid: Instituto de Estudios Políticos, 1947.

Villalba Bustillo, Carlos. *Los liberales en el poder: Del apogeo revolucionario a la decadencia clientelista.* Bogotá, Colombia: Ediciones Tercer Mundo, 1982.

Walton, John. *Urban Poverty in Latin America.* Washington, DC: Woodrow Wilson Center for Scholars, 1993.

Ward, Christopher. *Imperial Panama: Commerce and Conflict in Isthmian America, 1550–1800.* Albuquerque: University of New Mexico Press, 1993.

Weber, Max. *From Max Weber: Essays in Sociology.* Ed. and trans. H. H. Gerth and C. Wright Mills. New York, 1946.

Winkler, Max. *Investments of United States Capital in Latin America.* New York, New York: Kennikat Press, 1971.

Wood, Bryce. *The Dismantling of the Good Neighbor Policy.* Austin: University of Texas Press, 1985.

Woodward, Ralph. *Central America: A Nation Divided.* New York: Oxford University Press, 1985.

Zimbalist, Andrew, and John Weeks. *Panama at the Crossroads: Economic Development and Political Change in the Twentieth Century.* Berkeley: University of California Press, 1991.

Unpublished Secondary Sources

Aparicio, Fernando. "Panama: Society and Politics, 1885–1895." Master's thesis, University of Miami, 1991.

Cooley, John A. "The United States and the Panama Canal, 1938–1947: Policy Formulation and Implementation from Munich through the Early Years of the Cold War." Ph.D. diss, Ohio State University, 1972.

García, Pantaleón. "The Good Neighbor Policy in Panama: The Alfaro-Hull Treaty." Master's thesis, University of Miami, 1990.

Langley, Lester. "The United States and Panama, 1933–1941: A Study in Strategy and Diplomacy." Ph.D. diss., University of Kansas, 1965.

Pérez, Juan Manuel. "Panama: The Rise and Fall of Arnulfo Arias, 1931–1941." Ph.D. diss., Georgetown University, 1993.

Ward, Eliot Dunbar Christopher. "Imperial Panama: Commerce and Conflict in Isthmian America, 1550–1750." Ph.D. diss., University of Florida, 1988.

Published Secondary Sources: Articles

Alfaro, Ricardo J. "Enrique Adolfo Jiménez." *Revista Lotería* 16 (1971):84–87.

Amador Guerrero, Manuel. "Como se inició nuestra independencia." *Épocas* (October 25, 1947):9–14.

Aparicio, Fernando. "Significación, alcances y limitaciones de la experiencia porrista: 1912–1924." *Revista Humanidades* 3 (December 1993):149–54.

Bethell, Leslie. "From the Second World War to the Cold War: 1944–1954." In Abraham F. Lowenthal, ed., *Exporting Democracy: The United States and Latin America*. Baltimore, MD: Johns Hopkins University Press, 1991.

Bock, S., and P. Gans. "The Problems of Fuzzy Cause-Specific Death Rates in Mortality Context Analysis: The Case of Panama City." *Social Science & Medicine* 36 (1993):1367–71.

Borah, Woodrow. "Epidemics in the Americas: Major Issues and Future Research." *Latin American Population History Bulletin* 19 (Spring 1991):2–13.

Bort, John R., and Mary W. Helms, eds. "Panama in Transition: Local Reactions to Development Policies." *University of Missouri Monographs in Anthropology* no. 6. Curators of the University of Missouri, 1983.

Buchanan, Paul G. "The Impact of U.S. Labor." In Abraham F. Lowenthal, ed., *Exporting Democracy: The United States and Latin America*. Baltimore, MD: Johns Hopkins University Press.

Castillero Calvo, Alfredo. "Arquitectura y sociedad: La vivienda colonial en Panamá." *Revista Humanidades* 3 (December 1993):7–148.

———. "El movimiento anseatista de 1826." *Tareas* 4 (May–July 1961):4–25.

———. "El movimiento de 1830." *Tareas* 5 (August–December 1961):12–56.

———. "Transitismo y dependencia: El caso del Istmo de Panamá." *Revista Lotería* 210 (July 1973):17–41.

Clifford, J. Gary. "Both Ends of the Telescope: New Perspectives on FDR and American Entry into World War II." *Diplomatic History* 13 (Spring 1989):213–30.

Conte-Porras, Jorge. "Victoriano Lorenzo y la Guerra de los Mil Días como antesala de la independencia." *Boletín de la Academia de la Historia* 4 (July–September 1975):37–56.

Cook, Sherburne. "Historical Demography." In Robert Heizer, ed., *California: Handbook of North American Indians,* Volume 8. Washington, D.C.: Smithsonian Institution, 1978.

Correoso, Buenaventura. "Sucesos de Panamá (1886)." *Revista Lotería* 340–41 (July–August 1894):93–133.

Cronon, David E. "Interpreting the Good Neighbor Policy." *Hispanic American Historical Review* 39 (1959):55254.

Daley, Mercedes Chen. "The Watermelon Riot: Cultural Encounters in Panama City, April 15, 1856." *Hispanic American Historical Review* 70 (1990):85–108.

Darío Paredes, Rubén (Colonel). "Breve historia de la Policía Nacional y la Guardia Nacional." Panama City, Panama: n.p., n.d.

Devereux, Edward C. "Parsons's Sociological Theory." In Max Black, ed., *The Social Theories of Talcott Parsons: A Critical Examination.* Englewood Cliffs, NJ: Prentice Hall, 1961.

Dorsey, Steven D., John M. Hill, and M. E. Woods. "The Human Development Spectrum: Sub-Spectra and Social Indicators for Use in Development Project Planning, Design, and Implementation." *Social Indicators Research* 21 (1989):93–110.

Duncan, Jeptha B., and Octavio Méndez Pereira. "Una entrevista con el Dr. W. T. Burres." *Cuasimodo: Magazine Interamericano* 1 (June 1919):46–51.

Espinar, José Domingo. "Resúmen histórico que hace el general José Domingo Espinar de los acontecimientos políticos occuridos en Panamá en el año 1830, apellidados ahora revolución de castas por el gobernador señor José de Obaldía." *Boletín de la Academia Panameña de la Historia* 14 (July 1937):261–80.

Fonseca Mora, Ramón. "Movilización de los estudiantes leyes." *Diálogo social* 57 (June 9, 1974):35–37.

Furlong, William L. "Panama: The Difficult Transition towards Democracy." *Journal of Interamerican Studies and World Affairs* 35 (Fall 1993):19–64.

Gandásegui, Marco A. "La crisis de una alianza: La coyuntura panameña." *Caribbean Studies* 21 (1988):237–47.

———. "The Military Regimes of Panama." *Journal of Interamerican Studies and World Affairs* 35 (Fall 1993):1–17.

García, Pantaleón. "La administración del Ing. Florencio H. Arosemena: Crisis y Acción Comunal." *Revista Milenio* 1 (1995):79–112.

Herrera, Francisco. "Richard O. Marsh y su intervención en la política pana-meña." *Revista Milenio* 1 (1995):48–78.

Hogan, J. Michael. "Theodore Roosevelt and the Heroes of Panama." *Presidential Studies Quarterly* 19 (Winter 1989):79–94.

Howe, James. "La lucha por la tierra en la costa de San Blas (Panamá), 1900–1930." *Mesoamérica* 29 (June 1995):67–76.

Jones, Oakah L. "Cuna Rebellion and Panamanian Power, 1925." *Proceedings of the Pacific Coast Council on Latin American Studies* 12 (1986): 77–85.

Langley, Lester D. "United States–Panamanian Relations Since 1941." *Journal of World Affairs* (July 1970):223–25.

———. "The World Crisis and the Good Neighbor Policy in Panama." *The Americas: A Quarterly Review of Inter-American Cultural History* 24 (October 1967):137–52.

Leis, Raul. "The Cousin's Republic." *NACLA Report of the Americas* 4 (July–August 1988):26.

Major, John. "'Pro mundi beneficio'? The Panama Canal as an International Issue, 1943–8." *Review of International Studies* 9 (January 1983):17–34.

———. "Wasting Asset: The U.S. Re-Assessment of the Panama Canal, 1945–1949." *Journal of Strategic Studies* 3 (September 1980):123–46.

———. "Who Wrote the Hay-Bunau-Varilla Convention?" *Diplomatic History* 8 (Spring 1984):115–24.

Marco Serra, Yolanda. "El nacimiento del movimiento feminista en Panamá, 1923." *Revista Humanidades* 3 (December 1993):169–84.

McAlister, Lyle N. "The Military." In John J. Johnson, ed., *Continuity and Change in Latin America*. Stanford: Stanford University Press, 1964.

Mena García, María del Carmen. "La real hacienda de tierra firme en el siglo XVI: Organización y funcionamiento." *Revista Lotería* 30 (1985):85–95.

Migdal, Joel S. "Strong States, Weak States: Power and Accommodation." In Samuel P. Huntington and Myron Weiner, eds., *Understanding Political Development*. Boston, MA: Little, Brown, and Company, 1987.

Morris, Charles. "75 Years of Security History: The Panama Canal." *Security Management* 33 (1989):68–74.

Moss, Ambler H. "The Panama Treaties: How an Era Ended." *Latin American Research Review* 21 (1986):171–78.

Nordlinger, Eric A. "Political Development: Times Sequences and Rates of Changes." *World Politics* 20 (April 1968):494–520.

Paredes, Ruben Darío. "La policía en Panamá." Unpublished mimeograph in author's possession.

Perlmutter, Amos. "The Praetorian State and the Praetorian Army: Toward a Taxonomy of Civil-Military Relations in Developing Countries." *Comparative Politics* 1 (1969):382–404.

Pizzurno de Araúz, Patricia. "Los millones de la posteridad (1904–1954)." *Revista Milenio* 1 (1995):113–32.

Popkin, Barry M. "The Nutrition Transition in Low-Income Countries: An Emerging Crisis." *Nutrition Reviews* 52 (September 1994):285–98.

Porras, Belisario. "Reflexiones canaleras o la venta del istmo." *Tareas* 5 (August–December 1961):3–11.

Priestly, George. "Panama: Obstacles to Democracy and Sovereignty." *Radical Historical Review* 48 (1990):88–110.

Ricord, Humberto. "El Código de 1972: Cambio radical en la legislación laboral panameña." *Revista Jurídica Panameña* 2 (1974):140–54.

———. "La oligarquía panameña en el banquillo de los acusados." Included anonymously in Virgilio Araúz, ed., *Cinco ensayos*. Panama City, Panama: n.p., n.d.

Romero, Fernando. "El negro en tierra firme durante el siglo xvi." *Boletín de la Academia Panameña de la Historia* (January–June 1943):3–37.

Ropp, Steve. "Explaining the Long-Term Maintenance of a Military Regime: Panama before the U.S. Invasion." *World Politics* 4 (1992):210–34.

Schnoover, Thomas. "Max Farrand's Memorandum on the U.S. Role in the Panamanian Revolution of 1903." *Diplomatic History* 12 (fall 1988):501–6.

Scranton, Margaret E. "Consolidation and Imposition: Panama's 1992 Referendum." *Journal of Interamerican Studies and World Affairs* 35 (fall 1993):65–102.

Sosa, Tomás. "Breve reseña de la evolución demográfica de la ciudad de Panamá." *Anuario de estudios centroamericanos* 7 (1981):117–26.

Susto, Juan Antonio. "De la Guerra de los Mil Días: El puente de Calidonia." *Revista Lotería* 44 (July 1959):33–50.

Varg, Paul E. "The Economic Side of the Good Neighbor Policy." *Pacific Historical Review* 45 (1976):48–49.

Wearne, Phillip. "Noriega's Files." *New Statesman and Society* 3 (1990):20.

Wicks, Daniel H. "Dress Rehearsal: United States Intervention on the Isthmus of Panama, 1885." *Pacific Review* 49 (1980):581–608.

Wright, Almon. "The United States and Panama, 1933–1949." U.S. Department of State, Top Secret Research Report 499 (August 1952). Mimeographed. Richter Library, University of Miami.

Periodicals

El neogranadino (1856)
El Panamá América. Various issues.
Gaceta oficial. Various issues.
The New York Times. Various issues.
The Panama American. Various issues.
The Panama Star and Herald. Various issues.
Time. December 29, 1947:26.

Index

Page numbers in italic type refer to charts, graphs or maps.

About the Book and Author

We Answer Only to God

Politics and the Military in Panama, 1903–1947

Thomas L. Pearcy

Who can forget the televised drama of American troops tracking down Panama's leader, General Noriega, in 1989? How did that event come to pass? Narcopolitics—or money from illegal drugs influencing national affairs—is not the sole answer. The antecedents of the military's presence in the political life of Panama appear early in the twentieth century.

This book makes unprecedented use of Panamanian sources to study the military. It argues that their control of politics is not a temporary aberration but a natural result of the country's sociopolitical development. In exploring just how and when the military began dominating Panama's government, Pearcy fundamentally reinterprets the nation's modern history. He traces the slow and inevitable collapse of civilian rule during the first half of the century.

"Provides new insight into the intricate social and political circumstances of Panamá today."—Professor Fernando Aparicio, Universidad de Panamá

Thomas L. Pearcy is a professor of modern Latin American history at Brigham Young University.